Baseball Myths

Debating, Debunking, and
Disproving Tales from the Diamond

Bill Deane

THE SCARECROW PRESS, INC.
Lanham • Toronto • Plymouth, UK
2012

Published by Scarecrow Press, Inc.
A wholly owned subsidiary of The Rowman & Littlefield Publishing Group, Inc.
4501 Forbes Boulevard, Suite 200, Lanham, Maryland 20706
www.rowman.com

10 Thornbury Road, Plymouth PL6 7PP, United Kingdom

British Library Cataloguing in Publication Information Available

Library of Congress Cataloging-in-Publication Data

Deane, Bill.
  Baseball myths : debating, debunking, and disproving tales from the diamond / Bill
Deane.
     p. cm.
  Includes bibliographical references and index.
  ISBN 978-0-8108-8546-2 (cloth : alk. paper) — ISBN 978-0-8108-8547-9 (ebook)
  1. Baseball—Anecdotes. I. Title.
  GV873.D38 2012
  796.357—dc23

                                                                                    2012016453

Printed in the United States of America

For Jude,
My Muse

~

Contents

~

Introduction

The whole history of baseball has the quality of mythology.

—Bernard Malamud, author

This book was born back in 1995, when another author suggested we collaborate on a work about baseball myths. It sounded like a great idea. I had already done many articles and research projects that debunked myths in the history of the game and had a lot of fun doing them. I started gathering them together and telling people about this wonderful book we were writing.

For whatever reasons, my would-be coauthor soon stopped communicating with me and eventually decided to go his own way. I was left with a few dozen short chapters I had written, a bunch of half-baked ideas, and diminished enthusiasm for the project. Then, a series of personal setbacks and situations practically ground my efforts to a halt. I had occasional fits of progress, but, by 2007, I had only about half a book's worth of material to show for twelve years. To people asking how the book was coming, I'd respond that it was becoming more of a myth than any I had written about. Finally, I made a breakthrough and, except for one more hiccup, kept going until I reached the finish line. The myth became a reality.

I was debunking myths long before starting this book. While employed as senior research associate at the National Baseball Library (NBL) from 1986 to 1994, one of my early duties was documenting stories for Bruce Nash, Allan Zullo, and Bernie Ward, creators of the *Baseball Hall of Shame* book series. They brought to life stories of shameful escapades and humorously

xii Introduction

inept performances from the lore of baseball and wanted me to pin down the dates of these events for them. More often than not, my research proved than the oft-told tales could never have happened. The authors got to calling me "Killer." I only wish they or I saved or remembered this collection of debunked tales. Some of the chapters in this book arose from other NBL projects of mine: trying to prove for patrons that Dummy Hoy invented umpires' hand signals, or that Vic Wertz's 1954 World Series drive traveled 460-plus feet, for examples.

When I started writing this compilation, baseball books with footnotes were the exception; now they are the rule. I regret that this book does not follow that rule, but I have cited sources throughout the text wherever possible. (Well, maybe "regret" is too strong a word.)

Many people contributed ideas, items, and facts for this book. I wish to acknowledge the following, in alphabetical order: Marshall Adesman, Keith Allison, Mark Armour, Cliff Blau, Larry Boes, Gene Carney, Jim Charlton, Eddie Frierson, John Holway, Bill James, Pat Kelly, Herm Krabbenhoft, Doug Lyons, Jerry Malloy, Wayne McElreavy, Peter Morris, Rob Neyer, Clifford Otto, Pete Palmer, Doug Pappas, Wes Parker, John Pastier, Frank Russo, Bob Schaefer, Steve Schaeffer, Gabriel Schechter, Ron Selter, David Smith, Ted Spencer, Dana Swift, Dick Thompson, John Thorn, Stew Thornley, Jim Weigand, Mark Wernick, Tim Wiles, and Craig Wright. I deeply regret that some of these people did not live to see how it turned out.

~

CHAPTER ONE

Baseball's Infancy

Base ball is in its infancy.

—Dodgers' owner Charles Ebbets, 1911

Baseball has a reputation as a conservative sport, with very little change in its rules over the past century or more. But the game evolved drastically during its early decades. With frequent changes and haphazard record keeping, early baseball history became fertile for mythology.

Abner Doubleday Invented Baseball

"If baseball wasn't invented in Cooperstown, it should have been."

—historian John Thorn

Every schoolboy knows that General Abner Doubleday invented baseball in Cooperstown, New York. After all, why else would they have put the National Baseball Hall of Fame there? By now, most adults know there is something fishy about the story but couldn't tell you exactly what. The Doubleday myth has been debunked more times than any other legend associated with baseball, yet it lives on and spawns other myths. Some will tell you that the real birthplace of baseball is Hoboken, New Jersey, but couldn't name an inventor. How did this all begin?

The Mills Commission (1905–1907) started the ball rolling with its declaration that baseball was invented by Doubleday in Cooperstown in 1839.

Figure 1.1. Baseball Luminaries Take Time to Honor Baseball's Inventor (1939).
Source: Library of Congress

The commission was put together by noted sporting goods magnate Albert G. Spalding, to settle a long-running debate between himself and Henry Chadwick, a pioneering baseball writer and historian. The British-born Chadwick had written that baseball owed its origins to such English games as cricket and rounders, while the U.S. businessman Spalding claimed that the game was as American as apple pie. Spalding handpicked a committee of his cronies, seven elder statesmen with some connection to the game, to gather evidence on the subject. They collected voluminous correspondence but, as it turned out, made their conclusion based on the testimony of one man, Abner Graves. The elderly Graves claimed to have been a playmate of Doubleday's in Cooperstown, when the future Civil War general used a stick to diagram his new game, an improvement to "town ball," in the dirt. In a letter dated April 3, 1905, Graves wrote the following:

> The American game of "Base Ball" was invented by Abner Doubleday of Cooperstown, New York, either the spring prior, or following the "Log Cabin and Hard Cider" campaign of General [William Henry] Harrison for President, said Abner Doubleday being then a boy pupil of "Green's Select School" in Cooperstown, and the same, who as General Doubleday won honor . . . in the "Civil War."

In a follow-up letter, dated November 17, 1905, Graves fixed the date as "either 1839, 1840, or 1841" (although the Harrison campaign reference eliminates 1839 as a possibility) and described the game in detail, including a rule specifying 11 players on a side. This was just what Spalding and his cohorts were looking for: credible testimony that baseball was indeed of American origin, and invented by an American military hero to boot! They chose the 1839 date and announced it to the world.

Anyone who has taken the trouble to examine the evidence realizes that the Mills Commission's finding was ill advised at best. Abner Graves was only five years old in 1839, while Doubleday was twenty—a striking disparity for playmates. Furthermore, Doubleday was attending the West Point military academy between September 1, 1838, and 1842, and could not have been in Cooperstown at that time, unless he was AWOL (in fact, he never left West Point during those years). Doubleday, who died in 1893, never made any claims of inventing baseball and left behind dozens of journals, none of which mentioned the game. The evidence collected by the Mills Commission supposedly was lost in a fire, although Graves's letters survive (and, incidentally, the second one ends with, "I would rather have Uncle Sam declare war on England and clean her up rather than have one of her citizens beat us out of Base Ball"). Abner Graves, the star witness, later (1926) died in the Colorado State Insane Asylum.

But the public prefers fairy tales to facts, and the Doubleday legend was bound to live forever. Who really invented baseball? Probably no individual deserves that credit; the game evolved from various stick and ball games that had been played for centuries. It is the old "creation versus evolution" argument, and the early 1900s was the age of invention.

As baseball historian and author Peter Morris points out, it is possible that Graves was telling the truth but had his facts mixed up (and had them further mixed up by the Mills Commission). Although it was Graves who identified his playmate as the future general, there was an Abner Demas Doubleday—a younger cousin of the general (born May 1829)—who did indeed live in the Cooperstown area during the time in question. But even if Graves were telling the truth, so what? As Morris writes,

> It is quite possible that there was an actual game of ball in Cooperstown in or around 1839 in which the younger Doubleday proposed some changes to the rules previously adhered to in that region. Obviously, such an event does not entitle Doubleday to be recognized as the inventor of the game, nor anything more than the slightest footnote in the history of baseball.

As silly as Cooperstown's "Birthplace of Baseball" claim is, that of Hoboken, New Jersey, is off base as well. Hoboken *was* the site of the first match game played under the rules of the New York Knickerbocker Base Ball Club—the first team organized for the purpose of playing the sport—on June 19, 1846 (although they had been playing intrasquad games for nine months before that). Because of this, many people want Cooperstown to surrender its title and even its Hall of Fame to that dreary little city. But, it was the *New York* Knickerbockers, made up of gentlemen from *New York*, who established what came to be known as the *New York* Game of Base Ball. It so happened that they took a ferry to Hoboken's Elysian Fields for their first match game (against a team known as the *New York* Nine), simply because there was more space there. Does that make Hoboken the birthplace of baseball? If so, then the New York Mets were born in St. Louis, site of *their* first game.

Cooperstown celebrated its newfound notoriety. A village of 2,500 or so, with tourists attracted by its Otsego Lake, the town's previous claim to fame was being the birthplace and home of American novelist James Fenimore Cooper (*The Last of the Mohicans, The Deerslayer*), whose father founded the town. The author is buried a baseball's throw from Cooper Park (current home of the National Baseball Library), and a large statue of him sits in the middle of that park.

As the Mills Commission's news began to die on the vine, a local dentist named Ernest Pitcher began fund-raising efforts to erect a ball field at the site of Doubleday's mythical invention. Sportswriter Sam Crane and National League (NL) president John Heydler were two of the early supporters of this effort, increasing its recognition. Doubleday Field, as it is called, is owned by the Village of Cooperstown—not the Hall of Fame, as is commonly thought—and is now used for some 300 amateur, semipro, and professional games each year.

In 1934, Scottish immigrant Alexander Cleland, inspired by the progress on the field, proposed an idea to his boss, Stephen C. Clark. Clark was patriarch of the Clark Foundation, the philanthropic organization that owns most of Cooperstown. The Clark family had become wealthy through a partnership with Isaac Singer, inventor of the famous sewing machine (in 1989, *Forbes* magazine estimated the Clark empire fortune at $400 million plus). Cleland suggested a National Baseball Museum at Cooperstown, built in time for the Baseball Centennial celebration in 1939. Cleland predicted that "hundreds of visitors would be attracted." During the 1930s, times were tough all over, and any idea to promote tourism was a welcome thing. Clark offered his blessing and financial support to the idea and encouraged his employee to follow up on it. Shortly thereafter, a homemade 19th-century baseball was discovered in a farmhouse that supposedly had belonged to Abner Graves's family, a find that somehow lent credibility to the Mills Commission's report. Clark bought the ball for $5 and made it the centerpiece of an exhibit that evolved into the museum. It remains essentially the only museum artifact ever purchased by the National Baseball Museum.

Cleland approached the baseball hierarchy with his idea but found an enthusiastic backer in only one person: Heydler's successor as NL president, Ford Frick, who offered the "fullest cooperation in any project you may evolve." It was Frick who conceived the idea of a Hall of Fame as part of the museum and who sold the idea to the baseball establishment. Ironically, Frick went on to be voted into the shrine by the Veterans' Committee in 1970, 25 days after he resigned from the committee.

About this time arose the first serious attacks on the Doubleday myth. They were enough to prevent Doubleday from being inducted into the Hall of Fame, but it was too late to stop the museum from becoming a reality. For decades, Hall representatives clung to the Doubleday myth, or at least remained noncommittal to the evidence against it. Even into the 21st century, an essay in the *National Baseball Hall of Fame and Museum Yearbook* still reflected that line of thought. "From time to time over the years, various critics have challenged the speculation on Doubleday," reads the essay penned by former Hall vice president Bill Guilfoile. "Whatever may or may not be proved in the future concerning baseball's true origin is in many respects irrelevant at this time. . . . The Hall of Fame is in Cooperstown to stay."

More than a century after the Mills Commission's announcement, the commissioner of baseball still clings to the Doubleday myth. "As a student of history, I know there is a great debate whether Abner Doubleday or Alexander Cartwright really founded the game of baseball," wrote Bud Selig in an October 18, 2010, letter. "From all of the historians whom I have spoken with, I really believe that Abner Doubleday is the 'Father of Baseball.'"

Ninety Feet Is a Magical Distance

Ninety feet between bases is the nearest to perfection that man has yet achieved.

—Pulitzer Prize–winning sportswriter Red Smith

Everyone knows that the measurement between the bases in Major League Baseball is 90 feet, a distance established at baseball's birth and representing near perfection. In reality, the distance is less than 90 feet now, was even shorter in baseball's infancy, and has nothing to do with perfection.

It is commonly believed that the 90-foot distance was established by the original rules of baseball. The Hall of Fame plaque of Alexander Cartwright—key contributor to the first set of rules, drafted by the New York Knickerbocker Base Ball Club in 1845—names him as the man who "set bases 90 feet apart." But, a check of the Knickerbocker rules belies this claim. Rule number four states that, "The bases shall be from 'home' to second base, 42 paces; from first to third base, 42 paces, equidistant." In *Total Baseball* (2004), 19th-century baseball expert John Thorn says that,

> It has been presumed by scholars that when a three-foot pace is plugged in, the resulting baselines of 89 feet are close enough to the present 90 so that we can proclaim Cartwright's genius. In fact, the pace in 1845 was either an imprecise and variable measure—to gauge distances by "stepping off"—or precisely two and a half feet, in which case the distance from home to second would have been 105 feet and the Cartwright base paths would have been 74.25 feet.

The 90-foot distance did not enter the rule books until 1857, by which time Cartwright was out of the organized baseball picture.

Legendary baseball scribe Red Smith wrote that, "Ninety feet between bases is the nearest to perfection that man has yet achieved." It was a pet topic of Smith's. "Whoever first put the bases 90 feet apart qualifies as a genius, the Einstein of the baseball cosmos," Smith was often heard to say, according to fellow writer Roger Kahn. He continues, saying,

> Ninety feet is what makes the game work. How many times do you see a runner out by half a step? How seldom does a man beat out an infield hit? Almost every ground ball is an "out," just as it should be. Ninety feet between home plate and first base: one of the few examples of perfection on earth.

Commissioner Ford Frick expounded on the subject as well. "The establishment of the 90-foot distance between bases must be recognized as the greatest contribution to perfect competition any game has ever known," writes Frick in *Games, Asterisks, and People: Memoirs of a Lucky Fan* (1973). He continues saying,

> It is that specification on which our hitting and fielding records are based; that unchanging measurement of success or failure that has set the guidelines for heroes; the great reason why baseball, through the years, has qualified as the most mathematically perfect game ever devised by humankind.

This sentiment has been paraphrased by countless broadcasters and other followers of the game, saying things like, "On a ground ball, fielded cleanly, the infielder will throw out the runner by half a step, but if he bobbles it for a split second, the runner will be safe by half a step." The implication is that, if the bases were only, say, 85 feet apart, every ground ball would result in a hit.

Common sense tells us how ridiculous that is. The deeper infielders play, the more ground balls they can reach. Naturally, infielders play as deep as they can, depending on the field conditions, the speed of the batter, the situation, and their own arm strength, so that they can still throw out the batter at first base on a routine grounder. If the base paths were only 85 feet long, infielders would have to play a bit more shallowly, costing them a speck of range. If they were 95 feet long, fielders could play a bit deeper, enabling them to reach a few more balls than at the 90-foot distance. Batting averages would go slightly up or down, respectively, but it would hardly destroy the competitive balance of the game.

One need only look at different levels and variations of baseball for proof. In Little League, for example, the distance between bases is 45 feet, and, in slow-pitch softball, 65 feet. There is no shortage of close plays or destruction of competitive balance to be found.

So, the baselines have been 90 feet long for nearly a century and a half. But, the distances *between* bases are actually less than that, due to the width and positioning of the bases themselves. The distance from the edge of home plate to the edge of first base is about 87 feet, 9 inches; from first to second and second to third, 88 feet, 1½ inches; and, from third to home, 87 feet, 9 inches. And, prior to 1900, the distances were different still, varying due to changes in the size and positioning of bases.

Today's Reds Are Baseball's Original Pro Team

If the Reds were baseball's first team, who did they play?

—comedian George Carlin

The 1869 Cincinnati Red Stockings were baseball's first openly professional team. This paved the way for pro ball as we know it, and the Cincinnati Reds proudly carry the torch of their ancestors. Until 1997, the NL's opening game was traditionally held in Cincinnati because of this.

But today's Reds have no connection with the 1869 team, other than the fact that they play in the same city. In fact, if any team can trace its lineage to the Red Stockings, it is the Atlanta Braves! The 1869 team was led by brothers Harry and George Wright. Harry was the team's recruiter, manager, and center fielder, while George was its shortstop and best player. Both would wind up in the Baseball Hall of Fame as pioneers of the game.

The Red Stockings traveled the country, taking on all comers and emerging undefeated.

After enduring their first losses the following season, the team essentially disbanded in November 1870, reverting to an amateur team. Club president A. P. Bonte cited "enormous salary demands" in his decision. But, in the wake of the team's success, the first professional league—the National Association of Professional Base Ball Players—was organized in 1871. The original teams were located in Philadelphia, Chicago, Boston, Washington, New York, Troy, Fort Wayne, Cleveland, and Rockford—but not Cincinnati. The Queen City didn't have another pro team until 1876.

Harry and George Wright quickly found employment with the Boston team, and it was called the Red Stockings in honor of their former club. The Wrights weren't the only Cincinnati veterans to wind up in Beantown; of the nine starters on the 1869 club, six ultimately played for the Boston Red Stockings. Joining the Wright brothers on Boston were former Cincy teammates Charlie Gould, Cal McVey, Andy Leonard, and Charlie Sweasy (Sweasy had originally joined the Washington club, along with former Cincy players Fred Waterman, Asa Brainard, and Doug Allison).

With Harry Wright at the helm, the Red Stockings took four of five pennants before the league disbanded. Out of its ashes was formed the NL in 1876. The NL's Boston team, known as the Red Caps, still had Harry Wright as manager, George Wright at shortstop, and Andy Leonard in left field. The team eventually became known as the Braves, playing in Boston for 77 seasons, moving to Milwaukee in 1953, and finally settling in Atlanta in 1966.

There was also a charter NL team in Cincinnati, but it lasted only five seasons. The forerunner of the current Reds was born in 1882, playing in the rival American Association (AA) for eight seasons before switching leagues. Thus, today's Reds didn't join the Senior Circuit until 1890—the fifteenth year of NL play and 21 years after Cincinnati hosted the first professional baseball team.

Old Hoss Radbourn Pitched His Team's Last 27 Games in 1884, Winning 26

Charles "Old Hoss" Radbourn was one of the greatest pitchers of the 19th century, amassing 309 wins between 1881 and 1891. His crowning achievement came in 1884, when he earned a record 59 victories (long thought to be 60, and originally reported as 62), leading the Providence Grays to the NL championship. Old Hoss completed each of his 73 starts, totaling 678⅔ innings.

Most remarkably, according to his Hall of Fame plaque, "Radbourne (sic) pitched last 27 games of season, won 26." That's not quite true, although Radbourn's actual accomplishment is scarcely less remarkable. Between August 9 and September 18, Radbourn pitched 26 of the Grays' 27 games, winning 25; at the end of this streak, Providence still had 14 games remaining.

In those days, a typical team had only two full-time pitchers. Unless a pitcher was injured, the only way he could be replaced was if he switched positions with another player on the field. Teams played only about four or five games a week. Many, if not most, pitchers, including Radbourn, still threw underhand, although overhand pitching had been legalized that year. The pitching distance was only 50 feet (see the following chapter for clarification). Balls were rarely replaced, so pitchers didn't have to worry much about the long ball. In other words, it was a whole different ball game, easier for pitchers to amass a lot of innings.

In late July, Providence and Boston were battling neck and neck for the NL flag, when Grays' pitcher Charlie Sweeney jumped the team, leaving Radbourn to carry the load (although Ed Conley was available for spot starts). On August 8, Conley shut out Philadelphia, 6–0. Radbourn tossed the next six Grays' games, winning them all. Conley topped Detroit, 5–2, on August 20, with Radbourn playing shortstop and batting his usual cleanup. Old Hoss returned to the box the next day and didn't relinquish the position until September 25, by which time the Grays' pennant seemed assured, thanks to their 20-game winning streak between August 7 and September 6. The streak ended when Radbourn lost to Buffalo, 2–0, on September 9; he then ran off another eight wins in a row, before losing back-to-back starts on September 20 and 24.

Old Hoss pitched "only" five of the Grays' 12 regular-season games over the last three weeks of the season. Adjectives used to describe him during those appearances included "sore," "stiff," and "listless." Radbourn was said to be "suffering with lame cords in the arm and neck." Nevertheless, he won all five starts, then all three games of the first "World's Series" against the New York Metropolitans of the AA. And, predictably, Radbourn was never quite the same pitcher after 1884.

The Pitching Distance Was Increased from 50 to 60½ Feet in 1893

Many historians consider 1893 to be the dawn of "modern" baseball. That was the year the pitcher's area was moved back from 50 feet to the current

60½—an increase of 21%! Can you imagine facing Justin Verlander from 50 feet away? Actually, the difference was not nearly as great as it sounds. It's true that, since 1893, the pitcher starts his delivery 60'6" from the back of the plate. Prior to then, the pertinent rules read as follow:

- RULE 5. The pitcher's lines must be . . . five and one half feet long by four feet wide, distant fifty feet from the center of the home base.
- RULE 18. The pitcher shall take his position facing the batsman with both feet square on the ground, one foot on the rear line of the "box."

In other words, while the front of the pitcher's box was 50 feet away from home plate, the back of the box—where the pitcher had to start his delivery—was 55'6" away. And, since home plate at that time was a one-foot-square base within the diamond, much like first and third, the center of the base was about 8½ inches closer than the rear point—the point from which the modern pitching distance is measured. So, the pre-1893 pitcher was beginning his delivery about 56'2½" away from the back of home plate. Instead of a 21% leap in the pitching distance in 1893, the increase was a relatively modest 7.6%.

Mike Grady Made Four-Plus Errors on One Batted Ball

Legend has it that Mike Grady, playing third base for the New York Giants, set an all-time record for short-term fielding futility. Here's the story, as reported in an undated *Sports Digest* article found in Grady's National Baseball Library file:

Grady never was able to forget one day in 1899, when he was playing third base for New York. Grady often talked and laughed about the play, and the late Robert L. Ripley used the incident in one of his "Believe It or Not" cartoons a few years ago. As friends recall Grady telling it, the play apparently went something like this: The batter hit to Grady, playing third base, and was safe at first when Grady fumbled the ball for an error. However, Grady did try a belated throw across the diamond. The throw was wild, eluded the baseman, and the runner scampered on to second base—error no. 2. The runner continued toward third base, but the ball had been recovered and he would have been out if Grady held the return throw for the tag. Grady didn't hold the ball—for error no. 3. The runner then scrambled to his feet and started toward home, but the ball had rolled only a few feet from Grady and he recovered it. The runner was trapped in the ensuing rundown and should have been tagged out by Grady when he tried to dive back into third base. However, Grady muffed the play again; the runner got back to the base safely, jumped to his feet, and headed for home again. This time, Grady recovered the ball again and finally would have gotten his man at the plate, but the throw was wild for error no. 5 and a run.

Several other versions of the story have been found, some saying Grady was charged with "only" four errors on the play, the *Des Moines Daily News* (Iowa), January 4, 1906, saying six, but most agreeing he was playing third base for the Giants (the exception saying the Reds, whom he never even played for). The one purporting to be a first-hand account was in a 1918 issue of the *Sporting News*, where W. A. Phelon claimed he witnessed the incident in Chicago and heard the official scorer shout out, "Five errors for Grady!"

In fact, Grady played only 51 games at third base in his entire 11-year career and never made more than three errors in any game there, let alone in one at bat. Grady was mostly a catcher, appearing in 525 games behind the plate, but he also played every other position, except pitcher, between 1894 and 1906. Included were 246 games at first base, 29 games in right field, 14 in left field, 14 at shortstop, seven in center field, and five at second base. He certainly was no Brooks Robinson in his 51 games at the hot corner: He made 28 errors for an .826 fielding percentage, poor even for that era (the league average was .901).

But only once was Grady charged with more than two errors in one game at third base: three, against Cleveland on August 25, 1899. Could that have been the infamous day, with just the error count exaggerated? Nope. Cleveland scored four runs that day, and all four were earned. And the *Sporting Life*'s account of the game includes no mention of Grady.

Home Plate Is So Named
Because It Is Shaped Like a House

Why is the fourth base called home plate? Some have surmised that it is due to the base's pentagonal shape, which resembles a house. But the five-sided shape didn't come about until 55 years after the base was first called "home."

The term *home* dates back to the rules of the New York Knickerbocker Base Ball Club, first recorded on September 23, 1845. Rule number four states that, "The bases shall be from 'home' to second base, 42 paces; from first to third base, 42 paces, equidistant." It is likely the term was borrowed from other games played many years before.

A revised set of rules, adopted in 1857, specifies that,

> The bases . . . must be constructed as to be distinctly seen by the umpires and referee, and must cover a space equal to one square foot of surface . . . the home base and pitcher's point to be each marked by a flat circular iron plate, painted or enameled white.

The shape was changed to square, like the other bases, in 1868, and to the pentagonal shape in 1900.

Spalding's Official Base Ball Guide for that year explains the revision, saying, "The change made is undoubtedly an advantage alike to the pitcher and umpire, as it enables the pitcher to see the *width* of the base he has to throw the ball over better than before, and the umpire can judge called balls and strikes with less difficulty." And that's how the home became a house.

Negro Pitching Legend Rube Foster
Taught Christy Mathewson the Screwball

Christy Mathewson was one of the greatest pitchers in baseball history. Debuting in the majors in 1900, Mathewson had a cumulative won-lost record of 327–133 for the New York Giants between 1903 and 1914—an average record of 27–11. His innovative money pitch was called the "fadeaway," and is now known as the screwball. Legend has it that Matty learned the pitch from Negro pitching legend Rube Foster, c. 1902. Some even say Giants' manager John McGraw hired Foster to teach Matty the pitch. This story is propagated in such books as *Rube Foster: The Father of Black Baseball* (1981) and *Blackball Stars: Negro League Pioneers* (1988), by John Holway, and *The Crooked Pitch: The Curveball in American Baseball History* (1984), by Martin Quigley, and in the Ken Burns documentary *Baseball*. This supposedly explains Mathewson's transformation from a pitcher who was 34–34 in 1901–1902, to one who was 63–25 in 1903–1904.

The image is of a crafty veteran, not allowed to play in the all-white major leagues, imparting his wisdom to a neophyte slabsman—notwithstanding that Foster and Mathewson were born less than a year apart. And the improved won-lost records can be almost entirely attributed to the improvement of Matty's team. Table 1.1 gives his records for the four seasons in the context of the Giants' records (adjusted to remove his decisions), using a statistic I call "normalized winning percentage," which gives the pitcher's projected percentage if pitching for an average .500 team.

The late, great baseball researcher Dick Thompson punctured the Foster myth in the 1996 *Baseball Research Journal*. Thompson examined various

Table 1.1.   Christy Mathewson's Won-Lost Records, 1901–1904

Year	W	L	Pct.	Team W	L	Adj. Pct.	NWP
1901	20	17	.541	52	85	.320	.662
1902	14	17	.452	48	88	.324	.595
1903	30	13	.698	84	55	.563	.654
1904	33	12	.733	106	47	.676	.589

KEY: W = wins; L = losses; Pct. = winning percentage; NWP = normalized winning percentage (.500 + [(Pitcher Pct. - Team Pct.)/2 x (1.000 - Team Pct.)])

accounts about who taught Mathewson the pitch and determined that David O. Williams, a southpaw who pitched briefly in the majors, had the best claim. Williams's obituary in the April 25, 1918, *Hibbing Daily Tribune* (Minnesota) discusses his early baseball career in Pennsylvania, stating, "It was here that Williams taught Christy Mathewson, now manager of the Cincinnati nine, the 'fadeaway,' one of the freaks of the pitching art." This corroborated a claim made by Mathewson himself, in an article entitled, "How I Became a Big League Pitcher" in the May 1912 issue of *St. Nicholas Magazine*. Discussing his 1898 efforts for a semipro or amateur team in Pennsylvania, Matty writes, "In Honesdale, there was a left-handed pitcher named Williams who could throw an outcurve to a right-handed batter. Williams exhibited this curve as a sort of 'freak delivery' in practice, over which he had no control. He showed the ball to me and told me how to throw it." Research by Honesdale resident Keith Sutton shows that Christy Mathewson and Dave Williams were teammates on the 1898 Honesdale club.

Of course, it makes for a better story that Matty was taught the pitch by a Negro leagues' Hall of Famer, rather than a guy who pitched only 19 big-league innings. But, as Thompson writes,

> Foster's role is nothing more than a fable. . . . The Dave Williams who played for Boston in 1902 taught Christy Mathewson the fadeaway at Honesdale, Pennsylvania, in 1898. Matty said so, so did Williams. Fact must always remain more important than fascinating legend to true historians.

Concessionaire Harry M. Stevens, with Help from a Cartoonist, Introduced the Hot Dog

Famous concessionaire Harry M. Stevens is credited with introducing baseball's most popular stadium food. As Linda Stradley retells the story in her website, What's Cooking America:

> [T]he term *hog dog* was coined in 1902 [or 1907, by some other sources] during a Giants baseball game at the New York Polo Grounds. On a cold April day,

concessionaire Harry Mozley Stevens (1855–1934) was losing money trying to sell ice cream and ice-cold sodas. He sent his salesmen out to buy up all the dachshund sausages they could find and an equal number of rolls. In less than an hour, his vendors were hawking hot dogs from portable hot water tanks while yelling, "They're red hot! Get your dachshund sausages while they're red hot!" In the press box, sports cartoonist T. A. "Tad" Dorgan (1877–1929), a newspaper cartoonist for the *New York Evening Journal*, was nearing his deadline and desperate for an idea. Hearing the vendors, he hastily drew a cartoon of a frankfurter with a tail, legs, and a head, so that it looked like a dachshund. Not sure how to spell the word *dachshund*, he simply wrote "hot dog." The cartoon was a sensation, and the term *hot dog* was born.

Stradley also relates a rival claim, which credits Adolph Gehring for introducing wurst in a bun at a St. Louis game in 1903. But the canine terminology was in use long before either of these examples. For example, in the October 5, 1895, issue of Yale University's *Yale Record* appears this poem about a popular lunch wagon that sold sausages in buns:

Echoes from the Lunch Wagon

'Tis dogs' delight to bark and bite,
Thus does the adage run.
But I delight to bite the dog
When placed inside a bun.

As baseball historian and longtime Stevens attorney Larry Boes reports, Tad Dorgan wasn't even employed by the *New York Evening Journal* in 1902. Furthermore, *Dictionary of American Regional English* editor Leonard Zwilling found that the term *hot dog* was in print more than a decade before Dorgan first used it—and that Dorgan's earliest usage of the term was in relation to an event at Madison Square Garden, not the Polo Grounds.

Even Stevens himself didn't take credit for the innovation, although he kept it in the family. In a 1926 interview, Stevens said the following:

I have been given credit for introducing the hot dog to America. Well, I don't deserve it. In fact, at first I couldn't see the idea. It was my son, Frank, who first got the idea and wanted to try it on one of the early six-day bicycle crowds at Madison Square Garden. I told Frank that the bike fans preferred ham and cheese. He insisted that we try it out for a few days, and at last I consented. His insistence has all Americans eating hot dogs.

The World Series Was Named after a Newspaper

According to most sources, the World Series was born in 1903, when the NL's Pittsburg (no "h" in those days) Pirates played the American League's

(AL) Boston club (now known as the Red Sox) in a postseason series of games. Some say a newspaper, the *New York World*, sponsored the early championship games, which were named in honor of the paper.

The Fall Classic actually has roots going back nearly two decades before 1903, and the *New York World* had nothing to do with it. The AA (1882–1891) was a forerunner of the AL as a rival major league to the NL. Starting in 1884, the champions of each league met in a postseason series. The NL's Providence Grays swept the AA's New York Metropolitans that year to become what the *Sporting Life* called the "Champions of the World" (not as pretentious a claim in those days, since the United States was the only nation playing organized baseball). The rest of the press followed suit, thus labeling the games the "World's Championship Series," sometimes shortened to "World's Series." These series were played through 1890; the AA disbanded a year later.

As described earlier, the World's Series was resumed in 1903 and, after a hiatus the next year, became a permanent event (excepting the 1994 strike) in 1905. The apostrophe-s gradually disappeared (although it was still in some usage as late as the 1960s), with the event thus becoming the "World Series."

The late baseball historian Doug Pappas describes the *New York World* of a century ago as a "tabloid much given to flamboyant self-promotion." Nevertheless, not even they suggested any responsibility for the World Series' name. Pappas reviewed every issue of the paper for the months leading up to both the 1903 and 1905 Fall Classics and found no hint that the *New York World* was in any way linked with the World Series.

Dummy Hoy, a Deaf-Mute, Created Umpires' Hand Signals

What is history but a fable agreed upon?

—Napoleon

Umpires have been using hand signals to indicate balls and strikes and "safe" and "out" calls for more than a century. A common legend attributes this innovation to William Ellsworth "Dummy" Hoy, a fine deaf-mute big-league outfielder for 14 years. "Hoy was the reason umpires developed hand signals for outs, strikes, balls, fouls, et al.," according to *Sports Collectors Digest*. "Umpires began to use hand signals for his benefit in 1886." The *Sporting News* agrees that Hoy "was responsible for the system of hand signals universally adopted by umpires." The book *Baseball by the Rules: An Anecdotal Guide to America's Oldest and Most Complex Sport* (1987) states that, "he persuaded the authorities to introduce hand signals." A 1987–1988 off-Broadway

HOY, C. F. Washington

OLD JUDGE
CIGARETTES.
GOODWIN & CO., New York.

Figure 1.2.   Dummy Hoy, Hero to the Deaf Community.
Source: Library of Congress

play, *The Signal Season of Dummy Hoy*, was based on this legend. In reality, umpires' hand signals came about several years after Hoy retired and were designed for the benefit of fans.

Hoy did indeed rely on hand signals, but they came from his third base coach, not the umpire. According to the April 7, 1888, edition of the *Washington Evening Star* (Washington, D.C.), "When he bats a man stands in the captain's box near third base and signals to him decisions of the umpire on balls and strikes by raising his fingers."

Hoy died at age 99 in 1961. It was some time after that his supposed connection with umpire's hand signals began circulating. It probably started upon the release of the classic oral history *The Glory of Their Times: The Story of the Early Days of Baseball Told by the Men Who Played It* (1966), by Lawrence S. Ritter. In the book, the aging Sam Crawford recalls that Hoy "was the one responsible for the umpire giving hand signals for a ball or strike."

But, a thorough check of Hoy's voluminous clipping file at the National Baseball Library turns up only one article written during Hoy's long lifetime that mentions anything about hand signals. In *The Silent Worker*, April 1952, Hoy states that the "coacher at third kept me posted by lifting his right hand for strikes and his left for balls. This gave later day umpires an idea, and they now raise their right . . . to emphasize an indisputable strike." This indicates that this practice was adopted *after* Hoy's career, and, as far as we know, Hoy merely *assumed* that his coaches' signals were the inspiration for this idea.

The 1909 *Spalding's Official Base Ball Guide* provides more evidence against the Hoy myth. In a full-page essay entitled "Semaphore Signals by the Umpires," it is stated that,

Two or three years ago base ball critics in the East and West began to agitate the question of signaling by the umpires to announce their decisions. At first, the judges of play did not want to signal . . . now there is not an umpire [who doesn't use his] arms to signal. If he did not, two-thirds of the spectators in the immense crowds would be wholly at sea as to what was transpiring on the field.

There is no mention of Hoy, who had retired from pro baseball only five years earlier, in the essay.

NL umpires Bill Klem (who began his big-league career in 1905) and Cy Rigler (who started a year later) have both been credited with the innovation. Another source credits a fan, General Andrew Burt, who suggested the idea to AL president Ban Johnson in the first decade of the twentieth century. Klem's Hall of Fame plaque states that he was "credited with introducing arm signals indicating strikes and fair or foul balls." According to the May 1, 1905, edition of the *Evansville Courier*, Rigler introduced the practice in a Central League game there the previous day: "One feature of Rigler's work yesterday that was appreciated was his indicating balls by the fingers of his left hand and strikes with the fingers of the right hand so everyone in the park could tell what he had called." In a 1985 article in the *National Pastime*, Dan Krueckeberg asserts that, "When Rigler entered the National League a year later [September 27, 1906], he found that his raised-arm call had preceded him and was in wide use."

The idea actually preceded him by several years. The *Sporting Life* of January 27, 1900, announced the following:

A NOVEL IDEA, a Plan to Help Umpires for the Better Enunciation of Their Decisions. One of the disagreeable features that patrons of base ball are compelled to suffer is to listen to umpires with unintelligible voices, umpires from whose lips come the words, "strike," "ball," "foul," and others, with a mushy coating that makes them all sound alike, much to the disgust and confusion of the spectators in the stands. Mr. Warren J. Lynch, general passenger agent of the Big Four road, who is an enthusiast of the game, suggests *an idea* that will do away with the confusion occasioned by umpires of uncertain articulation. Mr. Lynch suggests that umpires shall call out when a ball is pitched and raise their right hands when a strike is pitched and raise their left hands in case of a foul. The system would be a simple one and would be certain to do away with the confusion that now follows the efforts of the umpire—although there is a question as to whether he really makes an effort—to inform the spectators just what the pitcher is doing. Close students of the game find *much interest* in following the balls and strikes as they are called on the batsmen. It adds greatly to the enjoyment that cannot be fully realized under existing conditions, and [that] could be brought about completely by the adaptation of the method suggested by Mr. Lynch.

The February 3, 1900, *Bangor Daily Whig and Courier* (Maine) comments on the proposal, which they said was "for the purpose of conveying [an umpire's] decisions to the spectators at games who occupy seats out of hearing of his voice." Interestingly, the article quoted Hoy, saying,

I think the idea is a splendid one. Such a rule, if established, will please not only the patrons of the game, but also the players. By reason of the distance the outfielders do not always hear the rulings of the umpires. The same thing applies to the occupants of the distant parts of the stands. . . . I have often been told by frequenters of the game that they take considerable delight in watching the coacher signal balls and strikes to me, as by those signals they can know to a certainty what the umpire with a not too overstrong a voice is saying.

But the idea did not become a reality that year.

There were apparently plans to try such a system as early as 1901. In the September 14 installment of that year, the *Sporting Life* reports that,

> Noiseless umpiring is to be attempted at [the Chicago White Sox] South Side park Monday afternoon. Impossible as this may seem at first hearing, it is to be attempted, and there are even bets that it will be a go. George W. Hancock, famed in Chicago as the man who invented indoor base ball [forerunner of softball], will be responsible for the success or failure of the scheme. The umpire is to wear a red sleeve on the right arm and a white one on the left; for an out [sic] he will hoist the right arm, for a ball the other. People at the far end of the park, unable to hear even that human buffalo, [AL umpire Jack] Sheridan, can see the colors, and there seems a good chance for the trick to make a hit.

However, the White Sox didn't play on any Monday afternoon after September 14 in 1901, and there is no indication that the colorful scheme was ever tried in the majors. And Hoy, a member of the White Sox that year, is not mentioned in the article.

The *Sporting Life* (March 30, 1907), reprinting an article from the *Chicago Tribune*, reports that,

> The *Tribune*'s agitation for a system of umpire's gestures to indicate decisions seems to be as far-reaching as popular. Chief Zimmer has been using signs for balls and strikes and delighting New Orleans [Southern Association] patrons. Today Collins, who officiated here, adopted the same system and used it successfully, with the result that the crowd forgave him for not calling everything the local twirler, pitched a "strike." To date [veteran NL arbiter] Hank O'Day appears to be the only opponent of the idea.

But, on April 12, 1907, in notes from Opening Day, the *Cincinnati Commercial-Tribune* reported that "Hank O'Day used the arm signals yesterday, and they were satisfactory. He raises his left hand for a ball. In case he raises neither hand, it is a strike." The *Chicago Tribune* of April 14, 1907, notes that,

> There is nothing but this habit of looking at baseball matters through the umpire's eyes to explain the failure of the big-league presidents to answer the public's demands by instructing their umpires to adopt a simple code of signals to indicate doubtful decisions on pitched balls, the same as on base decisions. The umpires objected to being overworked by the necessity of moving an arm to indicate a "strike." Consequently the public must continue to guess, until electric score boards are installed and perfected, and then miss some of the play while studying the score board.

The next day's *Chicago Tribune* reported that NL umpire Bill Carpenter had been a big hit with the fans by raising his right hand to indicate strikes. So, obviously, umpires' hand signals were in mass usage by 1907, although standardization was lacking.

There was at least one instance of umpires' hand signals being used in the minor leagues long before this. It involved a deaf player—but not Hoy. Ed Dundon, who had pitched in the major leagues in 1883–1884, was the innovator. The November 6, 1886, edition of the *Sporting News* reports that,

> Dundon, the deaf and dumb pitcher of the Acid Iron Earths, umpired a game at Mobile between the Acids and Mobiles, on October 20. . . . He used the fingers of his right hand to indicate strikes, the fingers of the left to call balls, a shake of the head decided a man "not out," and a wave of the hand meant "out."

The October 30, 1886, issue of the *New York Clipper* concurred with the description, saying, "Dundon, the deaf-mute pitcher, umpired a game in Mobile, Alabama, and gave entire satisfaction."

Frank Hough, in the December 27, 1909, *Philadelphia Inquirer*, recalls that 1880s umpire John Gaffney used crude hand signals to indicate balls and strikes. Peter Morris, in his *A Game of Inches*, also cites Gaffney as one of the umpires who used signals for the benefit of Paul Hines, who gradually lost his hearing during his 1872–1891 career. Morris also relates the story of AA umpire Robert McNichol, forced to use hand signals for the last two innings of an August 11, 1883, game after he was hit in the throat by a foul tip and lost his voice.

In a letter to the *New York Sun* in April 1889, two writers debated the merits of signaling umpires' calls. James Sullivan suggests that the umps use hand signals, but John Rooney argues that, "The umpire has enough to do in watching the game," saying he would resemble a "jack-in-the-box" if forced to use the system proposed by Sullivan. Rooney favored having someone using a "pleasant-sounding gong" to relay the ump's decisions.

And, the idea of umpires' signals was suggested even long before this. In a letter to the editor published in the March 27, 1870, *New York Sunday Mercury*, Cincinnati Red Stockings' manager Harry Wright writes,

> There is one thing I would like to see the umpire do at [a] big game, and that is, raise his hand when a man is out. You know what noise there is always when a fine play is made on the bases, and it being impossible to hear the umpire, it is always some little time before the player knows whether he is given out or not. It would very often save a great deal of bother and confusion.

There is no indication that Wright got the idea from seven-year-old Ohioan Billy Hoy. The consensus is that standardized umpires' hand signals first appeared in the big leagues around 1906, give or take a year. And Dummy Hoy, who last played in the majors in 1902, had nothing to do with them.

Nick Altrock Won a Game without Pitching a Ball

On May 1, 2003, Baltimore pitcher B. J. Ryan got credit for a win without throwing a pitch. He entered the game with two outs in the seventh inning, Baltimore losing 2–1, and Detroit rookie Omar Infante taking a big lead off first base. Ryan promptly threw over to first, and Infante was caught trying to advance to second, ending the inning. The O's scored three runs in the top of the eighth to take a 4–2 lead, and then Buddy Groom took over Baltimore's pitching chores. The Orioles held on to win, and, consistent with the scoring rules, Ryan was credited with the pitching victory—even though he hadn't pitched. This helped exhume the oft-told story that Nick Altrock was credited with a win without throwing a pitch, under almost identical circumstances, supposedly with the White Sox in 1906. This feat has been described in many sources, including "Ripley's Believe It or Not."

Trying to document this feat is a hard task. Record keeping was sloppy in the early part of the 20th century, when Altrock did most of his pitching. No official records survive for Nick's pre-1905 seasons, so we have to rely on the quasi-official "ICI" records (produced by 1960s computer nerds at Information Concepts, Inc.). The AL's official sheets for 1905 through 1972 were composed in longhand and are difficult to read, especially a century later. From 1905 through 1907, the AL didn't bother recording pitching lines on their official sheets, just dates and wins or losses. There are errors and discrepancies galore.

These are just stumbling blocks for an obsessive researcher, however. The following are my findings for each of the nine seasons Altrock is credited with at least one victory:

- 1898, Louisville (NL): Won three games, on July 21, August 15, and September 4, pitching at least eight innings each time. He had no appearances of less than one inning.
- 1903, Chicago (AL): Won five games, on July 16, August 4, August 20, September 22, and September 28. The first of these appearances was one and two-thirds innings, and the rest were nine each; he had no appearances all year of less than one inning. The *ESPN Baseball Encyclopedia* credits Altrock with only four wins that year.

- 1904, Chicago (AL): Won 20 games (*ESPN Baseball Encyclopedia* says 19), on April 16, April 20, May 1, May 23, May 26, May 29, June 2, June 15, June 24, June 27, July 1, July 9, July 26, July 30, August 6, August 10, August 25, September 5, September 21, and October 9. The June 2 win was five and two-thirds innings, the rest were nine each. He had no appearances with less than three innings.
- 1905, Chicago (AL): Won 24 games (*ESPN Baseball Encyclopedia* says 23), on April 16, April 28, May 14, May 19, May 26, June 7, June 10, June 25, July 4, July 6, July 21, July 24, August 14, August 22, August 25, August 27, September 8, September 14, September 17, September 20, September 25, September 27, and October 7. He pitched one inning on June 10 (with two strikeouts and a hit allowed) and one and one-third on September 20; the rest of the wins were complete games. The official sheets say he also pitched and won (with four fielding chances) on September 10, but he didn't; perhaps that accounts for the revision of his win total.
- 1906, Chicago (AL): Won 20 games, on April 20, April 22, April 26, April 29, May 24, June 16, June 18, June 20, June 23, June 28, July 4, July 11, August 16, September 9, September 12, September 14, September 16, September 24, September 25, and October 1. He pitched five innings on April 22, four on June 18, seven on June 23, seven or eight on August 16, and six on September 25; the rest were complete games.
- 1907, Chicago (AL): Won eight games (*ESPN Baseball Encyclopedia* says seven), on April 18, April 24, May 2, May 18, May 21, September 4, September 20, and September 28. All were complete or near-complete games; he had only one game with an assist as his only fielding chance but had two at bats in that game.
- 1908, Chicago (AL): Won three games (*ESPN Baseball Encyclopedia* says 5), on July 7, July 16, and July 25; there is also a handwritten note that says "6/7 win." Each of these four was nine innings or more. This is the only season in which the *ESPN Baseball Encyclopedia* credits him with more victories than the official sheets, leaving the possibility of the legendary win being among his other appearances; however, he had no games with fewer than four opposing batsmen.
- 1909, Washington (AL): Won one game, on July 7 (nine innings), and had no games with fewer than three opposing batsmen.
- 1918, Washington (AL): Won one game, on June 6 (seven and one-third innings), and had no games with fewer than three opposing batsmen.

Based on this research, we can't be 100% certain that Altrock's batterless win didn't happen, but I'm 99% certain that it didn't. Maybe it occurred in an exhibition game, or a minor league contest, or in the mind of a creative writer, but there's no evidence it happened in a major league game.

Besides Ryan, there have been at least four pitchers to get credit for a win without throwing a pitch:

1. In the second game of a Labor Day twin bill on September 7, 1914, Jim Bluejacket of the Brooklyn Federal League team performed the feat against Pittsburgh. According to the next day's *Brooklyn Eagle*, "Blue jacket (sic) did not pitch a single ball to a Pittsburg (sic) batter, but even at that he gets credit for winning the second game. He entered the fray in the eighth inning, with Monasky (sic) [Mike Menosky] on third and [Steve] Yerkes on first. Bringing his Indian cunning into play, he caught Yerkes napping off first and ended the inning. In the last half of the same round the local team scored the five runs that won the game."

2. On May 5, 1966, the Astros' Frank Carpin entered a 3–3 game against the Cubs in the top of the 13th inning, with runners on first and second. The runners promptly pulled off a double steal before Carpin threw a pitch. The dust had barely settled when the runner on third broke for the plate; Carpin stepped off the rubber and threw the runner out at home. Houston then scored in the bottom of the frame to give Carpin his final big-league victory.

3. On July 1, 1970, the Angels' Greg Garrett inherited a 2–1 deficit against the Brewers with two out in the sixth inning. Garrett promptly picked Tommy Harper off first base to end the frame. The Angels scored three in the top of the seventh, one on an RBI single by Bill Voss, batting for Garrett. Eddie Fisher hurled the last three innings to save the 4–3 victory for Garrett.

4. On July 7, 2009, the Rockies' Alan Embree entered a 4–4 game against the Nationals with two out in the eighth inning. Embree picked Austin Kearns off first, and the Rockies scored the go-ahead run in the bottom of the frame. Huston Street then pitched a scoreless ninth for the save.

Honus Wagner Objected to Tobacco Products

The most valuable baseball card in existence is the "T-206" Honus Wagner tobacco card. This item was produced in 1909, as part of a set of baseball cards distributed with various brands of American Tobacco Company cigarettes. A single Wagner card was recently auctioned for a price of $1,265,000.

HENRY RECCIUS

MANUFACTURER OF

Hans Wagner – 10c Cigar

Koda ✿ Bowler ✿ Our Favo
Farmers' and Gardeners' Fav
5c Cigars

Figure 1.3.   Obviously, Honus (or Hans) Wagner Was Not Averse to Endorsing Tobacco Products.
Source: National Baseball Hall of Fame Library, Cooperstown, New York

Although there are scarcer cards, only a few dozen of the Wagner cards are known to exist. This limited supply, combined with Wagner's greatness and popularity, make the card such a precious commodity. So few of them were produced because Wagner ordered production of the card halted. Why? Legend has it that the genteel sportsman objected to tobacco products.

The truth of the matter is that Wagner was a notorious user of both chewing tobacco and cigars. Among the many adjectives used to describe Wagner in *Superstars of Baseball* (1994, by Bob Broeg, a personal acquaintance of Wagner's) are "tobacco-gnawing" and "cigar-puffing." And, Wagner not only used tobacco products, but he also endorsed them. As shown in the figure 1.3, Henry Reccius of Louisville, Kentucky, manufactured the "Hans Wagner 10¢ Cigar," advertising the item with a likeness of Wagner in uniform. As the December 6, 1950, issue of the *Sporting News* points out, "It was quite a distinction for a sports personality to have a cigar named after him years ago, and Honus Wagner was one of the few who received this honor."

So, why *did* Wagner put the kibosh on the T-206 card? Some suggest the true reason was that he wasn't getting enough royalties.

Honus Wagner Viciously Tagged Out Ty Cobb on a Steal Attempt in the 1909 World Series

The 1909 World Series was ballyhooed as the meeting of each league's outstanding player: the Pittsburgh Pirates' veteran, gentlemanly 35-year-old shortstop, Honus Wagner, and the Detroit Tigers' prodigious, vicious 22-year-old outfielder, Ty Cobb. The two went on to combine for more than 7,500 hits and 1,600 stolen bases, along with 20 batting titles, with Cobb breaking many of Wagner's career records. Wagner came out on top in this matchup, however, outhitting the Georgia Peach, .333 to .231, and outstealing him, six to two, to pace the Pirates' World Series victory over the Tigers.

The tone was set in the first game, according to baseball lore. Here's the story, as told in Bob Broeg's *Superstars of Baseball*:

> When Ty Cobb reached first base the first time at Pittsburgh's brand new Forbes Field in the 1909 World Series, the fiery Detroit star cupped his hands and shouted to the Pirates' shortstop, "Hey, Krauthead, I'm coming down on the next pitch."
>
> "I'll be waiting," Wagner answered Ty the Terrible. In this first and only confrontation between players regarded by many as the best each major league ever has developed, Cobb came off a painful second best.

When Ty slid into second, spikes high, Wagner was there not only holding his ground to make the putout, but applying the tag so forcefully, trying
to stuff the ball down tyrannical Ty's throat, that Cobb wound up with a
lacerated lip.

This is a great story, but pure fiction. Cobb rarely reached first base during the World Series and didn't have many chances to steal, but he was
never thrown out trying. He was twice retired at second base during the
Series, but both were force-outs, not tag plays. Table 1.2 is a rundown of
Cobb's 29 plate appearances during the 1909 World Series and his base
running exploits, if any.

Table 1.2. Ty Cobb's 29 Plate Appearances during the 1909 World Series

G #	Inn.	Batting Result	Base Running Result
1	1	Walked*	Advanced to second on force-out; scored on single
	3	Grounded out	
	5	Reached on force	Stole second; stranded there
	7	Flied out	
2	1	Grounded out	
	3	Walked*	Advanced to third on double; stole home
	5	Grounded out	
	7	Singled	Retired at second on double play
3	1	Struck out	
	4	Grounded out	
	6	Reached on force	Forced out at second
	7	Singled*	Stranded at first
	9	Doubled*	Stranded at second
4	1	Hit by pitch	Reached second on error after caught in rundown; stranded
	3	Bunted out	
	4	Doubled	Stranded at second
	7	Bunted out	
5	1	Flied out	
	3	Grounded out	
	6	Singled	Scored from first on double
	8	Grounded out	
6	1	Struck out	
	3	Popped out	
	5	Grounded out	
	6	Doubled*	Stranded at second
7	1	Flied out	
	3	Grounded out	
	6	Grounded out	
	8	Flied out	

KEY: G # = World Series game number; Inn. = inning; * denotes a runner already occupied the next base

I did consider the possibility that the story is true, except that Cobb was *safe* on the play in question. Cobb did steal second in the fifth inning of Game 1. Certainly, had there been any trash talk between the two superstars, or any bloody injury resulting from the play, the press would have mentioned it. But they didn't, as proven by perusal of the *Sporting Life* and *Spalding's Official Base Ball Guide*. Ty Cobb may have been shown up by Honus Wagner in the 1909 World Series, but he wasn't beaten up. Cobb, in his own autobiography, dismisses the myth as well, expressing only respect for the great shortstop: "Spike Honus Wagner? It would have taken quite a foolhardy man."

Figure 1.4. Ty Cobb and Honus Wagner, Friendly Rivals.
Source: Library of Congress

In defense of Broeg, this story probably originated from Wagner himself. As the author says in the same book, "Separating fact from fancy about Wagner . . . is like trying to determine the veracious from the fallacious in the yarns the old man used to tell in those happy later years when he was a Pittsburgh landmark as a coach." According to Broeg, Wagner was once called for bluffing by a young teammate. Wagner replied, "That may be so, sonny, but I never told you anything that you can't repeat to your mother."

Tinker, Evers, and Chance Were a Great Double Play Combo

These are the saddest of possible words: "Tinker to Evers to Chance."

—columnist Franklin P. Adams

The second-most famous baseball poem of all time (after "Casey at the Bat") was penned by Franklin P. Adams in 1910. It reads as follows:

"Baseball's Sad Lexicon"

These are the saddest of possible words:
"Tinker to Evers to Chance."
Trio of bear cubs, and fleeter than birds,
Tinker and Evers and Chance.
Ruthlessly pricking our gonfalon bubble,
Making a Giant hit into a double—
Words that are weighty with nothing but trouble:
"Tinker to Evers to Chance."

Adams, a newspaperman, had moved from Chicago to New York (home of the Cubs' archrivals, the Giants) six years earlier. He was trying to fill up some column space for the *New York Evening Mail*, when he came up with this little ditty. He could never have dreamed that it would become a baseball poetry standard and help send Tinker, Evers, and Chance into the Baseball Hall of Fame.

Shortstop Joe Tinker (no "s" on his name), second baseman Johnny Evers (pronounced EE-vers), and first baseman Frank Chance played together in Chicago from 1902 through 1912. The Cubs won four pennants during that span, with the Giants also winning four (the teams finished one-two in five of those seasons). The three players were elected to the Hall of Fame together by the Hall's Old-Timers' Committee in 1946, certainly in large

Table 1.3.   Batting Statistics for Joe Tinker, Johnny Evers, and Frank Chance

Player	G	AB	R	H	HR	AVG
Joe Tinker	1,806	6,441	774	1,690	31	.262
Johnny Evers	1,784	6,137	919	1,659	12	.270
Frank Chance	1,288	4,299	798	1,274	20	.296

KEY: G = games played; AB = times at bat; R = runs scored; H = hits; HR = home runs; AVG = batting average

part due to the Adams poem. It has been suggested that the poet deserved enshrinement more than the players.

Tinker, Evers, and Chance were all solid players, but they were hardly immortals in their own rights. Table 1.3 gives their batting statistics. Combined, they accounted for 4,623 hits—barely more than Pete Rose had by himself—and a modest .274 batting average. Ah, but surely they were a great double play combination, as the poem attests.

Wrong. The trio of bear cubs played regularly as a double play combo for eight seasons, from 1903 to 1910. *The Cubs never led the NL in double plays during that period.* In fact, they never even finished second. Table 1.4 details the double play totals for the Cubs, the league leader, and the average of the eight NL teams during that span (disregarding the fact that the Cubs allowed fewer base runners than other NL teams in this era, thus presenting fewer double play opportunities).

Clearly, Tinker, Evers, and Chance were a more-or-less average double play combination who stuck together for a long time. As renowned baseball analyst and author Bill James says, "Tinker to Evers to Chance surely was not the greatest double play combination of all time, and probably was not the best in baseball at that time. They were good, but they were B/B+ good, not A/A+ material." But, perhaps because their names roll off the tongue better

Table 1.4.   Double Play Totals for the Cubs, the League Leader, and the Average of the Eight NL Teams, 1903–1910

Year	Cubs	NL Rank	Leader	AVG
1903	78	7th	111, Cardinals	90
1904	89	5th	93, three teams	89
1905	99	T-4th	122, Reds	100
1906	100	3rd	109, Pirates	93
1907	110	3rd	128, Braves	101
1908	76	3rd	90, Braves	75
1909	95	6th	120, Reds	99
1910	110	5th	137, Braves	117
AVG	95	5th	114	95

than "Wagner, Abbatichio, and Swacina," Tinker, Evers, and Chance gained immortality as a great double play combo.

Ty Cobb Psyched Joe Jackson Out of a Batting Title

I won a league batting championship that it seemed I was about to lose.

—Ty Cobb

Ty Cobb entered the 1911 season having won four straight batting crowns and a reputation as the most heartless man in pro baseball. This season, Cobb had a new challenger for the former title, in the person of Joseph Jefferson Jackson. Shoeless Joe, in his first full season, blasted the ball at a .408 clip, but Cobb set a career high at .420 to retain the crown. According to Cobb, in his 1961 autobiography *My Life in Baseball: The True Record*, with Al Stump, there was more than batsmanship involved:

I won a league batting championship that it seemed I was about to lose. With the 1911 season about finished, Shoeless Joe Jackson of Cleveland topped me nine points in the average; [it appeared] my string of four straight batting titles would be broken.

Jackson was a Southerner, like myself, and a friendly, simple, and gullible sort of fellow. On the field, he never failed to greet me with a "Hiyuh, brother Ty!"

So now we were in Cleveland for a season-closing six-game series, and before the first game I waited in the clubhouse until Jackson had taken his batting practice.

Ambling over, Joe gave me a grin and said, "How's it goin', brother Ty? How you been?"

I stared coldly at a point six inches over his head. Joe waited for an answer. The grin slowly faded from his face to be replaced by puzzlement.

"Gosh, Ty, what's the matter with you?"

I turned and walked away. Jackson followed, still trying to learn why I'd ignored him.

"Get away from me!" I snarled.

Every inning afterward I arranged to pass close by him, each time giving him the deep freeze. For a while, Joe kept asking, "What's wrong, Ty?" I never answered him. Finally, he quit speaking and just looked at me with hurt in his eyes.

My mind was centered on just one thing: getting all the base hits I could muster. Joe Jackson's mind was on many other things. He went hitless in the first three games of the series, while I fattened up. By the sixth game I'd passed him in the averages. We Tigers were leaving town, but I had to keep my psychological play going to keep Jackson upset the rest of the way.

So, after the last man was out, I walked up, gave him a broad smile and yodeled, "Why, hello, Joe—how's your good health?" I slapped his back and complimented him on his fine season's work.

Joe's mouth was open when I left.

Final standings: Cobb, .420 batting mark, Jackson, .408.

About the only accurate sentence in this account is the last one. Cobb had a double-digit lead in the batting race throughout the latter part of the season, the teams had no six-game series to end the campaign, and Jackson outhit Cobb in the last series they played against one another. Through September 9, Cobb was at .420 (213-for-507), Jackson at .406 (199-for-490). The Indians and Tigers played at Detroit on September 10, and at Cleveland on September 12 and September 13, the first time the teams had met since July 2. Cobb went 7-for-17 in the three games, merely holding his average at .420; Jackson had a hit in each game, but his 3-for-11 dropped him to .403. The teams parted until October 2, when they met at Detroit for another three-game series, the next-to-last series of the season for each team.

Cobb entered the series at .422 (245-for-580), Jackson at .407 (227-for-558). They played a game on October 2, and two on October 4. Cobb went 0-for-3 in the opener, while Jackson went 1-for-3. In the following double-header, Cobb went 3-for-7, Jackson 2-for-6. At the end of the day, Cobb's average was .420, Jackson's was .406.

The Tigers then hosted the St. Louis Browns for a season-ending four-game series, October 6 and 7 and two on October 8. Cobb didn't play in any of the games. Meanwhile, Jackson and the Indians entertained the White Sox for their final three games, two on October 7 and one on October 8. Jackson played in only one of the games and went 3-for-4 to finish at .408.

Cobb told a similar story 36 years earlier, but the details were quite different. In the 1925 book *Batting*, by F. C. Lane, Cobb says the following:

I remember, I think it was in 1916, that Joe Jackson started out at a tremendous pace. He was going to get me that year sure. He came into the clubhouse and told me he was going to get me. I laughed at him, whereupon he grew earnest and offered to bet. "All right, Joe," said I. "I will bet you $500 that I beat you out this season." He thought it over for a minute, but he didn't bet. That game I believe I made two or three hits, and he made but one. Next day I walked over to the bench where he was sitting. He spoke to me, but I did not answer him. I knew he would be puzzled. A little later I walked over again. I thought he might have imagined I didn't hear him speak, so I looked at him, straight in the eye, until I got very close. He spoke to me again, but I made no reply. . . . And he didn't make any hits at all that game. The final game, I walked over with a broad smile, clapped him on the back, and said, in the most friendly way, "Joe, Old Boy, how are you?" This seemed to astonish him more than anything else. All the rest of that season I had his goat, and I beat him out by 40 points.

Surely this story, just nine years after the fact, would hold up to investigation—but it doesn't. In 1916, Cobb batted .371 to Jackson's .341—and Tris Speaker unseated Cobb as the batting champ with a .386 mark. There was no other year in which Cobb beat out Jackson by 40 points, or anything within ten of that number.

Cobb's Tigers and Jackson's White Sox began the 1916 season in a four-game series (April 12–15) against one another; Cobb went 4-for-15 (.267), and Jackson was 5-for-13 (.385). By the time the two teams met for another four-game series a week later, Cobb had slipped to .231 (6-for-26) and Jackson to .300 (9-for-30). Surely this couldn't be the "tremendous pace" Cobb mentioned. Cobb went 3-for-4 in the opener, raising his mark to .300 and then sat out the next three games; Jackson was 2-for-15 in the series.

By the time the two teams reunited for another four-game set starting on Memorial Day, Cobb had boosted his average to .331 (45-for-136), while Jackson's had stagnated at .267 (36-for-135). Cobb was 5-for-15 in the series—but Jackson went 12-for-15. A month later, the teams met for yet another four-game series, June 29 through July 2. By this time, Jackson had opened up a nice lead over Cobb, .373 (85-for-228) to .345 (78-for-226). Could this be where Cobb wove his spell?

If he did, it must have had a delayed effect. Cobb went 4-for-13 in the series, while Jackson was 6-for-12. But by the time the teams met again on July 23 and 24, Cobb led, .356 (110-for-309) to .346 (113-for-327). Jackson went 3-for-11 in the two games; Cobb didn't play.

The Tigers and Sox were at it again from August 11 through August 13. Entering the series, Cobb led Jackson, .353 (129-for-365) to .347 (145-for-418). Cobb was 3-for-12, Jackson 3-for-9. The season's final game between the two teams was on September 2, by which time Cobb led by ten points, .363 (159-for-438) to .353 (172-for-487). Cobb went 1-for-4, Jackson 2-for-4. For the season, Cobb hit a modest .317 (20-for-63) against the White Sox, while Jackson batted a blistering .418 (33-for-79) against the Tigers. As is so often the case, the "True Record" from the memory of a former ballplayer does not hold up to historical scrutiny.

This is not the only story in the Stump biography that has been dismantled. In one of the most sensational, Cobb claims to have killed a man while defending himself in a 1912 mugging, but in a 1996 *National Pastime* article,

Doug Roberts proves that this could not have happened. In the 2010 *National Pastime*, William R. Cobb (not a descendant of Ty's) devotes 18 pages to investigating the book and the coauthor, concluding that Al Stump was a "proven liar, proven forger, likely thief, and certainly a provocateur who created fabricated and sensationalized stories."

Old-Time Relief Pitchers Were Nothing More Than Washed-Up Starters

> The only way you're ever going to see the ninth inning is . . . as a relief pitcher.
>
> —A's manager Dick Williams, to pitcher Rollie Fingers, c. 1971

The popular notion that old-time relief pitchers were nothing more than washed-up starters has some basis in fact, but is far from the whole truth. Aging or marginal starters were frequently used in mop-up roles, but critical relief appearances—including "save" situations—were typically entrusted to ace starting pitchers. For example, the first three men to reach double figures in the save column were Hall of Fame starters still in the prime of their careers: Mordecai "Three Finger" Brown, Ed Walsh, and Chief Bender.

Brown shattered the record of eight when he notched 13 saves for the 1911 Cubs. It was the fourth straight season he had led the NL in that category, while compiling won-lost records of 29–9, 27–9, 25–14, and 21–11. Walsh reached ten while going 27–17 for the White Sox in 1912. It was the fifth time he had led the AL in saves. And Bender recorded 13 saves to go along with 21 wins for the 1913 Philadelphia A's. Brown retired in 1916 with a record 49 career saves, safely ahead of second-place Walsh (35) and third-place Bender (32).

It should be noted that "saves" were not officially recorded before 1969; however, researchers for the first edition of Macmillan's *Baseball Encyclopedia* compiled them retroactively for pre-1969 pitchers. The criteria were very lenient, though; all a reliever had to have done was finish a winning game (whether it be 3–2 or 23–2) without earning the win himself, and he was awarded an ex post facto save.

The first true closer was Frederick "Firpo" Marberry of the Washington Senators. In each of his first three full seasons, from 1924 to 1926, Marberry led the AL in both games and saves, and he upped the career saves record to 101 before he was through. But Marberry wasn't a washed-up starter, either; he was a 25-year-old rookie on a championship team.

Thanks in part to Marberry's success, the practice of using top starters as bullpen aces declined in the 1920s. The practice had a resurgence in the 1930s, when the Depression cut roster sizes, and such eminent starting hurlers as Lefty Grove, Carl Hubbell, and Dizzy Dean led their leagues in saves in different years. The practice was still around as late as the 1950s, when the Yankees' Allie "Superchief" Reynolds often put out fires between starts.

The fact is, using unsuccessful starters as relief aces is a relatively recent phenomenon. Most of the great relievers of the 1950s through the 1980s who did try their hands at starting were utter failures in that role: Former all-time saves leader Lee Smith was 0–5 with a 4.62 ERA as a starter; Hall of Famer Goose Gossage was 9–22, 4.49; and Hall of Famer Rollie Fingers was 7–17, 4.12. Some other bullpen heroes who struggled as starters included Elroy Face (8–13, 4.92), Mike Marshall (5–14, 4.95), Tug McGraw (7–23, 4.77), Lindy McDaniel (22–31, 4.65), and, more recently, Mariano Rivera (3–3, 5.94) and Eric Gagne (10–13, 4.70). In fact, until 1988, not a single pitcher with 150 or more career saves was above .500 as a starter.

Grover Land Hit a 65-Foot Home Run

One of the oddest home runs in major league history, according to baseball lore, was hit by Grover Land and traveled only about 65 feet. The feat has been described in the *New Baseball Catalog* and *USA Today Baseball Weekly* (December 5, 2000), among other places. In a Federal League game in 1914 or 1915, according to the story, there was only one umpire on hand for a game involving Land's Brooklyn team. In such a situation, the ump normally stationed himself near the pitcher's mound, so he could call balls and strikes, as well as plays on the field. On this hot day, the arbiter was growing weary of having to jog to the sidelines for new baseballs every time one was hit out of play. Finally, he gathered a bunch of balls and set them up in a neat pile behind the mound.

Land proceeded to hit a shot into the pyramid of spheres, scattering them like a rack of pool balls. Grover circled the bases as the opponents and umpire tried to ascertain which was the actual ball in play. The ump had no choice but to award Land a home run.

The only problem with the story is that Grover Land, in 910 at bats over parts of seven seasons, never hit a major league home run. The Federal League also operated as a nonmajor outlaw circuit in 1913, but Land played for Toledo (AA) and Cleveland (AL) that year. Rob Neyer pursued the possibilities that Land was actually credited with a double or triple, or that the game failed to go into the books due to a protest, but came up empty.

Incidentally, those same *New Baseball Catalog* and *USA Today Baseball Weekly* articles describe another "strange but true" home run, hit by Jimmy McAleer. The ball supposedly got stuck in a tomato can in the outfield, and McAleer scored before outfielder Hugh Duffy could retrieve and return the ball (still in the can) to home plate. Strange but untrue. McAleer was credited with only 11 homers in his career, just two (September 10, 1892, and May 30, 1896) of which were hit against Duffy's teams. Neither of those are listed in the Society for American Baseball Research's Home Run Log as inside the park, and the *Sporting Life* didn't find either homer worthy of mention in their game accounts.

Christy Mathewson Died as the Result of a Gassing Incident in World War I

> A simple story, however inaccurate, is preferred to a complicated explanation, however true.
>
> —baseball author Leonard Koppett

Beloved Hall of Fame pitcher Christy Mathewson died on October 7, 1925, at the tender age of 45. Neither his good looks, his education, nor his athleticism could spare him from tuberculosis (TB). It is said that Matty's lungs had been weakened by a gassing incident during World War I; however, there is no evidence of a particular incident, and, in fact, it appears that the story is based almost entirely on his wife's amateur medical opinion.

Mathewson resigned as manager of the Reds on August 27, 1918, to accept a U.S. Army post. While traveling to Europe, he contracted the flu (a deadly disease at the time) and also got horribly seasick. Mathewson was stationed in France as a captain until 1919, when he returned to baseball as a Giants' coach (he had been formally replaced as Reds' manager on January 30, 1919, when he failed to answer a cable). Matty's health problems became so bad by July 1920, that he went to Saranac Lake for recuperation. That's where he died five years later.

Christy's widow, Jane Stoughton Mathewson, offered her opinion as to the source of her husband's health woes, saying the following:

> I think the beginning of it was in France. . . . He had influenza there. Besides, as assistant gas officer to the 28th Division, he demonstrated lethal gas shells to the students and inhaled much of the gas. When he came back, the first severe cold he developed settled into a cough he could not shake off. In the summer of 1919 he developed a strange lassitude that he could not shake off.

Actor and baseball researcher Eddie Frierson—creator of the critically acclaimed one-man show *Matty: An Evening with Christy Mathewson*—has another theory, saying, "I find it odd that he himself never mentioned that as the cause—even while sick and giving detailed interviews late in his life," reports Frierson. "I am 99% positive that he had the bug years before going to war." Matty's effectiveness had dropped noticeably starting in 1914, due to mysterious pain in his left (nonpitching) side, one his doctors—suspecting a muscular problem—couldn't pinpoint. Three years later, Christy's brother Hank died of TB. Frierson has discussed this at length with TB experts, who unanimously theorize that the pain was caused by a lesion rubbing on the inside of Matty's rib—in other words, that he already had TB then, four years before he ever set foot in France. It then lay dormant for a number of years, they speculate, until it was revived by the stress of managing, travel, war, the flu, losing his job, or any one or more of a number of things.

But, that's not the version you'll find in the history books. Christy Mathewson, the All-American Boy, was a casualty of war. It appears that the press latched onto Mrs. Mathewson's diagnosis and put it in the books.

Charles Comiskey Gypped Ed Cicotte out of a 30-Win Season and Bonus

Eddie Cicotte won 29 games for the White Sox in 1919, leading the team to the AL pennant. But Cicotte also led the team's surprising loss in that year's World Series to the Reds, dropping two games in the midst of what became known as the Black Sox Scandal. According to the book *Eight Men Out: The Black Sox and the 1919 World Series* (1963), part of Cicotte's motivation to throw the World Series was the Sox' penny-pinching team owner, Charles Comiskey. Comiskey supposedly promised Cicotte a $10,000 bonus if he won 30 games in 1917, but Comiskey kept Cicotte out of the rotation at the end of the season, grounding him at 28 victories that year (the movie version moves the bonus offer to 1919).

There is no evidence in Cicotte's transaction cards (donated by Major League Baseball to the National Baseball Hall of Fame in 2002) or the contemporary *Chicago Tribune* of such a bonus, and it is incredible just at face value. In the final season of a three-year pact, Cicotte was earning just $5,000 per annum in 1917, and had never won even 20 games in a season, let alone 30.

A bigger problem with this story is that the AL did not even keep track of pitchers' wins and losses in those years. According to *Total Baseball*,

In 1913, [league president] Ban Johnson not only proclaimed the ERA (earned run average) official, he became so enamored with it that he also instructed

American League scorers to compile no official won-lost records. This state of affairs lasted seven years, 1913–1919.

(Of course, the records have been calculated retroactively since then.) In other words, it is not likely that Cicotte or Comiskey even knew how many wins he had in 1917 or 1919, let alone that any bonus would have been offered for reaching a certain victory total.

Through August 22, 1917, Cicotte lost four straight decisions, giving him an 18–11 record. The White Sox had only 34 games to play, so certainly no one was thinking of Cicotte as a candidate to win 30 games at that point. But Eddie went on a roll. Over the next 25 days, he won eight straight games, including two victories in long relief; however, when he lost his next game, September 19 against the last-place A's, his record stood at 26–12 and the Sox had just ten games to go. With the pennant virtually decided, there was no reason for Cicotte to pitch in more than two of those games—and that's how many he pitched, winning both of them to finish 28–12. Cicotte wound up pitching 19 more innings than any other pitcher in the league; there is no evidence that he was being denied a chance to win 30 games.

In 1919, however (by which time Cicotte's salary was still just $952.50 per month, equivalent to $5,715 for a full season), Cicotte spent two weeks on the bench in September. After a sloppy victory (six walks) over Cleveland on September 5, he did not pitch again until September 19. The *Cleveland Plain Dealer* reported on September 17 that Cicotte "told friends that it [his arm] was not lame, but very tired." Following his return, the *Sporting News* quoted Cicotte as saying that his "arm has responded to rest and treatment the last two weeks." Cicotte got two starts following his 29th victory on September 19. On September 24, Eddie was roughed up for 11 hits and five earned runs in seven innings against the Browns, escaping with a no-decision. On September 28, he hurled just two innings against Detroit in a World Series tune-up. Again, there is little evidence that Comiskey tried to prevent Cicotte from reaching 30 wins by benching him in September. And even if he did, it would be a stretch to use that as an excuse to justify Cicotte's role in the fix, since the conspiracy was probably hatched in August.

The Reds Hit an Inordinate Number of Triples toward Joe Jackson's Position in the 1919 World Series

Shoeless Joe Jackson and seven of his teammates were banned from baseball for allegedly conspiring with gamblers to throw the 1919 World Series. In what has been dubbed the "Black Sox Scandal," the heavily favored White

Sox lost to the Reds, five games to three (the World Series was best of nine from 1919 to 1921). Defenders of Jackson point out that he led all World Series batters in hits, homers, batting, and slugging, while fielding 1.000. Others have picked apart Jackson's performance, claiming he did not hit in the clutch and that he may have made misplays in the field that were not scored as errors.

Lloyd Johnson makes this claim in Bill James's *The Baseball Book* (1990), saying, "During the series, *three* triples were hit to left field where Jackson was playing. (Triples normally are rarely hit to left field; almost all triples go to right field and right-center.)" In fact, the Reds' three-baggers were hit where "almost all triples go." In *Burying the Black Sox: How Baseball's Cover-Up of the 1919 World Series Fix Almost Succeeded* (2006), Gene Carney describes (from contemporary newspaper accounts) each of the Reds' seven triples in the 1919 World Series, writing the following:

> Game One, 4th inning: Dutch Ruether's tremendous drive to left center bounced back off the temporary wire fence into [center fielder Happy] Felsch's hands.
>
> Game One, 7th: Jake Daubert caught one on the end of his bat and hit it so far to right field that it hopped into the crowd on the first bound. This was a ground rule triple.
>
> Game One, 8th: Ruether slugged a wonderful drive far over Felsch's head, which rolled clear to the concrete wall in deepest center.
>
> Game Two, 4th: Larry Kopf hammered the first ball for a clean three-bagger to left center.
>
> Game Five, 6th: Edd Roush whaled the ball over Felsch's head for three bases. Hap misjudged the ball, then let the ball trickle off his left hand.
>
> Game Six, 4th: Shano Collins overran [Greasy] Neale's safe hit to right field and the ball rolled far enough to give the batter a triple.
>
> Game Eight, 5th: Kopf smashed a triple to right field, the ball eluding [Chick] Gandil.

There may have been a few suspicious triples by the Reds in that World Series (both Felsch and Gandil were also named in the conspiracy), but it doesn't appear that Jackson had anything to do with them. Incidentally, it is commonly said and written that baseball's first commissioner, judge Kenesaw M. Landis, punished Jackson and the other Black Sox by "banning them from baseball for life." In fact, all Landis said was that nobody accused of such deeds would *play* pro ball. His edict, delivered hours after the Black Sox were acquitted of conspiracy in a court of law in 1921, was as follows:

Regardless of the verdicts of juries, no player that throws a ball game; no player that undertakes or promises to throw a ball game; no player that sits in a conference with a bunch of crooked players and gamblers where the ways and means of throwing games are planned and discussed, and does not promptly tell his club about it, will ever play professional baseball.

And, since all of the Black Sox players are long dead, yet still theoretically on baseball's "Ineligible List" (see page 176), the ban has proven to be much longer than "for life."

CHAPTER TWO

~

The Truth about Ruth

I always thought Babe Ruth was a cartoon character. I really did.

—Don Mattingly, upon being compared to former Yankees' stars

More than six decades after his death, George Herman "Babe" Ruth remains the best-known figure in baseball history. Although many of his records have been surpassed, some—like his .690 career slugging percentage—remain unapproached. It should not be necessary to make up stories about someone like that, yet nobody in the annals of the game has spawned more mythology.

The Owner of the Red Sox Sold Ruth to Finance His Theatrical Production, *No, No, Nanette*

New York theater owner and producer Harry Frazee owned the Boston Red Sox from November 1, 1916, until July 11, 1923. He and his partner, Hugh Ward, acquired the team for $1,000,000 in the midst of a dynasty—four world championships in seven years—and sold it for $1,150,000 as a last-place club beginning a historic run of futility. Frazee dismantled the team during this period, trading and selling off most of his best players, mostly to the Yankees. The biggest deal of this series was announced on January 5, 1920: the sale of Boston superstar Babe Ruth to the Yanks for the unheard-of price of $100,000, plus a $300,000 loan. Legend says Frazee did this to finance his theatrical production, *No, No, Nanette*.

While Frazee did sell off his stars and finance productions, the sale of Ruth had nothing to do with bankrolling *No, No, Nanette* or any other play.

41

That musical debuted in 1924—nearly five years after the sale of Ruth, and more than a year after Frazee sold the Red Sox. Until three decades ago, the prevailing Boston lament was to the effect of, "If only *No, No, Nanette* had come along a few years earlier, the Red Sox could have afforded to hold on to Ruth and others and remained a contending team." But, in August 1979, award-winning writer Jim Murray mangled the story, writing that the Ruth sale was made to finance *No, No, Nanette*. It was repeated that November in Joe Giuliotti's Red Sox beat column in the *Sporting News* and has been floating around ever since.

It is likely that Murray was inadvertently twisting something he read in a book published in 1979. George Sullivan's *The Picture History of the Boston Red Sox* details the "Rape of the Red Sox," including Frazee's sale and trade of such stars as Ernie Shore, Duffy Lewis, Dutch Leonard, Carl Mays, Babe Ruth, Waite Hoyt, Wally Schang, Harry Hooper, Everett Scott, Joe Bush, Sam Jones, Stuffy McInnis, Roger Peckinpaugh, Muddy Ruel, and Herb Pennock in a four-year span. "Ironically," writes Sullivan, "his financial crisis passed the year after he sold the Sox. One of his stage productions struck it rich as an international success. *No, No, Nanette* would net him more than $2 million."

But, by the end of the 1910s, Frazee was struggling just to retain ownership of the Boston club. Despite fielding a world championship team, he lost money in 1918. The schedule was cut from 154 games to 126 due to World War I, and Boston's home attendance plunged 36%. The World Series attendance was just 128,483 in six games, down 45% from 1917. Then, despite Ruth's heroics in 1919 (a record-breaking 29-homer season, not to mention a 9–5 pitching log), the team sunk to a 66–71 record in another shortened season, its worst finish since 1907.

"There is no getting away from the fact that despite his 29 home runs, the Red Sox finished sixth last year," Frazee pointed out, calling Ruth's dingers "more spectacular than useful." Frazee added that, "What the Boston fans want . . . is a winning team, rather than a one-man team that finishes in sixth place."

In addition, the baseball owners were facing $864,000 in settlements and judgments due as the result of the 1913–1915 Federal League's antitrust lawsuit. Frazee claimed that previous owner Joseph Lannin was responsible for the Boston club's share (between $50,000 and $70,000) of this amount, under a "hold harmless" clause of the 1916 contract for preexisting indebtedness. Lannin disagreed.

Furthermore, Frazee's purchase of the team in 1916 was encumbered by a $262,000 note held by Lannin and secured against Fenway Park. The note came due after the 1919 season, and Frazee initially defaulted on it. To add to all this, Frazee had overdrawn his salary and owed the Red Sox more than $11,000. And he needed $100,000 to put down on purchase of the Harris Theatre in New York.

Meanwhile, Ruth, following his record-breaking year, was asking that his salary be doubled to $20,000, notwithstanding the two years remaining on his three-year contract. Frazee was counseled by manager Ed Barrow, later to join the Yankees himself after the 1920 season, not to cave in to Ruth. If the reserve clause fell with the Federal League case on appeal, Boston's contract with Ruth might prove worthless, anyway. And, with Ruth's excessive lifestyle, there was concern that he would flame out before too much longer. "Ruth had become simply impossible, and the Boston club could no longer put up with his eccentricities," said Frazee after the deal. "I think the Yankees are taking a gamble." Although the quote would come back to haunt him, many baseball observers agreed at the time.

The Yankees, on the other hand, were not suffering as much as other teams. Having legalized Sunday baseball, their 1919 home attendance was 619,164, just shy of the league high and 48% more than the Red Sox total. And so, in December 1919, Frazee sold Ruth's contract for the record-breaking sum of $100,000: $25,000 down and the remainder to be paid with $10,000 interest over three years. But the key for Frazee was Yankees' owner Jacob Ruppert's loan of $300,000, to pay off the mortgage debt to Lannin, with the loan again secured by the Fenway property. It was a deal that Frazee believed he had to make to save his ownership of and investment in the team.

Ironically, the Red Sox rose one notch in the standings in 1920, while the Yankees remained in third place. But the long-term effect of the shift of stars from Boston to New York was profound. While the Yankees won pennants more often than not, the Sox wouldn't win another flag until 1946, or another World Series until 2004. As the years rolled on, some pointed to the Ruth sale as the start of this futility record, dubbing it the "Curse of the Bambino."

The "curse" itself has qualities of myth. When the Sox finally returned to the World Series in 1946, they lost it in seven games to the Cardinals. Over the next half century, the Red Sox made it to the postseason six more times but were beaten at the end each time, including three more heartbreaking seventh-game Fall Classic defeats. But was it a curse, or was it because the teams they played were simply better? Judge for yourself:

Table 2.1. **Red Sox Records versus Records of Teams Played**

Year	Series	Boston Record	Opponent	Record	Difference
1967	World Series	92–70	Cardinals	101–60	−9½
1975	World Series	95–65	Reds	108–54	−12
1986	World Series	95–66	Mets	108–54	−12½
1988	ALCS	89–73	Athletics	104–58	−15
1990	ALCS	88–74	Athletics	103–59	−15
1995	ALDS	86–58	Indians	100–44	−14

Ruth Replaced George Halas as the
Yankees' Right Fielder

What Hall of Famer did Babe Ruth replace as the Yankees' right fielder? The supposed answer to this trick question is George Halas. "Papa Bear," who went on to a long career as an NFL player, coach, and executive, landing him in the Pro Football Hall of Fame's inaugural class, played right field for the Yankees in 1919, the year before Ruth joined the team. The trivia question is even trickier than we thought: It's not accurate.

Halas made his big-league debut for the Yankees on May 6, 1919, and he played right field in four games over the next week, going 2-for-17. After that, he was relegated to the bench, pretty much limited to eighth- or ninth-inning appearances. Halas participated in just nine more games in his career (not eight, as the record books show): five as a pinch hitter, three as a pinch runner, and one as a right fielder, remaining in another game in center. He went 0-for-5 in those appearances, dropping his career average to .091, and his last game was on July 5, 1919. The Yankees' principal right fielder throughout that season was Sammy Vick, who played 100 of the team's 141 games at that position. Vick remained on the Yankees through the 1920 season (51 games) before being traded to the Red Sox.

And, while Ruth was mainly a right fielder, he saw a lot of action at other positions, too. In 1920, he played 85 games in right, 36 in left, 20 in center, two at first base, and one as a pitcher. In his career, Ruth played almost as many games in left field (1,057) as in right (1,131). The Yankees would station him wherever the sun was the least problem: right field at Yankee Stadium, left in most other parks.

The Yankees Adopted Pinstripes to
Make Ruth Look Slimmer

Babe Ruth was dealt from the Red Sox to the Yankees in 1920. Legend has it that the Yanks adopted pinstripes to make their portly new star appear slimmer. According to *Baseball: The Biographical Encyclopedia* (2000), Jacob Ruppert, Yankees' owner from 1915 to 1939, "designed the Yankees' distinctive uniform to hide Babe Ruth's increasing girth." This repeated a claim in Robert Creamer's 1974 book, *Babe: The Legend Comes to Life*: "Because of Ruth's bulk, Ruppert decided to dress the Yankees in their now traditional pinstripe uniform. The natty, clothes-conscious Ruppert felt that the new uniform would make Ruth look trimmer."

In reality, Ruth was still a solidly built athlete when he joined the Yankees, packing a modest 198 pounds on his 6-foot, 2½-inch frame. He often reached double figures in triples and stolen bases. He didn't let himself go to pot until the mid-1920s, when physical problems caused him to miss 58 games at the age of 30. A renewed fitness program enabled the Babe to shed most of the unwanted pounds and regain his status as baseball's dominant slugger.

And the pinstripes? The Yankees adopted them in 1912, when Ruppert was a Manhattan congressman and Ruth was still a teenager in reform school.

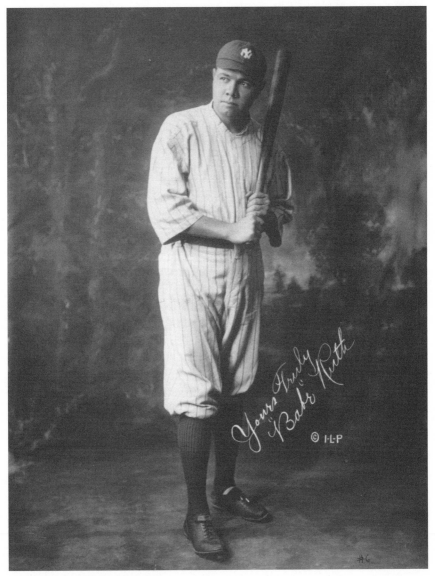

Figure 2.1. Not Much Baby Fat on the Young Babe.
Source: Library of Congress

The Baby Ruth Candy Bar Was Not
Named after the Yankees' Slugger

The Baby Ruth candy bar has been popular for nearly a century. One might think that it was named after slugger George "Babe" Ruth, but the manufacturers (the Curtiss Candy Company) have long insisted that wasn't the case. They say the name was inspired by President Grover Cleveland's daughter, Ruth, who was born in 1891 while Grover was in the White House.

However, the candy bar was introduced in 1921, when Babe Ruth was approaching the peak of his fame, and some 17 years after Ruth Cleveland died of diphtheria at the age of 12. There is no reasonable doubt that the bar was named after the baseball Babe, and it would seem that the manufacturers were trying to avoid paying him royalties. Curtiss filed for a federal trademark for Baby Ruth in December 1923, and the company secured it in May 1924. Ironically, when Babe Ruth introduced his "Babe Ruth's Home Run Bar" in 1926, Curtiss brought a trademark interference claim against his company, prevailing in 1931.

In more irony, Nestle USA, which now owns Baby Ruth, has had some joint marketing ventures with Major League Baseball. And Babe Ruth's name is licensed by the Curtis Management Group.

Ruth Won Only One MVP Award in His Career

It has often been noted that the great Babe Ruth won only one MVP Award in his 22-year career. Even when the Babe hit 60 homers in 1927, it was teammate Lou Gehrig who walked home with the award. The implication is that Ruth, despite his staggering statistics, was not considered by the experts as such an asset to his team.

Perhaps someone forgot to tell you that Ruth was not even eligible for the 1927 award, and, in fact, that he was really eligible for only two MVP Awards before his 36th birthday. The first version of the AL MVP Award was the Chalmers Award, starting in 1911. The next was the American League Award (1922–1928). Finally, in 1931, came the Baseball Writers' Association of America's MVP Award—the version still in existence today.

The Chalmers Award was discontinued in 1914, the same year Ruth played in four games as a 19-year-old recruit. For the next seven seasons, there was no MVP Award. If there had been, Ruth would have been a contender for all seven, and a certain winner of a few:

- 1915: As a rookie pitcher for the world champion Red Sox, Ruth not only posted an 18–8 record with a 2.44 ERA, but he batted .315 and led the team with four home runs.

- 1916: Ruth was the ace of another world championship team, going 23–12 and leading the AL in games started (41), shutouts (9), and ERA (1.75). He again was tops on the team in homers, with three.
- 1917: The Babe led the league with 35 complete games, while going 24–13 with a 2.01 ERA for the second-place Sox. He also batted .325, the best on the team.
- 1918: In perhaps the greatest double-duty season ever, Ruth led the AL with 11 homers and a .555 slugging percentage, while going 13–7, 2.22 on the mound. Boston won another world title.
- 1919: Ruth set a new record, with 29 home runs in a single season, also leading the league in total bases (284), runs (103), RBI (114), on-base percentage (.456), and slugging (.657). He even led league outfielders in fielding percentage (.996) and went 9–5 as a pitcher.
- 1920: Now with the Yankees, Ruth shattered his own mark, with 54 homers—more than any other AL *team*. He also topped the circuit in runs (158), RBI (137), walks (150), and OBP (.532), while posting the highest slugging percentage (.847) in the first 125 years of major league history.
- 1921: Ruth had arguably the best individual season in baseball history, setting modern records in runs scored (177), extra-base hits (119), and total bases (457). He also led the league in homers (59, another new record), RBI (171), walks (145), OBP (.512), and slugging (.846). The Yanks won their first pennant.

When the AL Award finally came into existence in 1922, Ruth had his worst season (although he still led the league in slugging), missing 44 games due mostly to a league suspension. He didn't get a single vote in the balloting, partly because voters could name only one player on each team. The Bambino made up for it in 1923, however, leading New York to its first world championship and earning unanimous selection for the AL Award.

And, in so doing, he disqualified himself from the next five trophies. A provision for the AL Award specified that no player could win it more than once. From 1924 to 1928, Ruth would have been a strong contender in all but one season (1925, when he missed 58 games due to illness and suspensions). Judge for yourself:

- 1924: Ruth led the AL in total bases (391), runs (143), homers (46), walks (142), batting (.378), OBP (.513), and slugging (.739). The AL Award went to Washington pitcher Walter Johnson, who posted a 23–7 record for the league champions, topping the circuit in wins, percentage (.767), shutouts (6), and ERA (2.72).
- 1926: Babe batted .372 and led the league in total bases (365), runs (139), homers (47), RBI (146), walks (144), OBP (.516), and slugging

(.737), as the Yankees won the pennant. The award went to first sacker George Burns, who batted .358 with four home runs for the second-place Indians, leading the league in hits (216) and doubles (64).

- 1927: Ruth again broke his own record by hitting 60 homers (including 17 in September), also leading the AL in runs (158), walks (137), OBP (.486), and slugging (.772). He hit .356 with 164 RBI as the Yankees won the world championship. Teammate Gehrig copped the AL Award after leading in total bases (447), doubles (52), and RBI (175). New York writers, seeking to rectify things, gave Ruth a special "Player of the Year" trophy.

- 1928: Ruth led the AL in runs (163), total bases (380), homers (54), RBI (142), walks (137), and slugging (.709), as the Yankees won another world title. The AL Award went to the second-place Athletics' catcher, Mickey Cochrane, who batted .293 with ten homers and 57 RBI.

There was no official AL MVP Award in 1929 or 1930, although Ruth finished in the top ten in unofficial polls both years. By the time the modern MVP Award came to be in 1931, Ruth was 36 and no longer *the* dominant player in the game. He finished fifth in MVP voting in 1931 and tied for sixth the following year, the last time he was mentioned in the balloting. So Ruth indeed won "only" one MVP Award in his career, but it could very easily have been six or eight.

Ruth Promised and Delivered a Home Run to Johnny Sylvester

Boy Regains Health as Ruth Hits Homers.

—headline in the *New York Times*

Babe Ruth was a one-man wrecking crew in Game Four of the 1926 World Series. In a game played at St. Louis on Wednesday, October 6, Ruth hit two-out solo home runs in the first and third innings, walked and scored in the fifth, hit a two-run blast in the sixth, and walked in the eighth, leading the Yankees to a 10–5 victory over the Cardinals that evened the Series at two games each.

Legend has it that Ruth promised a home run to an ailing boy, Johnny Sylvester. In the movie *The Babe Ruth Story*, Ruth (played by the athletically inept William Bendix) is shown visiting the boy in his hospital room and making the vow. When the Bambino delivered not just one but three homers, it inspired Sylvester's miraculous recovery.

There really was a sick boy named Johnny Sylvester, and he really was inspired by Ruth's exploits, but Ruth's contact with the boy was limited to an autograph on a baseball mailed from Missouri to New Jersey and received after Game Four was over. The legend owes its origin to an article that appeared in the October 8, 1926, edition of the *New York Times*. Datelined October 7, in Essex Falls, New Jersey, and headlined "Boy Regains Health as Ruth Hits Homers," the article reads in part,

> John Dale Sylvester, 11 years old, to whom physicians allotted 30 minutes of life when he was stricken with blood poisoning last week, was pronounced well on the road to recovery this afternoon, after he had contentedly listened to the radio returns of the Yankees' defeat of the Cardinals. His father, Horace Sylvester Jr., vice president of the National City Bank, and the physicians, are convinced that John owes his life to messages of encouragement [that] the boy received Wednesday from Babe Ruth and other world series (sic) players. They had learned of his plight and of his request for autographed baseballs from his father.
>
> The physicians say that the boy's return to health began when he learned the news of Ruth's three homers in the fourth game of the series. His fever began to abate at once, and the favorable course was hastened today after he had listened to the radio returns, clutching the autographed baseballs, which he received by air mail on Wednesday night.

Ruth Didn't Really Call His Shot in the 1932 World Series

Of course I didn't see him point. Nobody else saw him point, because he didn't. . . . Charlie would've thrown it right at his head. I knew that and so did all of the ballplayers.

—Dorothy Root, widow of pitcher Charlie Root

One of the most enduring legends in baseball history is Babe Ruth's "Called Shot." In the 1932 World Series, Ruth supposedly pointed toward the Wrigley Field fence and then deposited the next pitch over that very spot for his 15th and final Fall Classic home run. Some facts are clear: Ruth's Yankees were engaged in an acrimonious battle with the Cubs and had won the first two games at Yankee Stadium. Now in Chicago, Game Three of the World

Series was knotted at four in the top of the fifth inning, when Ruth—who had homered earlier in the game—strode to the plate to face Charlie Root.

This is where it gets a little hazy. Ruth evidently was the target of jeers and produce missiles and carried on some sort of pantomime act during his at bat. After taking one or two balls and two strikes, he made some sort of gesture and then hit a titanic home run over the fence in right center. But, what exactly was the gesture? There seem to be as many versions of the event as there were witnesses. The following is a sampling of quotes, most made decades after the fact:

- "Ruth pointed toward the center field fence, but he was pointing at the pitcher. . . . Someone asked him, 'Babe, did you call that home run?' Babe answered, 'No, but I called Root everything I could think of.'"— Yankees' teammate Ben Chapman
- "What Ruth did then was hold up his hand, telling them that was only two strikes, that he still had another one coming and that he wasn't out yet. When he held up his hand, that's where the pointing came in. But he was pointing out toward Charlie Root when he did that, not toward the center field bleachers. . . . I can tell you just what would have happened if Ruth had tried (calling his shot)—he would never have got a pitch to hit."—Cubs' second baseman Billy Herman
- "Ruth's finger just happened to be pointing to center field when he indicated he had one strike remaining."—Yankees' teammate Frank Crosetti
- "I really didn't notice it, but I seem to recall that the story originated in New York several days after the game."—*Chicago American* writer James Gallagher
- "I had a good friend who was at the game, and he swore to me later that Ruth pointed to the bleachers. 'Forget it,' I'd tell him, 'I don't want to hear about it.' . . . [Cubs' pitchers Guy] Bush and Bob Smith . . . tyrated (sic) Ruth because he had two strikes. They said 'What are you going to do now?' Then Ruth pointed his finger at the Cubs bench and said 'I've got the big one left.'"—Cubs' pitcher Burleigh Grimes
- "He held up those two fingers. He may have been pointing out to right-center field, but he was calling out, 'That's only two strikes, only two strikes.' He wasn't calling his shot, he was just holding up the two fingers, suggesting that he had one strike left."—Cubs' third baseman Woody English
- "[Cubs' pitcher Guy] Bush, leading the tirade from our bench, turned a blast on the Babe. . . . Babe pointed straight away and turned to-

ward our dugout—no doubt for Bush's benefit. . . . I hesitate to spoil a good story (but) the Babe actually was pointing to the mound. As he pointed, I heard Ruth growl [to Bush], 'You'll be out there tomorrow, so we'll see what you can do with me.'"—Cubs' first baseman–manager Charlie Grimm

- "The gestures were meant for Bush. Ruth was going to foul one into the dugout, but when the pitch came up, big and fat, he belted it."—Yankees' on-deck hitter Lou Gehrig
- "If he'd pointed to the bleachers, I'd be the first to say so."—Cubs' catcher Gabby Hartnett
- "Ruth did point, sure. He definitely raised his right arm. . . . He indicated (where he'd already) hit a home run. But as far as pointing to center, no he didn't. . . . You know darn well a guy with two strikes isn't going to say he's going to hit a home run on the next pitch."—Cubs' shortstop Mark Koenig
- "I'm not going to say he didn't do it. Maybe I didn't see it. Maybe I was looking the other way."—Yankees' manager Joe McCarthy
- "I thought Ruth raised his finger to indicate the number of strikes, and did not make a pointing gesture."—*Chicago Herald Examiner* writer Edgar Munzel
- "Of course I didn't see him point. Nobody else saw him point, because he didn't. . . . Charlie would've thrown it right at his head. I knew that and so did all of the ballplayers."—Dorothy Root, widow of Charlie Root and spectator at the game

Okay, so we're agreed that Ruth didn't really call his shot? Well, Munzel adds that sports editor Davis Walsh shouted, "Hey, he hit it exactly where he had pointed!" Photographic evidence shows that Hartnett's back was turned when Ruth made his gesture. And Gallagher's claim that the story was concocted several days later is belied by the next morning's newspapers:

- "Very soon the crowd was to learn its lesson. A single lemon rolled to the plate as Ruth came up in the fifth and in no mistaken motions, the Babe notified the crowd that the nature of his retaliation would be a wallop right out of the confines of the park."—*New York Times* writer John Drebinger
- "He pointed to the spot where he expected to send his rapier home."—*New York Daily News* writer Paul Gallico
- "Ruth Calls Shot as He Points Homer No. 2 in the Side Pocket."—*New York World-Telegram*

- "Babe Calls His Shots. . . . Then with a warning gesture on his hand to [the Cubs], he sent the signal for the customers to see. 'Now,' it said, 'this is the one.' And that one went riding in the longest home run ever hit in the park."—*Chicago Sunday Tribune* writer Westbrook Pegler

And, then there are these versions:

- "Ruth pointed with his bat in his right hand, to right field, not center field. But he definitely called his shot."—Yankees' teammate Lefty Gomez
- "At that point, Ruth stepped from the box, dusted his hands, and then raised his right arm, with one finger extended, in the now famous gesture. . . . At that moment, there was no doubt in my mind, or in the minds of any of the writers who were covering the Yankees. The Big Guy had done it again. He had called his shot, and in the most spotlighted arena imaginable."—sportswriter and future Major League Baseball commissioner Ford Frick
- "When Babe got back to the bench, [the Yankees' Herb] Pennock said, 'Suppose you would have missed. You would have looked like an awful bum.' Ruth . . . laughed. 'I never thought of that,' he said."—Yankees' trainer Doc Painter
- "Don't let anyone ever tell you that Babe didn't point. In our hotel room that night Babe told me what a sucker he had been to point. 'Look how many ways they could have gotten me out,' he said."—Yankees' coach Cy Perkins
- "Ruth had the bat in his left hand and I thought—now, I'm going to be honest with you—I thought he pointed to the right-center or center field bleachers. Charlie Root pitched the ball just as soon as Ruth stepped back into the box, and when he did, Ruth hit the ball clear out of the ballpark. . . . I believe that Ruth meant to call the home run. He was so mad, see. I believe that he pointed, and I'll always believe that he pointed."—Cubs' pitcher Guy Bush
- "Don't let anybody tell you differently. Babe definitely pointed."—Cubs' broadcaster Pat Pieper
- "Before the next pitch, the Babe stuck up his hand—elevated his arm with his palm up, pointing over Root's head out to the center field bleachers. The next pitch came in and he creamed it!"—Ray Kelly, Ruth's personal mascot
- "Now Babe raises that finger again and looks out at Charlie. He gets his sign from Gabby. Into the windup. Here's the one-and-two pitch.

A swing—a long drive. It's toward that center field corner. That ball [several syllables drowned out by crowd noise] out of Wrigley Field in almost the exact spot that Babe had been pointing to. . . . As he comes into third, he thumbs his nose in the direction of the Cubs' dugout."—sportscaster Quin Ryan's play-by-play of the incident

- "Yes, he pointed to the fence, and I have a mental picture of the ball going out of the park in center field, through a tree loaded with small boys seeing the game. I had just [made an out] and returned to the bench, got a drink of water. . . . Our old coach, Jimmy Burke, was fussing at Babe for taking the strikes, and I sat down by Jimmy. . . . Ruth, after two strikes, got out of the batter's box, dried his hands off, got back in the box with his bat in his left hand, and two fingers of his right hand pointed in the direction of center field, looking at the Cubs' bench all the time. Then, on the next pitch, he hit a low ball, like a golf ball, that rose all the way to the tree. . . . Regardless of what anyone says or writes, that is the way I saw it all happen. . . . I will always remember that Series, and that one special game."—Yankees' teammate Joe Sewell

But we no longer have to rely solely on the eyewitness accounts. Two home movie films of the event have surfaced in recent decades, one taken by Matt Kandle, the other by Harold Warp. Of course, there is no sound to accompany the grainy images, but Ruth clearly makes a cocking and pointing gesture of some sort just before hitting the mammoth home run. From the body language, one can easily imagine Ruth engaging in some trash-talk exchange with Root and his teammates, driving home his point with his finger—something along the lines of, "Just throw the damn ball in there and let's see what happens."

Did Ruth point to the outfield wall and announce, "I'm going to hit the next pitch over that fence"? Probably not. But he did make a brazen gesture toward his opponents and follow it up with a long, game-winning home run. That's about as close to a called shot as any of us will ever see.

CHAPTER THREE

~

The Lively Ball Era

Baseball saw a surge in scoring—and popularity—starting in the 1920s. The subject of the previous chapter had a lot to do with both, but he wasn't the only reason—and he wasn't the only one subject to mythology.

A Lively Baseball Was Introduced in the 1920s

> We are too much accustomed to attribute to a single cause that which is the product of several, and the majority of our controversies come from that.
>
> —Roman emperor Marcus Aurelius (A.D. 121–180)

In 1918, the penultimate year of the "Deadball Era," the major leagues averaged just 7.27 runs per game for all teams combined. Only 235 home runs were hit by the 16 teams. But, in 1920, those numbers leaped up to 8.72 runs per game and 630 homers. By 1930, they were up to 10.27 runs per game and 1,565 four-baggers. The entire National League, including pitchers, batted .303 that year. Any time there is a profound change in the sport's scoring patterns, the baseball itself becomes the focus of attention, and this era was no exception. Legend has it that a new, lively "rabbit ball" had been introduced to the bigs, leading to the hitter-happy 1920s and 1930s.

In fact, there was no substantial change to the ball. Tests conducted during the 1920s failed to reveal significant changes in its composition. For example, widely publicized experiments done by Columbia University professor Harold A. Fales (reported in the *New York Times* on July 16, 1925) concluded that 1914, 1923, and 1925 balls had similar elasticity. He did note the "tighter, thinner, and all but seamless cover" of the 1925 ball, whose countersunk seams prevented pitchers from getting a good grip on the sphere.

There were actually several factors that coalesced around 1920, changing the balance of power from the pitchers to the hitters, including the following:

- *Frequent replacement of baseballs.* Before 1920, a ball was typically used until it was literally falling apart. An average of fewer than ten balls per game were used, and, in at least one game (Reds 9, Cubs 6, June 29, 1913), a single baseball lasted the entire contest. The pellets became soft and discolored, difficult to hit with any authority. In 1920, umpires were instructed to replace balls more frequently. According to the *New York Times* of August 19, 1920, as the season progressed, the owners were concerned about the extra expense of using a lot of balls, and American League president Ban Johnson issued a notice ordering umpires to "keep the balls in the games as much as possible, except those [that] were dangerous." That was the case until the Indians' Ray Chapman was killed by a pitched ball that month. It was theorized that Chapman had a difficult time picking up the darkened ball in the afternoon shadows in New York. From then onward, umpires were instructed to replace scuffed and soiled balls at all times. As noted writer F. C. Lane observed in 1921, "several dozen balls are called into play in the course of a game where two or three would have sufficed when Christy Mathewson was in his prime." By 1931, AL records showed 17,772 balls used in 618 games, an average of 29 per game.

  A related change came about in 1921. Historically, fans were obliged to return foul balls hit into the stands, but that changed after an incident at the Polo Grounds on May 16 of that year. A fan named Reuben Berman was arrested when he refused to turn over a foul ball he retrieved, and he sued the Giants for $2,000. The case came before the New York Supreme Court on July 27, 1921, and Berman won. Soon afterward, fans in all big-league parks were allowed to keep balls hit into the stands. Batters were quick to take advantage of the new policy. In a 1921 *Atlanta Constitution* article, Cliff Wheatley notes that batters were deliberately fouling off pitches to get new balls put into play.

- *The Babe Ruth style of offense.* Thanks in great part to the usage of balls, the Deadball offensive philosophy was to go for one run at a time. There were bushels of sacrifice bunts and stolen base attempts. F. C.

Lane credited Ty Cobb as the leader of this style, saying, "Under his magnetic leadership, batters tried for safe hits rather than long hits. The concentration on batting average encouraged them in this. The records gave a man as much credit for a bunt that was beaten out by an eyelash as they did for a three-base hit." Babe Ruth almost single-handedly changed this approach. Ruth's batting heroics showed the effect of bunching runs on the scoreboard, both in respect to winning games and drawing fans. As Lane wrote in 1921,

every so often some superman appears who follows no set rule, who flouts accepted theories, who throws science itself to the winds and hews out a rough path for himself by the sheer weight of his own unequalled talents. Such a man is Babe Ruth in the batting world, and his influence on the whole system of batting employed in the major leagues is clear as crystal . . . almost every batter who has it in him to wallop the ball, is swinging from the handle of the bat with every ounce of strength that nature placed in his wrists and shoulders. . . . Ruth has not only slugged his way to fame, but he has got everybody else doing it. . . . Babe has not only smashed all records, he has smashed the long-accepted system of things in the batting world and on the ruins of that system he has erected another system.

And, perhaps not coincidentally, slugging percentage and RBI were adopted as official statistics in 1920.

Incidentally, there were considerably fewer pitches per game during the Deadball Era—not only because there were fewer batters reaching base, but there were fewer pitches per batter. A pitch-by-pitch analysis of the 1919 World Series, as compared to that of the 1997 Fall Classic, suggests that the modern game requires about 36% more pitches per contest. In other words, a pitcher who tossed 225 innings in 1997 threw about as many pitches as one who labored 305 frames in 1919. And the Deadball pitcher didn't have to give 100% on every pitch, because there was little fear of the long ball; he could pace himself and save his best stuff for the crucial batters and situations. The old-time pitchers didn't rack up so many innings and complete games because they were tougher, they did so because the game was easier.

- *Outlawing of the spitball and similar trick pitches.* During the Deadball Era, pitchers devised all sorts of freak pitches, using saliva, paraffin, resin, talcum powder, and emery boards, among other things, to deface the ball and make it break unpredictably. There were no rules against this until February 9, 1920, when the major leagues' Joint Rules Committee banned the pitchers' use of all foreign substances or other alterations to the ball.

Certain pitchers would be grandfathered and allowed to use the spitball for the remainder of their careers, but the overall effect was obvious.

• *Improved technology in ball making.* George Reach, head of the company that manufactured the official AL baseball, repeatedly denied that any deliberate alterations had been made since the introduction of the cork-center ball in 1910. "In all that time we have never been requested by the league officials to make any change whatever in the baseball we manufacture, nor have we made any changes of our own volition." Reach did say that, thanks to the end of material shortages caused by World War I and technological advances, "We are manufacturing the best ball now we ever made." Reach cited a higher grade of yarn (imported from Australia), which had more spring and could be wound tighter, coupled with mechanical improvements in the winding and sewing machines.

Center Fielder Johnny Mostil Caught a Foul Ball

Ty Cobb used to say that Chicago had two traffic cops and one outfielder, and all the "cops" would do would be to wave Mostil to come on through.

—White Sox player/manager Eddie Collins

Johnny Mostil played for the White Sox for parts of ten seasons and was their regular center fielder in all but one season between 1921 and 1928. Although he batted .301 lifetime and twice led the AL in steals, he is remembered mostly for his defense. Stationed between the slow-footed left fielder Bibb Falk and aging right fielder Harry Hooper, Mostil had to cover a lot of ground, and he did, leading the league in range factor in 1922, 1923, 1926, and 1928. To top it off, according to baseball lore, Mostil became the only center fielder ever to catch a foul ball.

Surely such a unique event would have merited contemporary press coverage, yet a look through Mostil's clipping file at the National Baseball Library reveals no contemporary references to such an event, and only two mentions at all. One is just an anonymous typewritten statement, reading, "Johnny Mostil, centerfielder of White Sox, is reported once to have caught a foul ball in an AL game while playing centerfield." Real hard evidence there! The other is in Mostil's December 26, 1970, *Sporting News* obituary, which reads,

It was in a minor league park in 1925 that he made one of the most unusual plays in baseball history—a center fielder catching a foul fly. During an exhibition in Nashville, Falk was playing left field, and he never won a foot race with anything or anybody. A long, high fly drifted over to the left field foul area, and Mostil took after it. Falk just watched, and Mostil kept running until he caught it.

The White Sox did play one preseason game in Nashville in 1925, on April 7, but neither the *Sporting News*, the *Chicago Tribune*, the *Chicago Daily News*, nor other sources, mention any notable play by Mostil in that game. At least two books repeat the story but place it in a different year and city. *The White Sox Encyclopedia* (1997), by Richard C. Lindberg, claims that "in a spring training game played in Birmingham in 1924, the fleet-footed Mostil snared a foul fly down the left field line—while playing center." In *Eddie Collins: A Baseball Biography* (2008), by Rick Huhn, Collins is quoted as saying, "In an exhibition game with Birmingham of the Southern Association, Johnny, a center fielder, actually caught a foul ball. Bibb Falk stepped aside to let him make the catch, and he got it."

However, Mostil was a holdout through most of spring training in 1924, and the White Sox did not play any preseason games in Birmingham that year. The *Sporting News* issues from March through mid-April of both 1924 and 1925 make no mention of a notable defensive play by Mostil in spring training in either year or in any city.

But wait, there's more! In Arch Ward's "In the Wake of the News" column of April 10, 1951, is yet another version:

> Ted Lyons, the Detroit coach, is telling scribes in the Tiger training camp that his old White Sox colleague, Johnny Mostil, was a better outfielder than Joe DiMaggio. In an exhibition in Nashville one day, Lyons offers by way of argument, Mostil, the center fielder, caught a foul in right field. The veteran Harry Hooper, assigned to right, told Mostil he had a charley-horse, adding: "Take anything you can get that comes out this way." Johnny got to a fly over the foul line.

Now we're back in Nashville—but in *right* field instead of left! And since Lyons debuted with the Sox in July 1923, and Hooper left after the 1925 season, that would suggest it happened in spring training of either 1924 or 1925, which we've already checked.

Last but not least, the May 6, 1963, edition of the *Christian Science Monitor* has a column by Ed Rumill, quoting Mostil at length about the play. Mostil said it happened at Nashville, in right field, where Hooper was stationed. "I didn't think anything about it at the time," Mostil concludes, "but Eddie Collins told the sports writers traveling with the team that it was a foul ball. Maybe it was. I wouldn't know. I was moving too fast."

Note that all of these detailed accounts were written decades after the fact, and all place the event in an exhibition game, not an official big-league game. Some have it happening in Nashville, some in Birmingham, some in left field, some in right. This has all the elements of a story that started out as, "With Falk and Hooper at his sides, one of these days Mostil is going to catch a foul ball!"—and over the years, people came to claim or believe it actually happened.

Of course, this doesn't prove that Mostil never caught a foul ball while playing center somewhere; you can't prove a negative. But it seems to indicate that, if he did, it did not happen in a major league championship game.

A Headache Cost Wally Pipp His Career

Practically everyone knows the story of Wally Pipp. The veteran first baseman took the day off on June 2, 1925, saying he had a headache, and rookie Lou Gehrig was inserted into his spot. Gehrig went on to play 2,130 consecutive games en route to the Hall of Fame, and Pipp's career was over. To this day, people in all walks of life express fear of taking a day off in fear of becoming another "Wally Pipp story." Pipp apparently created the story himself, telling it on the banquet circuit for decades. Like many baseball tales, it has ingredients of truth but is more fiction than fact: There is no mention in any contemporary account about a Pipp headache; Miller Huggins was simply shaking up the lineup of a slumping team. And Pipp was not pushed into retirement until three years later.

The 1925 Yankees were off to a terrible start, including five losses in a row through June 1. Babe Ruth had missed all of April and May due to a mysterious ailment, reportedly an ulcer, and the rest of the club was not picking up the slack. Pipp, the Yankees' first sacker since 1915, was among the slumping (three homers, .244 average), and manager Miller Huggins had already dropped him from fourth to sixth in the lineup. Wally was particularly ineffective against southpaws, like the Senators' scheduled starter on June 2, George Mogridge. According to the next day's New York Times, "Miller Huggins took his favorite lineup and shook it to pieces." Pipp (age 32) was replaced, but so were second baseman Aaron Ward (28) and catcher Wally Schang (35). On June 8, the New York Times reported that,

> Miller Huggins's withdrawal of Ward, Pipp, and the Schang-[Steve] O'Neill combination was an admission that the absence of Ruth was not the only thing wrong with the club. Not all of these men are through—Ward least of all, but they were in a slump, and Huggins did the obvious thing by injecting a little youth into the team.

John Kieran of the New York Herald-Tribune writes that, "The old order, as the late Lord Tennyson observed, yieldeth place to new, and the new sun rises, bringing in the new day." The *Sporting News* said that, "Huggins has arrived at the inevitable conclusion that he is carrying too many fading stars and that now is the time to lay a new foundation."

Gehrig, not yet 22, had played in 12 of the Yankees' 42 games before June 2, and his streak had actually started on the previous day, when he flied out as a pinch hitter. He went 3-for-5 on June 2, and didn't miss another game until 1939.

Pipp remained on the Yankees bench for the next month, until he suffered a fractured skull when hit by a pitch in batting practice on July 2 (there were no batting helmets in those days). No doubt this incident helped create the headache story. On February 1, 1926, the Yankees sold Pipp to the Reds, where he played 277 of 310 games in 1926–1927, before being phased out during the 1928 season. It was a Hall of Famer who pushed Pipp out to pasture, but it was George Kelly, not Lou Gehrig.

Babe Herman Tripled into a Triple Play

He never tripled into a triple play, but he once doubled into a double play, which is the next best thing.

—sportswriter John Lardner

In the two decades between their pennants of 1920 and 1941, the Brooklyn Dodgers were a pretty woeful team. They finished in the bottom half of the league 14 times in an 18-year span and became known as the "Daffiness Boys" for their entertainingly inept play. No incident better captured this mood than the one on August 15, 1926, when the Dodgers had three runners on base—the *same* base. Baseball lore has it that Babe Herman tripled into a triple play.

As the quote above indicates, it's well known by now that Herman's base-running blunder wasn't as bad as reported. It's not even unique; there have been several similar plays since. But, there are at least as many versions of the Herman incident as there were base runners that day.

It happened in the seventh inning of a 1–1 game against the Boston Braves. Brooklyn had Hank DeBerry on third, pitcher Dazzy Vance on second, and Chick Fewster on first with one out as Herman stepped to bat. This is where the story gets fuzzy.

According to the book *The Baseball Hall of Shame* (1985), Herman

lined a hard shot to right for a sure double, maybe a triple. . . . [Vance] held up until he saw the ball carom off the wall. He then headed for third with Fewster right on his heels. And behind them both, rounding second, came the galloping Herman, head down, arms pumping.

Coach Mickey O'Neill saw trouble brewing so he yelled at Herman, "Back! Back!" Vance thought the coach was talking to him, so he hustled back to third base just in time to meet Fewster arriving from second. Then Herman came sliding in and found himself hugging not only the bag, but Fewster and Vance as well.

Disgusted with the whole mess, Fewster walked off toward the dugout. . . . Third baseman Eddie Taylor . . . proceeded to tag everyone in the neighborhood. . . . Second baseman Doc Gautreau then grabbed the ball, chased down Fewster, and tagged him too. . . . The umpires ruled that Vance was safe at third since he got there first. Fewster was tagged out, and Herman was called out for passing Fewster on the base path.

Since there was one out before Herman batted, the double play ended the inning. And, since Babe had reached second base safely on his hit before the baserunning fiasco, he was credited with a two-base hit.

Another book, *Uncle Robbie* (1999), agrees with most of those details, except it says that, "Herman's drive hit the left field wall," and that Fewster was tagged out not on his way to the dugout, but to the outfield. "He went to retrieve his glove from behind second base. . . . [Gautreau] got the ball and chased Fewster, who ran zigzag patterns in the outfield trying to escape. He was finally cornered and tagged." For those wondering what Fewster's glove was doing in the field, until 1954 that's where players left them between innings.

An article by Herbert Simons in the January 1942 issue of *Baseball Magazine* has elements of both versions, with a different coach:

Herman sent a towering fly to right field. Because it was doubtful whether the ball would hit the fence or be caught, the runners held their bases. Nothing, however, could hold Herman. When the ball finally hit the fence, the other runners all broke. . . . Vance rounded third from second, and Fewster was on his way to third from first when Otto Miller, coaching at third, was astonished to see Herman, too, on his way to third. Frantically he shouted, "Go back." . . . Vance thought the order meant for him, and so, halfway home, he headed back for third. Fewster . . . bewildered by Vance's antics, pulled up a dozen feet short of third. Herman roared past him. Fewster shrugged his shoulders and started walking back for his glove. Gautreaux (sic) dashed over to third and tagged both Vance and Herman. The latter was out for conduct unbecoming a base runner in passing Fewster. . . . Vance was acquitted, however, and entitled to hold his base. . . . Fewster [was] out in the grass retrieving his glove for the next inning. Gautreaux immediately started after him, and the startled Fewster headed for the right field fence. He almost got there before Gautreaux tagged him for the final out of the inning, although technically, of course, he was out long before that for having run out of the baseline.

Beans Reardon, an umpire in the game, recalled the play in *The Men in Blue* saying the following:

> Now I got three men standing on third, and every one of them is being tagged. I said, "Damn it, wait a minute, I got to figure this out." Finally I said, "The bag belongs to Vance, so Fewster, you're out, and so are you, Turkey Neck [Herman], for passing the runner on the baselines. That's it. The side's out. Let's play ball, fellas."

Herman, quoted by Jim Murray in the *Los Angeles Times* in 1972, remembered the play a little differently still:

> George Mogridge hung a curve, and I hit it four feet from the top of the wall in right. . . . Vance runs halfway to third, then he runs around third, then he starts to run back. Fewster is on third, so he starts back to second.
>
> Now, I got the throw beat, and I slide into second. Safe. Right? So, now, somebody hollers to Jimmy Cooney, the shortstop, and he throws home. Al Spohrer chases Vance back to third. Now, I go to third on the rundown, and, naturally, I slide into third. . . . Now, I was called out for passing Fewster, but Vance is on third and it's his bag by the rules. Spohrer begins tagging everybody. . . . Fewster wanders out to right field to get his glove, and (Gautreau) chases him and tags him out.
>
> You see, there never were three men on third exactly.

Well, maybe not, but Al Spohrer wasn't there, either. He didn't reach the major leagues until 1928.

To sort it out, I went to the contemporary newspapers. According to a special dispatch to the *Boston Globe*,

> Herman lashed his double against the right field wall. . . . [Vance] thought that [right fielder] Jimmy Welsh was going to catch the ball and tarried close to the bag before he started to run.
>
> He attempted to score, and seeing the throw to the plate had him trapped started back for third. Fewster and Herman kept tearing around the bases before they realized what had happened, and Chick and Babe both pulled in to third as Vance managed to get back safely in the rundown. The ball was put on both Fewster and Herman, thereby completing an exceedingly unusual twin killing.

It was scored 9–4–2–5–4: right field to second base to catcher to third base and back to second. Incidentally, the box score indicates that Beans Reardon was umpiring at first base, not third. And, lost in the confusion, DeBerry had scored what proved to be the winning run for the Daffiness Boys.

Grover Alexander Clinched the 1926
World Series despite Nursing a Hangover

Won 1926 world championship for Cardinals by striking out Lazzeri
with bases full in final crisis at Yankee Stadium.

—Grover Cleveland Alexander's Baseball Hall of Fame plaque

It was a classic confrontation suitable for fiction. Yankee Stadium. Game
Seven of the World Series. Three–two score. Bases loaded. Twenty-two-year-
old rookie slugger, destined for the Baseball Hall of Fame, at bat. Thirty-nine-
year-old veteran pitcher, also destined for the Hall, comes in to pitch, despite
having gone nine innings the day before. A long foul ball. And then—strike
three! But it was all true. The only fiction was added to the story after the fact:
that the pitcher, Grover Cleveland "Pete" Alexander, was hungover or still
drunk after celebrating the previous day's victory; that Lazzeri missed a grand
slam homer by inches; that the strikeout ended the game.

The Yankees, on the verge of historic greatness, had won the first game
of the World Series, but Alexander held the Murderers' Row to four hits in
winning Game Two, 6–2. The Yanks came back to win two out of three in
St. Louis, including an extra-inning victory in Game Five, returning home
needing just one win in two tries. But Alexander stopped them again on
October 9, knotting the Series with a 10–2 triumph. It would all come down
to Game Seven the next day.

New York started the scoring with a third-inning home run by Babe Ruth
off Jesse Haines, but the Cards came back with three runs in the top of the
fourth. The Yankees scored one in the sixth and were threatening for more
in the seventh. Earle Combs led off with a single to left-center and was
sacrificed to second. Ruth was intentionally walked. After a force-out and a
walk to Lou Gehrig, the Yanks had the bases loaded with two out and Tony
Lazzeri due up against the tiring Haines. Lazzeri had set a professional record
with 60 home runs in the Pacific Coast League the year before and collected
18 homers (third in the AL) and 114 RBI (second) in his rookie big-league
season. Although hurlers were expected to finish what they started in those
days, Haines had developed a blister on his finger, and St. Louis player/man-
ager Rogers Hornsby decided it was time for a pitching change.

In came Alexander, showing no particular urgency. With the count 1–1,
Alexander went against the scouting report and laid in a fastball, which Lazzeri pulled deep and foul. Lazzeri then struck out on an off-speed pitch out
of the strike zone to end the threat. The confrontation was so dramatic that
it overshadowed everything else Alexander had done throughout his career,

which would end in 1930 with 373 wins and 90 shutouts. More than half of Alex's Hall of Fame plaque is devoted to that one strikeout.

But the game wasn't over: Alexander still had six outs to get while clinging to a 3–2 lead. He made it look easy, not allowing a ball out of the infield. In the eighth, Joe Dugan grounded to short, Pat Collins fouled to first, and pitcher Herb Pennock popped to second. In the ninth, Earle Combs and Mark Koenig each grounded to third, bringing up Ruth. Alexander walked the Bambino on a close 3–2 pitch. Then came one of the most inexplicable moments in baseball history. With the number four hitter up and the team down to its last out, Ruth tried to steal second base. He was thrown out, ending the World Series and making the Cardinals world champions.

So, obviously, that part about the strikeout ending the game is false. So is the implication (on his Hall of Fame plaque, among other places) that Alexander won the game: He merely saved it. But what about the stories that Alex, an alcoholic, thinking that his year's work was over after the Game Six victory, had drunk himself into oblivion the night before, and had the hangover to prove it?

Alexander didn't refute his problems with alcohol, but he steadfastly denied being under the influence on that day. He told writer Frank Conniff,

> After the sixth game, Hornsby called me aside in the locker room. "Pete," he said, "if there's a guy on the team who's earned the right to celebrate, it's you. But there's one game left, and I may need you. Try to get a good night's sleep tonight in case I have to call on you tomorrow."

Alexander told writer Frank Graham that he stayed with Hornsby that night: "We had dinner together and went back to his room and sat around, and finally we went to bed. The next morning he told me he was going to start Haines, and that if Jess got into trouble he might call on me." Noted journalist Joe Williams wrote,

> I present Hornsby's testimony that Alex retired after an early dinner, did not leave his room, and as far as anybody knows did not even partake of a nightcap. . . . Do you think for a second [Hornsby] would have called on a bleary-eyed, jumpy-nerved, wabbly (sic) veteran, as Alex is always pictured, in such a critical spot and with the stakes so high? Of course not.

Cardinals' third baseman Les Bell gave a vivid account to author Donald Honig a half century later, saying, "when you hear those stories about how Alec didn't think he might have to pitch the next day and was out all night celebrating and how he was hungover when he came in, that's a lot of bunk."

According to Les, Alexander was at the hotel (which would not have had a bar during Prohibition) the whole evening. He had a game plan when he entered Game Seven: to take his time going to the mound, working on the rookie's nerves; to get ahead of Lazzeri by having him foul off an inside fastball; and to set down the rest of the order until Ruth represented the last hope with no one on base, "so when the big son of a bitch comes up there the best he can do is tie the ball game." Bell also downplays Lazzeri's foul, which some say missed by inches of being a grand slam. "I was standing on third base and I'll tell you—that ball was foul all the way."

Bell continues, saying,

> If you stop to think about it, no man could have done what Alec did if he was drunk or even a little soggy. Not the way he pitched that day, and not the way his mind was working. Everybody knows that he was a drinker and that he had a problem with it, but he was not drunk when he walked into the ball game that day. No way.

The Yankees Beat the Pirates in the 1927 World Series before the Games Even Started

Many people still consider the 1927 New York Yankees the greatest team of all time. With Babe Ruth and Lou Gehrig combining for 107 homers and 339 RBI, the Yanks went 110–44, winning the pennant by 19 games, then swept the Pittsburgh Pirates, led by diminutive brothers Paul and Lloyd Waner, in four straight in the World Series.

Legend has it that the Pirates were beaten the day before the World Series even started. According to Fred Lieb, in *The Story of the World Series: An Informal History* (1949),

> After the Pirates worked out, [manager Donie] Bush extended the courtesy of the field to his rivals. The Pirates dressed, and most of them remained in the [Forbes Field] stands to observe the New Yorkers go through their exercises. And the Yankees put on a pyrotechnic display that had many of the Bucs whoozy. Ruth and Gehrig hit balls into and over the distant right-field stand as if it were a softball park, and [Bob] Meusel and [Tony] Lazzeri gave the left-field stands a similar treatment. Little 140-pound Lloyd Waner turned to his brother Paul and asked, "Gee, they're big guys; do they always hit that hard?"

The awestruck Pirates then continued to watch as the Yankees beat them to a pulp once the games began.

But Lloyd Waner remembers it differently in *The October Heroes: Great World Series Games Remembered by the Men Who Played Them* (1979), by Donald Honig:

> If you want to know the truth, I never even saw the Yankees work out that day. We had our workout first, and I dressed and was leaving the ball park just as they were coming out on the field. I don't think Paul stayed out there either. We never spoke of it. I know some of our players stayed, but I never heard anybody talk about what they saw.

A check of contemporary accounts, the *Sporting News*, the 1928 *Reach*, and *Spalding Official Baseball Guides*, further belies the Lieb version. Most observers had considered the Yankees and Pirates a pretty even match, and even following the World Series few recognized the Bronx Bombers as one of the all-time juggernauts. After all, Pittsburgh had won the 1925 Fall Classic, and the Yankees were essentially the same team that had lost the 1926 Series. Most ascribed the Yanks' sweep to the fact that the Bucs—particularly their pitchers—were weary from their pennant drive. There was mention that the Yankees seemed to get all the "breaks"—an error here, a wild pitch there—and speculation that the Pirates might have done better with future Hall of Famer Kiki Cuyler in the lineup, rather than in his manager's doghouse. There was absolutely no indication of the Pirates being intimidated, nor any mention of a batting practice story.

The Yankees hit only two homers in the World Series, and two of their wins were by one run, 5–4 in the opener and 4–3 in the finale. And the frightened Waner brothers batted a collective .367.

For Five and a Half Years, Chuck Klein Was as Great a Hitter as Baseball Ever Saw

While I did get some homers on high flies over the fence, I also lost a lot because line drives that would have cleared the fence in other parks ricocheted off the wall at Baker Bowl.

—Chuck Klein

Chuck Klein exploded into the major leagues in 1928 as if he were Babe Ruth and Ty Cobb rolled into one. No other player has ever begun a career with statistics like Klein had during his first five and a half seasons (see table 3.1). For good measure, the Phillies' slugger also led the NL in stolen bases once and

Table 3.1. Chuck Klein's Major League Statistics during His First Five and a Half Seasons

Year	AB	R	H	TB	2B	3B	HR	RBI	AVG	SLG
1928	253	41	91	146	14	4	11	34	.360	.577
1929	616	126	219	405	45	6	**43**	145	.356	.657
1930	648	**158**	250	**445**	**59**	8	40	170	.386	.687
1931	594	**121**	200	**347**	34	10	**31**	**121**	.337	**.584**
1932	650	**152**	**226**	**420**	50	15	**38**	137	.348	**.646**
1933	606	101	**223**	**365**	**44**	7	**28**	**120**	**.368**	**.602**
Total	3,367	699	1,209	2,128	246	50	191	727	.359	.632

KEY: AB = times at bat; R = runs scored; H = hits; TB = total bases on hits; 2B = doubles; 3B = triples; HR = home runs; RBI = runs batted in; AVG = batting average; SLG = slugging average. **Bold** indicates league leadership.

outfield assists three times, and he won the *Sporting News* MVP Award in 1931 and 1932 and the Triple Crown in 1933.

The rest of Klein's career was not nearly so spectacular, and he retired with 300 homers and a .320 lifetime average. He was finally elected to the Hall of Fame by the Veterans Committee in 1980, nearly four decades after he had hit his last home run. Some say he should have made it to Cooperstown much sooner, while others feel that he didn't deserve enshrinement at all.

The controversy boils down to what Klein did, in the context of where he did it: an old Phillies' park called Baker Bowl. As noted sportswriter Joe Williams once said, "On his home grounds in Philadelphia [Klein] was a man-eating tiger. In precincts less congenial to his grooved swing, [he] gratefully compromised on a more conventional cuisine." According to Red Smith, "It was felt that Lady Godiva could hit .334 with 27 home runs in that chummy playground, with or without spikes."

Baker Bowl, also known as the Hump, the Cigar Box, and the Band Box, among other things, was first used by the Phillies in 1895. Renamed two decades later after Phils owner William F. Baker, the stadium held fewer than 20,000 people and was the site of two disasters (other than the teams that played there). On August 8, 1903, stands near the left field bleachers collapsed, killing 12 people and injuring more than 200 others. On May 14, 1927, the right field stands collapsed, resulting in one death and dozens of injuries. The last game at Baker Bowl was played on June 30, 1938. The field was torn down in 1950, and it has been replaced by a parking lot and car wash, among other things.

The park had many unique features. It was situated on an elevated piece of ground, with a railroad tunnel underneath the outfield section (hence the nickname "the Hump"). A 15-foot-wide embanked bicycle track rimmed the outfield. A swimming pool was housed in the basement of the center field clubhouse. Policemen on milk crates routinely surrounded the field, and sheep grazed in the outfield grass between games.

Figure 3.1. Chuck Klein, Putting Up Dominant Numbers.
Source: National Baseball Hall of Fame Library, Cooperstown, New York

The most notable feature was in right field. A 60-foot-tall tin wall (raised from 40 feet in 1929) stood there just 280½ feet from home plate. It sported a prominent soap ad, saying "The Phillies Use Lifebuoy" ("and they still stink," grumbled frustrated fans). More significantly, the right-center power alley was only 300 feet away from home. As Red Smith once wrote, "If the right fielder had eaten onions at lunch, the second baseman knew it." Left-handed sluggers like Chuck Klein regularly rattled drives off the wall, or popped flies over it.

Charles Herbert Klein was born on a farm near Indianapolis, Indiana, on October 7, 1905. In high school, the blue-eyed blond competed in track and basketball, in addition to baseball. After graduation, he went to work in an Indianapolis foundry, playing semipro ball on weekends. Adolph Stallman, a prohibition agent, spotted Klein on the sandlots and recommended him to the owner of the Evansville minor league club. There, Klein began his pro career in 1927, moving up to the Central League the following year, and arriving in Philadelphia in late July 1928.

Klein's heroics from then through 1933 didn't seem to help his team much. The Phillies averaged just 62 wins per year during this period, only once reaching .500 (as a result, they often faced secondary pitching, which may have contributed to Klein's imposing stats). Under the theory that, "We could have finished seventh without you," the Phils dealt Klein to the Chicago Cubs on November 21, 1933. The Cubs, certain that the strong slugger would carry them back into the World Series, gave up a reported $125,000 (a whopping sum during those Depression days) and three players to get him.

Noted writer Daniel M. Daniel expressed reservation about the Cubs' acquisition, reporting a common belief that, "Klein was purely a Baker Bowl hitter and that, taken away from that . . . neighborly right field fence, his average would shrink all out of proportion." As Joe Williams said a quarter-century later, "If there had been any way to include the cozy right field wall, the Cubs would have had themselves a hot deal. As it turned out, they got the least important part of Klein's equipment."

Following a decent start in 1934, Klein injured his leg and, playing hurt, hit only one home run after the All-Star break. The Cubs finished in third place, with 86 wins, just as they had in 1933. In 1935, Chicago staged a remarkable 21-game string of wins in September to overtake the leaders and clinch the pennant, but Klein had nothing to do with it. Hitless in five straight games, he was benched for the remainder of the streak. Only an injury to Fred Lindstrom allowed Klein into the World Series lineup.

In May 1936, the disappointed Cubs sent him back to his old team. As Chicago manager Charlie Grimm related many years later, "Away from the Philadelphia bandbox, Chuck was a different player . . . his averages and power production not only fell off . . . but he couldn't cover the ground in Wrigley Field, either."

After three more seasons with the Phils (during which the team vacated Baker Bowl in favor of Shibe Park), Klein was released and picked up by

Pittsburgh in 1939. Within a year he was released again and reacquired by the Phillies. From 1940 to 1944, he served the club variously as a reserve outfielder, pinch hitter, and coach. His meager .192 average during this period lowered his career mark to .320. On August 18, 1941, Klein hit his 300th and final major league homer, making him only the second National Leaguer to reach that milestone.

Klein never received more than 27% of the vote in any Hall of Fame election held by the Baseball Writers' Association, indicating that there was considerable doubt about his credentials among those who saw him play. He operated a Philadelphia tavern after his playing days and died in Indianapolis on March 28, 1958.

Not everyone has attributed Klein's heroics entirely to the Baker Bowl fence. Gene Torpey, his brother-in-law, said, "That wall probably took away from him as many home runs as it gave him. . . . I don't know how many times I saw it stop his high line drives and hold them to singles and doubles." Klein himself concurred, saying, "Those four home runs [hit at Pittsburgh's Forbes Field on July 10, 1936] weren't hit at Baker Bowl. And, while I did get some homers on high flies over the fence, I also lost a lot because line drives that would have cleared the fence in other parks ricocheted off the wall at Baker Bowl." Analyst Bill James, in his first edition of *The Bill James Historical Baseball Abstract*, writes, "You just can't ignore *that much* statistical evidence. . . . I've become convinced that Klein was significantly over . . . the level of unquestioned excellence but marginal greatness." And, as the *Philadelphia Inquirer*'s Allen Lewis notes, "Others have played in parks that were made to order for them and it has not been held against them." Apparently, other members of the Hall of Fame's Veterans Committee finally came to agree in 1980, the year after Lewis joined the committee.

In Klein's era, there were no statistical services analyzing data the way the Elias Sports Bureau and STATS, Inc., has in recent times. Consequently, the seven decades of arguments about Klein's home-park advantage have depended upon limited observation and speculation. I finally ended the speculation with thorough research. The eye-opening results appear in table 3.2.

These numbers should speak for themselves, but to summarize: During those first 5½ seasons, his ticket to Cooperstown, Klein hit a modest .295 (as compared to the overall league average of .283), with 60 home runs on the road. At home, he hit an incredible .422, with 131 homers. He had seasonal *home* totals of 92 runs, 143 hits, 270 total bases, 32 doubles, 29 homers, 109 RBI, a .467 average, and a .799 slugging percentage in various years. Per 154 games played, Klein averaged 44 home runs, 158 RBI, and a .397 average at the Cigar Box, 18–80–.277 elsewhere. Prorated for an equal number of games at each NL park,

Table 3.2. Chuck Klein's Major League Statistics at Baker Bowl versus at Other Ballparks

			Chuck Klein at Baker Bowl							
Year	G	AB	R	H	2B	3B	HR	RBI	AVG	SLG
1928	37	145	28	56	6	3	9	26	.386	.655
1929	71	304	65	119	25	2	25	78	.391	.734
1930	77	326	91	143	32	3	26	109	.439	.794
1931	74	297	79	121	22	7	22	78	.407	.751
1932	77	338	92	143	26	7	29	97	.423	.799
1933	72	285	62	133	28	2	20	81	.467	.789
1934	11	41	11	14	2	0	3	11	.341	.610
1935	11	46	15	16	1	1	5	14	.348	.739
1936	64	264	47	82	17	3	9	45	.311	.500
1937	57	201	48	77	16	0	13	39	.383	.657
1938	27	95	12	25	3	1	3	16	.263	.411
Total	578	2,342	550	929	178	29	164	594	.397	.708

			Chuck Klein in Other Parks							
Year	G	AB	R	H	2B	3B	HR	RBI	AVG	SLG
1928	27	108	13	35	8	1	2	8	.324	.472
1929	78	312	61	100	20	4	18	67	.321	.583
1930	79	322	67	107	27	5	14	61	.332	.578
1931	74	297	42	79	12	3	9	43	.266	.418
1932	77	312	60	83	24	8	9	40	.266	.481
1933	80	321	39	90	16	5	8	39	.280	.436
1934	104	394	67	117	25	2	17	69	.297	.500
1935	108	388	56	111	13	3	16	59	.286	.459
1936	82	337	55	102	18	4	16	60	.303	.522
1937	58	205	26	55	4	2	2	18	.268	.337
1938	102	363	41	88	19	1	5	45	.242	.342
1939	110	317	45	90	18	5	12	56	.284	.486
1940	116	354	39	77	16	2	7	37	.218	.333
1941	50	73	6	9	0	0	1	3	.123	.164
1942	14	14	0	1	0	0	0	0	.071	.071
1943	12	20	0	2	0	0	0	3	.100	.100
1944	4	7	1	1	0	0	0	0	.143	.143
Total	1,175	4,144	618	1,147	220	45	136	608	.277	.450

KEY: G = games played; AB = times at bat; R = runs scored; H = hits; 2B = doubles; 3B = triples; HR = home runs; RBI = runs batted in; AVG = batting average; SLG = slugging average

Klein's career totals would include 1,892 hits, 244 homers, 1,017 RBI, and a .294 average—not bad, but hardly Cooperstown material.

Even his fielding statistics benefited from a park illusion. By most accounts, Klein had limited defensive skills, yet he set a modern record, with 44 outfield assists in 1930. But, remember, Klein had much shorter throws to make than the average right fielder. As Edward Burns wrote in the June 13, 1938, *Chicago Tribune*, "The right fielder who plays most of his games at Baker Bowl has a better chance . . . to make assists than any outfielder on any other team in the National League." The numbers bear that out: Thirty-two of Klein's record-setting assists were made in Philadelphia, and, during his Baker Bowl days, he made 119 assists at home, with just 43 on the road. Longtime Philadelphia baseball fan Ed "Dutch" Doyle—who claimed to have witnessed all or part of 500 of Klein's 578 games at the Hump—explained that Klein was adept at playing caroms off the tin wall, often nabbing runners trying to take extra bases on such hits.

Klein was not the only player to benefit from Baker Bowl's dimensions. Gavvy Cravath, who missed winning seven consecutive homer crowns during the Deadball Era by one dinger, hit 92 of his 117 Phillie homers at the Baker Bowl (Cravath, a right-handed hitter, learned to direct his hits toward the opposite field). Lefty O'Doul batted .426 in 189 games there, including a remarkable 1929 season, in which he hit .453 with 144 safeties in 76 home games. The Giants' Mel Ott hit .412 at Baker Bowl, with 40 homers and 160 RBI in just 121 games (then, he failed to homer in 71 games at Shibe Park).

We must remember that a park doesn't make statistics by itself. Klein still had to hit and throw the ball himself and should be given some credit for learning to take advantage of his circumstances. Hell, .422 is a decent average for slow-pitch softball! But a true star should be able to hit anywhere. Players like Ty Cobb, Rogers Hornsby, Babe Ruth, Ted Williams, and Stan Musial each got some help from his home park, but each of them also managed to hit over .325 on the road during his career. A ballpark doesn't make an MVP or a Hall of Famer. Well, not usually, anyway.

Al Simmons's Holiday Cost Lefty Grove
His 16-Game Win Streak

Lefty Grove was practically unbeatable in 1931. The Philadelphia Athletics' ace rolled up a 31–4 pitching record with a 2.06 ERA, as compared to the league's 4.38. And each of Grove's four defeats was tainted, but none received more ink than a loss to the lowly St. Louis Browns on August 23. Grove entered the day with 16 consecutive victories, which matched Walter Johnson's and Joe Wood's AL mark. Lefty wanted the record all to himself and certainly pitched well enough to claim it. He hurled the complete game, allowing seven hits and one run, striking out six and walking none. The lone tally came in the third inning. With two outs, Fred Schulte reached on a bloop single. Oscar Melillo then sent a drive toward left field. Substitute outfielder Jimmy Moore, battling the sun, mistakenly took two steps in before reversing direction, and the ball tipped off his glove and rolled to the fence for an RBI double. It turned out to be the game's only run, and Grove's streak was over.

After the game, Grove practically destroyed the clubhouse in a temper tantrum. He was mad not at Moore, but at regular left fielder and future Hall of Famer Al Simmons, for skipping the game. "If Simmons had been here and in left field," Grove fumed, "he would have stuck that ball in his back pocket." Grove lived another 44 years and never forgave Simmons for taking the day off. So, history remembers that Al Simmons, playing hooky, cost Grove the record.

The Browns' Dick Coffman had shut out the mighty A's on just three hits. Every sports fan knows you can't win if you don't score, so it's unfair to heap the blame on Simmons or Moore. But, more to the point, Simmons wasn't just absent for the day. Nursing an infected toe, he hadn't played since August 15, and he wouldn't play again until September 6. Moore played left in all 20 A's games in between, recording 37 putouts, two assists, and one error. He was no Al Simmons, but few were.

A Broken Toe Ruined Dizzy Dean's Career

We all know the story. Dizzy Dean, just 27 years old, was the best pitcher in baseball until the 1937 All-Star Game. Then, in the third inning of that July 7 contest, Earl Averill sent a screaming line drive that slammed into Dean's left foot, breaking his big toe. Dean tried to come back too soon after the injury and, favoring his toe, injured his shoulder. He was never the same after that and won only 17 more games the rest of his career.

But Craig Wright, in his excellent online subscription series "A Page from Baseball's Past" (baseballspast.com), makes a persuasive case that Dean's arm was on the way out before the toe injury, a victim of overuse at a young age. "The injury was a minor contributor at most in the emergence of Dean's shoulder problem, which had the classic symptoms of a rotator cuff injury," writes Wright.

It is well known today that pitching too much at a young age is a pretty sure recipe for career-altering arm problems. Dean would wind up with 150 career victories, the last at age 30. Since World War I, only 16 pitchers have won 150 or more games before the age of 30—and most of them were pretty much washed up by then. The two leaders are Hal Newhouser, who had 188 wins before that birthday and only 19 thereafter, and Catfish Hunter, who had 184 and 40, respectively. Wes Ferrell (175–18), Don Drysdale (170–39), Dwight Gooden (157–37), Lefty Gomez (153–36), and Ken Holtzman

(151–23) followed similar patterns. Just four of the 16 pitchers had as many as 100 wins after age 30, and only Greg Maddux made it to 300 victories.

But the baseball cognoscenti didn't start making the connection between youthful overwork and mid-career arm problems until the 1980s, a half century too late for Old Diz. Turning pro at the age of 20 in 1930, Dean hurled a total of 311 innings in three leagues. The next year, it was 304. As a rookie with the 1932 Cardinals, Dizzy led the NL, with 286 innings. In 1933, he collected 293 frames and a league-leading 26 complete games. In his greatest season, 1934, including World Series action, Dean amassed 338 innings and 26 complete games. He led the league in both innings pitched and complete games in both 1935 (325, 29) and 1936 (315, 28). And this was all in the high-scoring 1930s, making for more pitches per inning than other times in baseball history.

Dizzy was right back at it in 1937. He went ten innings while tossing a 13-hit shutout in his first game of the season, April 20. He followed with complete game victories on April 25, April 30, May 5, and May 9. Wright estimates that he averaged 135 pitches per start over those five outings, fresh out of spring training. Not surprisingly, in hindsight, he began to experience arm fatigue. Over the next two months, Dean was a modest 7–7 with a 3.30 ERA, sometimes getting pounded, other times pitching well, including a shutout on July 4, three days before the Midsummer Classic. It was his 14th complete game of the season, giving him 150 innings pitched.

Interestingly, Dean had announced that he wasn't even going to the All-Star Game. "I'd like to do something for myself for a change," he said. "All I've been doing is running here and there for somebody else, and I'm sick and tired of it all. Not only that, I've got a sore arm." Of course, he did go, pitching the first three frames and allowing two runs. The last pitch he threw was to Averill who, incidentally, didn't get a hit on the liner. The ball caromed off Dean's toe to second baseman Billy Herman, who threw Averill out at first base to end the inning.

Dean returned to action exactly two weeks later, going the distance in a 2–1 loss on July 21. Four days later, he toiled ten and a third innings in a no-decision. He pitched only sporadically after that. After the All-Star Game, he was just 1–3, although his ERA (3.59) was not much higher than in the two-month stretch before the fateful game.

"The truth is that Dean's shoulder was already starting to act up before he broke his toe," writes Wright. "It is far more likely that Dizzy was simply another case of a great young pitcher being pushed too hard, and breaking down in what was expected to be mid-career."

Mel Ott Owed All of His Success to the Polo Grounds

The 170-pound Ott hit 511 homers. They weren't really homers, they were pop flies—seven-iron shots—into the 250-foot overhang in the Polo Grounds upper deck. . . . If he had played anywhere else, no one would have heard of him.

—author John Holway

Who hit the most home runs in one ballpark? It was Mel Ott, who hit 323 of his 511 career four-baggers at New York's Polo Grounds. Ott, a left-handed hitter for the Giants from 1926 through 1947, held the NL record for career homers until 1966, and he was a shoo-in Hall of Fame selection. But he benefited greatly from his park's right field fence, only 257 feet from home plate (contrary to the previous quote, there was no overhang in right field). In Ott's last seven seasons, 100 of his 123 homers (including all 18 in 1943) were hit at home. He slugged .589 at home and only .370 on the road during this period and didn't score a run in his last 37 road games. One is liable to think that his home park kept him in the major leagues.

The Polo Grounds may have extended Ott's career and turned him into a world-class home run hitter, but he was a world-class *hitter* all by himself. Over his first nine seasons, Ott batted a resounding .343 on the road, as compared to .286 at home. He hit .300 or better on the road every year from 1928 through 1940. In 1928, he set NL single-season records for runs (79) and RBI (87) on the road. For his career, Ott batted 14 points better on the road and hit significantly more singles (971 to 834), doubles (306 to 182), and triples (51 to 21) away from home. And even as a home run hitter, Ott was no phony. He led the league in *road* homers five times. Had he played an equal number of games in each NL park during his career, he is projected to have hit 410 career homers. That *still* would have been the NL record until 1963.

In the interest of full disclosure, it should be noted that a great part of Ott's success on the road was due to Baker Bowl, the Philadelphia park (see the section on Chuck Klein). In 121 games there, Ott batted .412 with 40 homers and 160 RBI. At Shibe Park, the Phillies' new home beginning in 1938, Ott hit just .220 and failed to hit a home run in 71 games. Table 3.3 lists Ott's complete home and road breakdowns.

Ted Williams Risked His .400 Average on the Last Day of the 1941 Season

The major leagues' last .400 hitter was Ted Williams in 1941. The young Red Sox slugger finished the season with 185 hits in 456 official at bats,

Table 3.3. Mel Ott's Major League Statistics at the Polo Grounds versus at Other Ballparks

Year	G	AB	R	H	2B	3B	HR	RBI	AVG	OBP	SLG
						Mel Ott at the Polo Grounds					
1926	12	14	3	7	0	0	0	0	.500	.500	.500
1927	37	79	14	26	3	2	1	9	.329	.398	.456
1928	59	204	29	59	8	2	9	33	.289	.372	.480
1929	75	266	59	79	12	1	20	65	.297	.417	.575
1930	76	257	67	92	10	2	21	64	.358	.484	.658
1931	70	245	49	57	7	1	20	57	.233	.354	.514
1932	77	270	53	77	15	2	24	66	.285	.415	.622
1933	74	267	45	70	9	1	13	48	.262	.360	.449
1934	75	270	49	69	8	1	16	49	.256	.366	.470
1935	79	292	59	99	11	2	19	60	.339	.442	.586
1936	75	250	58	83	12	1	18	64	.332	.463	.604
1937	75	263	48	71	10	1	15	45	.270	.390	.487
1938	71	241	65	76	12	2	20	58	.315	.469	.631
1939	64	198	46	61	7	2	15	44	.308	.465	.591
1940	75	256	42	71	13	0	12	39	.277	.399	.469
1941	73	236	51	82	11	0	19	50	.347	.488	.636
1942	77	269	70	94	10	0	23	62	.349	.468	.643
1943	65	211	41	50	6	0	18	34	.237	.399	.521
1944	65	203	51	51	5	1	21	46	.251	.409	.596
1945	72	242	52	83	13	0	18	49	.343	.440	.620
1946	18	41	2	3	0	0	1	3	.073	.208	.146
1947	4	4	0	0	0	0	0	0	.000	.000	.000
Total	1,368	4,578	953	1,360	182	21	323	945	.297	.421	.558

(continued)

Table 3.3. *(Continued)*

| | | | | Mel Ott on the Road | | | | | | | |
Year	G	AB	R	H	2B	3B	HR	RBI	AVG	OBP	SLG
1926	23	46	4	16	2	0	0	4	.348	.362	.391
1927	45	84	9	20	4	1	0	10	.238	.273	.310
1928	65	231	40	81	18	2	9	44	.351	.419	.563
1929	75	279	79	100	25	1	22	87	.358	.478	.692
1930	72	264	55	90	24	3	4	55	.341	.431	.500
1931	68	252	55	88	16	7	9	58	.349	.431	.575
1932	77	296	66	103	15	6	14	57	.348	.432	.581
1933	78	313	53	94	27	0	10	55	.300	.372	.482
1934	78	312	70	121	21	9	19	86	.388	.459	.696
1935	73	301	54	92	22	4	12	54	.306	.370	.525
1936	75	284	62	92	16	5	15	71	.324	.434	.574
1937	76	282	51	89	18	1	16	50	.316	.424	.557
1938	79	286	51	88	11	4	16	58	.308	.416	.542
1939	61	198	39	61	16	0	12	36	.308	.432	.571
1940	76	280	47	84	14	3	7	40	.300	.413	.446
1941	75	289	38	68	18	0	8	40	.235	.324	.381
1942	75	280	48	68	11	0	7	31	.243	.361	.357
1943	60	169	24	39	6	2	0	13	.231	.381	.290
1944	55	196	40	64	11	3	5	36	.327	.438	.490
1945	63	209	21	56	10	0	3	30	.268	.378	.359
1946	13	27	0	2	1	0	0	1	.074	.107	.111
1947	0	0	0	0	0	0	0	0	—	—	—
Total	1,362	4,878	906	1,516	306	51	188	916	.311	.407	.510

KEY: G = games played; AB = times at bat; R = runs scored; H = hits; 2B = doubles; 3B = triples; HR = home runs; RBI = runs batted in; AVG = batting average; OBP = on-base percentage; SLG = slugging average. Note: On-base percentage here does not account for sacrifice flies.

good for a .406 average. It is often noted that Williams could have sat out the final doubleheader of the season to preserve his .400 mark, but instead he gallantly played and went 6-for-8, raising his average six points. In fact, Williams's average was .3996 before the doubleheader. Although it could be rounded up, the media didn't consider it a true .400 mark. And, once Ted got a hit on his first at bat, he was never in danger of sinking below .400 on a subsequent at bat.

On September 27, 1941, Williams went 1-for-4 against the last-place Philadelphia Athletics. This left him with 448 at bats and 179 hits for the season. The Red Sox finished the next day with a doubleheader against the same A's. According to the Associated Press wire story in the September 28 papers, "Ted Williams, striving to become the first major leaguer in 11 years to hit .400 for a season, made only one hit in four official chances yesterday and dropped just below .400." The *New York Times* had it in the headlines: "Williams at .3996 as Red Sox Win, 5–1; Star Batter below .400 Goal."

When Ted hit safely on his first time up on September 28, his average climbed to .4009. Had he made an out his next appearance, his batting average would have been an even .400, so there was no risk in remaining in the game at that point. Instead, he got a second hit (upping his mark to .4022), a third (.4035), and a fourth (.4049), before being retired on his last at bat of the first game (.4040). He had essentially clinched a .400 average; even a 0-for-4 performance in the second game would have left him at .4004. Instead, he went 2-for-3, beginning with a hit (.4053) and then another (.4066), before making an out in his final at bat of the year (.4057). Ted Williams was a great hitter, and his 1941 campaign was one of the greatest in baseball history. But there was no real gallantry or risk in what he did on the season's final day.

Bill Veeck Tried to Buy the Phillies and Stock It with Black Players, Years before Jackie Robinson

In his 1962 autobiography with Ed Linn, *Veeck—as in Wreck*, Hall of Fame executive Bill Veeck reveals his extraordinary plan of two decades before. In the book, Veeck writes the following:

> I had tried to buy the Philadelphia Phillies and stock it with Negro players well before I went into the [military] service. I had made my offer to Gerry Nugent, the president of the fast-sinking club, and he had expressed a willingness to accept it. . . . The players were going to be assembled for me by Abe Saperstein and Doc Young, the sports editor of the *Chicago Defender*, two of

the most knowledgeable men in the country on the subject of Negro baseball. With Satchel Paige, Roy Campanella, Luke Easter, Monte Irvin, and countless others in action and available, I had not the slightest doubt that in 1944, a war year, the Phils would have leaped from seventh place to the pennant.

Veeck goes on for nearly two pages about his plan, how commissioner Kenesaw Landis and NL president Ford Frick (who "was bragging all over the baseball world . . . about how he had stopped me from contaminating the league") squashed the idea, and how the Phillies wound up being sold to lumber dealer William Cox "for about half of what I had been willing to pay." Thus, Veeck lost his chance to become organized baseball's racial crusader years before Branch Rickey and Jackie Robinson broke the color line.

David M. Jordan, Larry R. Gerlach, and John P. Rossi puncture this myth in great detail in the 1998 edition of the Society of American Baseball Research's *The National Pastime*. Some of the sticking points include the following:

- It couldn't have happened in 1944. Cox bought the Phillies on February 18, 1943, some three months after longtime owner Nugent put the team up for sale. And, incidentally, the 1942 Phils had finished in eighth (not seventh) place out of eight teams for the fifth year in a row.
- Two of the four players Veeck names were not available to play at the time. Irvin was in military service, and Easter did not begin his pro career until 1946.
- The sports editor of the *Chicago Defender* was Fay Young, not A. S. "Doc" Young.
- The story has never been corroborated by anyone else, even though it was supposedly known "all over the baseball world." All published versions of it can be traced back to Veeck.
- It is inconceivable that Nugent would turn over his franchise to the NL for $26,000 plus assumption of the team's debts (estimated at $330,000), and say that he was "entirely satisfied" by this resolution, rather than sell to a buyer who offered $500,000 (Cox, whom Veeck claimed paid about half of what he had offered, bought the team from the NL for approximately $250,000).
- Veeck's right-hand man, Rudie Schaffer, was with Veeck when he visited Nugent in the fall of 1942 to discuss a possible deal. In 1994, Schaffer recalled the meeting "wasn't a very productive one" and said that he knew of no subsequent communications between Veeck and Nugent.

- None of the contemporary major black newspapers—including the *Amsterdam News, Baltimore Afro American, Chicago Defender, Cleveland Call and Post, Kansas City Call, Los Angeles Sentinel, Newark Afro American, New York Age, New York People's Voice, Philadelphia Afro American, Philadelphia Tribune, Pittsburgh Courier, St. Louis Argus,* and *Washington Afro American*—which campaigned hard for the integration of the major leagues during this period, mentioned Veeck's thwarted plan.
- When Veeck reached the major leagues by buying the Cleveland Indians in 1946, there was only one mention of a previous effort to buy the Phillies: by Red Smith of the *New York Herald Tribune,* who wrote that Veeck backed out because, "at the last moment he decided the risk was too great to take with his friend's money."
- When Veeck integrated the AL in 1947, there was no mention by Veeck or anyone else of a previous plan to integrate the game. In fact, just in 1946, Veeck had been quoted as saying, "in my opinion, none of the present crop of Negro players measure up to big-league standards."

There has been criticism of the authors' rush to judgment, and some new finds about the earliest mentions of the story, but the authors' key points and logical conclusion remain intact. Bill Veeck probably was interested in buying the Phillies after the 1942 season. He may even have thought about integrating the team if he did so. But the story as recorded by Veeck appears to be a complete fabrication by the master of self-promotion.

Veeck's credibility is further diminished in checking another book of his, *The Hustler's Handbook.* In one story, Veeck tells how Mickey Vernon "owned" legendary pitcher Satchel Paige, who finally gave up trying to get him out: "I have seen Satch come into the game with the bases loaded and his team two runs ahead and deliberately walk Vernon, forcing in a run." In fact, a check of games in which Paige pitched against the Senators and walked at least one, and Vernon had at least one walk and one RBI, turns up only four occasions in which Paige walked Vernon, twice intentionally—but none came with the bases loaded. Furthermore, in the 32 documented confrontations between the two players, Vernon batted a modest .276 (as compared to his overall lifetime average of .286) against Paige, hardly an indication of ownership.

Elsewhere in the book, Veeck tells a taller tale about Paul Waner nursing a hangover, writing the following:

I once saw Paul line a sure triple into the right-center field gap at Wrigley Field, take a wide turn around second base, and go sliding into the bull pen mound in the left field foul grounds, no more than 60 feet away from his destination . . . he won the game in the tenth inning by lining a home run into the right field bleachers.

But Waner actually hit only three homers at Wrigley Field in his entire career, only one of which was relatively late in the game: on July 8, 1934, in the seventh inning. But that was during an 11–4 victory, and Waner had no other extra-base hits in the game.

Leo Durocher Said, "Nice Guys Finish Last"

Hall of Fame manager Leo Durocher had a lot of quotable quotes during his half century in the game, but only one made it to *Bartlett's Familiar Quotations*. And, as Yogi Berra might put it, Leo never really said what he said. On July 5, 1946, "The Lip" was managing the Brooklyn Dodgers in a series against the rival New York Giants. "Why don't you be a nice guy for a change?" suggested broadcaster Red Barber, as *New York Journal-American* reporter Frank Graham recorded the conversation. Durocher launched into a 474-word diatribe about nice guys in general, including a barb aimed at the Giants' dugout: "Look over there. Do you know a nicer guy than Mel Ott? Or any of the other Giants? Why, they're the nicest guys in the world. And where are they? In last place!" The *Sporting News* reprinted the article on July 17, with the headline, "'Nice Guys' Wind Up in Last Place, Scoffs Lippy." By the time it reached *Bartlett's Familiar Quotations*, Durocher's monologue had been boiled down to four words: "Nice guys finish last."

Enos Slaughter Scored from First Base on a Single to Win the 1946 World Series

Baseball lore tells us that Enos Slaughter's greatest moment—and Johnny Pesky's worst—came in Game Seven of the 1946 World Series. With two out in the eighth inning, Slaughter scored all the way from first base on Harry Walker's single, giving the Cardinals a 4–3 lead that they would not relinquish. Pesky, the Red Sox shortstop taking the relay throw from the outfield, turned toward second base instead of home, holding the ball in shock while Slaughter scored. Some say this play is what put Slaughter in the Baseball Hall of Fame, and keeps Pesky out of it

The sun-blanched film footage is difficult to make out, but it tells a little different story. Slaughter was off with the pitch and got a big jump. Walker drove the ball to left-center field, where backup Leon Culberson was stationed (Culberson had pinch run for Dominic DiMaggio when the center fielder par excellence suffered a charley horse in the top of the eighth). Culberson fielded the ball and lobbed it to the cutoff man, Pesky.

Pesky turned to his *left*—toward home—and hesitated for a nanosecond, before flinging the ball to the catcher, far too late to get Slaughter. Clearly visible in the footage, as Pesky pivots, is Walker pulling into second base. That's why he was credited with a double, not a single.

Slaughter, quoted in *The World Series*, said,

Pesky got hit with a bum rap. . . . Because of the steal sign, I already had a pretty good jump on the pitcher when Walker hit this little floater into center field. The play was in front of me, so I could easily see that nobody was going to catch the ball. In fact, the ball was still in the air when I came into second base. I knew third base was a cinch, and I began to think I might make it all the way, especially since I knew that Culberson was not a strong thrower. Pesky had to go out to take the outfielder's throw, and he couldn't see me, what with his back to the plate. It was up to his teammates to yell to him, but nobody did. You couldn't blame Pesky. By the time he turned around and got ready to throw, I was just a step or two away from the plate.

So, Enos Slaughter gained immortality from doing something base runners do every day: scoring from first base on a two-out double. And Johnny Pesky—not pitcher Bob Klinger, who gave up both Slaughter's single and Walker's double in his two-thirds of an inning of work, nor Culberson, who threw the ball with no apparent urgency—was given the goat horns.

Joe DiMaggio Was One of the Best Outfielders Ever

Repetition carries conviction against which truth cannot stand.

—Red Smith

There is no question that Joltin' Joe DiMaggio was a devastating hitter; the stats and the stories are unanimous on that point. But, they part company when it comes to defense: Baseball lore insists that Joe D. was one of the best, if not *the* best, defensive outfielders of all time. He prowled Yankee Stadium's center field, it is said, with the instincts of a tiger, the reflexes of a cobra, the range of a cheetah, and the grace of a gazelle—a one-man Bronx Zoo—not to mention the hurling strength of a cannon and the precision of a neurosurgeon. There were no Gold Glove Awards

Figure 3.2. Joe DiMaggio, Gracefully Snaring an Imaginary Drive.
Source: National Baseball Hall of Fame Library, Cooperstown, New York

in DiMaggio's day, but Rawlings presented him with their first "Lifetime Achievement Award for Fielding Excellence" in 1992.

The statistics tell a different tale: DiMag led the AL just once each in fielding percentage, putouts, and assists. Of course, missing some 20 games a year, as Joe did, makes it tough to lead in the latter two categories. To be fair, I took his career fielding statistics and prorated them based on an average *full* season

(154 games, in that era), finding that Joe averaged 404 putouts, 14 assists, and nine errors per year. Next, I did the same for his contemporaries. I found eight major league center fielders from Joe's 1936 to 1951 era who played in at least 1,000 games apiece. Their 154-game averages appear in table 3.4.

Granted, men who play 1,000 games in center field tend to be better than your average big-league outfielders. Still, of the eight, Joe D. ranks just fifth in putouts (indicating range), fourth in assists (arm strength), and seventh in fielding percentage (sure-handedness). Two flyhawks—his brothers, Dom and Vince—outperformed Joe in all three categories. So, tell us, how in hell could Joe DiMaggio have been the best outfielder in history, if he was only the third-best in his own *family*?

Still not convinced? Fielding stats can be misleading, you say. They don't tell us, for instance, how many bases an outfielder saves by cutting off balls headed for the gap, or by holding runners in respect for his arm. The only baseball stat that really counts, after all, is "runs."

Fair enough. If an outfielder is really helping his team defensively, then it should show up on the scoreboard: The team should allow fewer runs, over a period of time, when he is on the field than when he isn't. Joe DiMaggio missed 292 games on the field in his 13-year career, during which—in theory—the Yankees were forced to insert their fourth-best outfielder in his stead. And, over a 292-game span, the difference between an outfielder reputed to be one of the greatest, and ones regarded as only the fourth-best on their own club, ought to show up on the scoreboard in a big way, don't you think?

But it didn't. Researching the number of runs scored against the Yanks with and without Joe D. in the outfield, from the AL's official day-by-day statistics, shows a different story. The methodology is not foolproof, but it

Table 3.4. Averages over 154 Games for Joe DiMaggio and Contemporary Center Fielders

Player	PO	A	E	PCT
Sam Chapman	420	13	13	.972
Doc Cramer	389	12	8	.979
Dom DiMaggio	433	16	10	.978
Joe DiMaggio	404	14	9	.978
Vince DiMaggio	405	18	8	.981
Mike Kreevich	433	12	8	.982
Terry Moore	404	13	6	.985
Stan Spence	402	15	7	.984

KEY: PO = putouts; A = assists; E = errors; PCT = fielding percentage. Note: Dom DiMaggio's percentage rounds to .9783, Joe's to .9780.

is better than any other measure of fielding we have available for that era. Table 3.5 demonstrates the figures.

The figures show that the Yankees allowed 4.07 runs per game with the Yankee Clipper in the outfield, as compared to 4.03 per game without him. This suggests the team actually did *better*, defensively, with a replacement-level outfielder in the garden, than with the great DiMaggio. Actually, using weighted averages, it is almost a dead heat: 4.02 to 4.03. Either way, there is absolutely no evidence that DiMag was anything special, defensively. There is a word to describe these findings, and its definition is "of only ordinary or moderate quality; neither good nor bad." The word is *mediocre*.

This would have come as no surprise to Tris Speaker, considered the greatest center fielder of pro baseball's first 75 years, if not all time. Said Speaker about DiMaggio in 1939, "Him? I could name 15 better outfielders!" But it leaves unexplained how an ordinary defensive player could have gained universal reputation as an all-time great fielder. Author Roger Kahn gives a clue, in his book *The Era* (1993), in which he writes the following:

> The three New York ball clubs underwrote New York baseball journalism years ago and promotional copy . . . was the return. The teams paid expenses for baseball writers on the road: hotel, Pullman berths, a weekly meal allowance. "Loans" were common. The teams served free meals and drinks to sportswriters

Table 3.5.　The 1936 to 1951 Yankees with and without Joe DiMaggio in the Outfield

Year	With			Without		
	G	OR	AVG	G	OR	AVG
1936	138	656	4.75	17	75	4.41
1937	150	652	4.35	7	19	2.71
1938	145	659	4.54	12	51	4.25
1939	117	425	3.63	35	131	3.74
1940	130	572	4.40	25	99	3.96
1941	139	564	4.06	17	67	3.94
1942	154	507	3.29	0	0	—
1946	131	467	3.56	23	80	3.48
1947	139	510	3.67	16	58	3.63
1948	152	622	4.09	2	11	5.50
1949	76	297	3.91	79	340	4.30
1950	137	613	4.47	18	78	4.33
1951	113	453	4.01	41	168	4.10
Total	1,721	6,997	4.07	292	1,177	4.03

KEY: G = games played; OR = opposing runs; AVG = average runs per game. Note: DiMaggio was in military service from 1943 to 1945.

before and after every home game. Favored journalists, who wrote with scarlet passion, drew special rewards, say a free trip to Florida for the wife and children during spring training. In this climate, most New York baseball writers were not in fact reporters. They were hairy-legged cheerleaders sans pompoms.

And, in the era before television became a part of life, the newspapers often dictated public perception of the players. The fans were told that DiMaggio was a great fielder and had no reason to disbelieve it.

It could be that the writers truly believed what they wrote about Joe's "D." The most learned observers would be hard pressed to discern the difference between an outfielder who catches 2.8 fly balls per game and another who gets 2.6. Since fielding statistics are typically ignored or dismissed, appearances are all-important. A graceful or flashy fielder might get more attention than he deserves, and a great hitter might erroneously be credited with being a great fielder. It is something sociologists call the "halo effect": the tendency to attribute positive traits to individuals known to possess other (but unrelated) positive traits.

And that, I believe, is what happened with Joe DiMaggio. Once he was identified as a great fielder, writers, players, and fans observed him with that preconceived notion and came to believe it. Or, as Red Smith once put it, "Repetition carries conviction against which truth cannot stand."

Jackie Robinson Was the First Black Player in the Major Leagues

Instrumental in easing acceptance of Jackie Robinson as baseball's first black performer.

—Hall of Fame public relations director
Bill Guilfoile on Pee Wee Reese's Hall plaque

Pee Wee Reese was "Instrumental in easing acceptance of Jackie Robinson as baseball's first black performer," according to Reese's Hall of Fame plaque. "History was made in 1947, when Jackie Robinson became the first African American to compete in Major League Baseball." So said the December 1996 edition of CMG *Worldwide Report*, publication of the Curtis Management Group, which represents Robinson's estate in marketing ventures. CMG was preparing to commemorate the 50th anniversary of this "first." They were at least 63 years late.

The first known African American major leaguer appeared 35 years before Robinson was born. On May 1, 1884, catcher Moses F. "Fleet" Walker made his debut for the Toledo Blue Stockings. Toledo was a member of the American Association (AA), considered by historians to be the second major league in baseball history. The AA started operation in 1882, six years after the NL, and rivaled the NL for the next ten seasons before disbanding after the 1891 season. The two leagues even competed in seven "World's Championship Series"—forerunner of the modern World Series—between 1884 and 1890.

Walker played in 42 of Toledo's 110 games that season, batting a respectable .263 (the league average was .240). On July 15, Fleet was joined on the team by his brother, Welday Walker. Welday, an outfielder, played in only five games, and neither brother appeared in the majors after 1884. The big leagues remained practically all white for the next 62 seasons.

Besides the Walkers, more than 130 African Americans played minor league ball between 1878 and 1899. Many of them, including second baseman/pitcher Bud Fowler, infielders Frank Grant and Sol White, and pitcher George Stovey, were evidently good enough to play in the majors but were never given the chance. This was due to the "color line," the unwritten rule that barred blacks from the big leagues for six decades.

African American pro ballplayers faced prejudice and hostility from fans in most cities, and even teammates, but especially from opponents. A quote from an unidentified International League player, published in the *Sporting News* in 1889, gives some idea what they were up against:

> While I myself am prejudiced against playing in a team with a colored player, still I could not help pitying some of the poor black fellows that played in the International League. Fowler used to play second base with the lower part of his legs encased in wooden guards. He knew that about every player that came down to second base on a steal had it in for him and would, if possible, throw the spikes into him. He was a good player, but left the base every time there was a close play in order to get away from the spikes.
>
> I have seen him muff balls intentionally, so that he would not have to try to touch runners, fearing that they might injure him. Grant was the same way. Why, the runners chased him off second base. They went down so often trying to break his legs or injure them that he gave up his infield position the latter part of last season and played right field. This is not all.
>
> About half the pitchers try their best to hit these colored players when [they are] at the bat. . . . One of the International League pitchers pitched for Grant's head all the time. He never put a ball over the plate but sent them in straight and true right at Grant. Do what he would he could not hit the Buffalo man, and [Grant] trotted down to first on called balls all the time.

Hall of Famer Adrian "Cap" Anson made perhaps the most decisive move in the drawing of the color line. Anson, the first baseman and manager of the Chicago NL club, was one of the most popular and respected players in the game. On July 14, 1887, Chicago was scheduled to play a much-awaited exhibition game against the International League's Newark Little Giants and their famed "colored battery" of George Stovey and Fleet Walker. But Anson refused to field his team against any black players. For the game to go on as scheduled, Stovey and Walker were benched for the game.

That day, the International League's board of directors held a secret meeting in Buffalo to discuss the fate of African American players, whose participation in the league had already contributed to various dissent. According to the July 15, 1887, *Newark Daily Journal*—in an article entitled "The Color Line Drawn in Baseball"—the "board finally directed Secretary White to approve of no more contracts with colored men." Twenty years later, Sol White wrote a history of black baseball, blaming Anson for the color line.

Although Anson undoubtedly played a large role in this development, he does not deserve all the "credit." As historian Robert Peterson writes in his landmark book *Only the Ball Was White* (1970), "Anson's animus toward Negroes was strong and obvious. But that he had the power and popularity to force Negroes out of baseball almost singlehandedly, as White suggests, is to credit him with more influence than he had, or for that matter, than he needed."

Whatever the reason, the extinction of black players from pro baseball came swiftly after 1887. By the twentieth century, until Jackie Robinson came along, the major and minor leagues were as white as the baselines. Judge Kenesaw M. Landis, commissioner of baseball between 1921 and 1944, has been charged with deliberately keeping the color line intact during his regime. Hall of Fame manager Leo Durocher called Landis out on this in July 1942, and Landis responded that integration was up to the team owners. But it wasn't until after Landis's 1944 death that any owner took a chance.

Robinson made his debut on April 15, 1947. There is a perception that he was the lone representative of his race for two full years, but, in fact, six other black players joined him in the major leagues in 1947–1948, with Larry Doby starting just 80 days after Jackie.

Despite the color line, it is quite possible that other players of African American ancestry infiltrated the big leagues before Robinson. If a team owner found a talented player of questionable race, he might try to pass off the player as, say, a Native American or Cuban. Outfielder Bill Smith (1873); first baseman Bill White (1879); catcher Sandy Nava (1882–1886); pitcher Bumpus Jones (1892–1893); outfielder George Treadway

(1893–1896); catcher Chief Meyers (1909–1917); outfielder/infielder Tex McDonald (1912–1915); catcher Mike Gonzalez (1912–1932); pitcher Gus Bono (1920); pitcher Jose Acosta (1920–1922); the Miller brothers, Bing (outfielder, 1921–1936) and Ralph (pitcher, 1921); second baseman/first baseman George Grantham (1922–1934); outfielder Bobby Estalella (1935–1949); pitcher Hi Bithorn (1942–1947); and pitcher Tommy de la Cruz (1944) are among pre-1947 players believed or rumored to have had black ancestry, yet had light enough skin to "pass" as white. Other players were callously nicknamed "Nig" for their Negroid features including pitcher George Cuppy (1892–1901), catcher Charles Fuller (1902), catcher Jay Justin Clarke (1905–1920), infielder John Perrine (1907), and pitcher Gerard Lipscomb (1937). Rumors have included even the immortal Babe Ruth.

Only one thing is certain: Jackie Robinson was not the first.

Bill Bevens and Cookie Lavagetto Ended Their Careers on the Near No-Hitter in the 1947 World Series

Game Four of the 1947 World Series was one for the ages. The Yankees' Bill Bevens was working on a no-hitter until, with two outs in the bottom of the ninth inning (and two on base via walks), the Dodgers' Cookie Lavagetto slammed a two-run double to cost Bevens the no-hitter and the game, 3–2. It is often said that this was the last major league pitch thrown by Bevens, and the last swing taken by Lavagetto.

Not quite. While neither Bevens nor Lavagetto played in the majors after 1947, both saw more action in this World Series. Lavagetto struck out in Game Five, flied out and grounded out in Game Six, and popped out in Game Seven. And Bevens pitched two and a third scoreless innings in the final game of the Fall Classic, good enough to earn the clinching victory under modern scoring rules.

A Boston Writer Cost Ted Williams the 1947 AL MVP Award

Then it came out that one Boston writer didn't even put me in the top ten on his ballot. A tenth-place vote would have given me two points and the Most Valuable Player Award . . . the writer's name was Mel Webb.

—Ted Williams, in My Turn at Bat (1969)

In 1947, Ted Williams had another remarkable season. The Red Sox slugger won his second Triple Crown, leading the league in home runs (32), RBI (114), and batting (.343), as well as runs (125), walks (162), on-base percentage (.499), and slugging percentage (.634). Yet, when the AL's MVP balloting was announced, Williams had lost out to the Yankees' Joe DiMaggio, whose numbers (20 homers, 97 RBI, .315) were far less imposing. To add to Williams's frustration, he lost the honor by just one point in the voting, 202–201. And one of the 24 voters didn't even list Williams—meaning that the writer didn't think Ted was one of the ten most valuable players in the league. That inexplicable decision helped cost Williams the MVP Award.

To add insult to injury, the writer in question was a Boston scribe, according to Williams. In his autobiography with John Underwood, *My Turn at Bat*, Ted writes, "Then it came out that one Boston writer didn't even put me in the top ten on his ballot. A tenth-place vote would have given me two points and the Most Valuable Player Award . . . the writer's name was Mel Webb." Williams recalled feuding with the *Boston Globe* writer earlier in the season, giving that as the probable reason for Webb's snub. Actually, a tenth-place vote would have been worth just one point, creating a tie for first place. But, more to the point, Mel Webb wasn't the culprit—because he didn't even have a vote in the election.

Three beat writers from each of the eight AL cities—Boston, Chicago, Cleveland, Detroit, New York, Philadelphia, St. Louis, and Washington— did the voting. Voting, then as now, was done on a 14–9–8–7–6–5–4–3–2–1 basis: writers were to name ten players in descending order of perceived value, with a first-place vote worth 14 points, a second-place nomination nine, on down to one point for a tenth-place vote. Prior to 1938, a first-place vote was worth only ten points and, under that system, Williams would have won the 1947 MVP handily, 189–170.

Evidence indicates that the three Boston voters in 1947 were Joe Cashman of the *Boston Daily Record*, Jack Malaney of the *Boston Post*, and Burt Whitman of the *Boston Herald*, all staunch supporters of Williams who voted in several MVP elections each. There was a lot of flak in the contemporary Boston press about the outrageous election result, but very little of it was focused on the one voter who omitted Terrible Ted. Harold Kaese of the *Boston Globe* suggested that Williams's snub actually came from Chicago, Cleveland, Detroit, or St. Louis, writing about a "Mid-Western writer who couldn't even see Ted ranked with the top ten!"

Analysis of the voting shows that Williams's loss was far more than a case of being left off one ballot. Ted received just three of 24 first-place votes, ten seconds, three thirds, five fourths, a fifth, and a seventh. DiMaggio, on the other hand, got eight first-place nods, five seconds, four thirds, a fourth, an eighth, a ninth, and a tenth—and was left off three ballots himself. The only man to be named on every ballot was Cleveland shortstop Lou Boudreau, who had one first-place vote and finished third overall, with 168 points. Other first-place nominations went to Yankees' reliever Joe Page (seven); Yanks' first baseman George McQuinn (three); and Athletics' shortstop Eddie Joost (two), a .206-hitter who was named on only one other ballot. In a similar anomaly, Yanks' rookie Yogi Berra, who played just 83 games, received two second-place votes but wasn't mentioned on any of the other 22 ballots. Page, the first relief pitcher to get any support in an MVP election, finished fourth in the voting, with 167 points. Tigers' third baseman George Kell was fifth at 132, and McQuinn was sixth with 77, with 34 players in all receiving points. Writers could also list "honorable mention" candidates beyond the top ten; 21 players received such nominations, but they weren't worth any points, and neither Williams nor DiMaggio was listed among these mentions. It was obviously a wide-open election with a lot of curious results.

Yes, Ted Williams probably deserved the MVP Award in 1947—and 1941 and 1942 as well, along with the two he did win in 1946 and 1949. But, we can't blame Mel Webb for the injustice.

The 1948 Braves Won the Pennant Only because of Spahn and Sain

Back will come Spahn, followed by Sain, and followed, we hope, by two days of rain.

—*Boston Post* writer Gerry Hern

The Boston Braves won the NL pennant in 1948, their first in 34 years, and their last before their move to Milwaukee. Thanks to a well-known refrain, it is commonly believed that the Braves were a two-man team. Pitchers Warren Spahn and Johnny Sain anchored the team's pitching staff, and Braves' fans supposedly hoped for foul weather when they weren't scheduled to pitch. "Spahn and Sain, and pray for rain," went the popular ditty, truncated from a Gerry Hern poem published in the *Boston Post* on September 14, 1948:

> First we'll use Spahn, then we'll use Sain,
> Then an off day, followed by rain.
> Back will come Spahn, followed by Sain,
> And followed, we hope, by two days of rain.

Hern was inspired by the stretch-drive performance of the two pitchers. On September 6, Spahn and Sain led the Braves to a doubleheader sweep of the rival Dodgers, 2–1 and 4–0. Two off days and two rainouts followed, and by the time the Braves played again on September 11, their aces were ready to go again—and they again led Boston to a twin bill sweep. Thus began a span of 13 days during which Spahn and Sain pitched eight of the Braves' ten games, winning them all.

But in fact, Spahn and Sain accounted for only 39 of the team's 91 victories in 1948, and their winning percentage was lower than the rest of the teams' pitchers. The Braves won the pennant thanks to a well-balanced blend of offense and defense. Sain did have what was probably his best year in 1948. He went 24–15 with a 2.60 ERA, leading the NL in games started (39), complete games (28), innings pitched (314⅔), and victories, and finishing second behind Stan Musial in MVP balloting. Spahn, on the other hand, had an off year, arguably the worst of the first 17 full seasons of his Hall of Fame career. His ERA was 3.71, the highest he posted between 1942 and 1964, and barely better than the league average, and his record was a modest 15–12.

Combined, the two pitchers were 39–27 (.591), while the rest of the staff was 52–35 (.598). According to Craig Wright, the 1948 Braves were the first team to win an NL pennant with their top two starters combining for a lower winning percentage than the rest of the staff. Spahn and Sain accounted for 43% of the team's victories, a percentage surpassed by the top duos of three other NL teams (Giants, Reds, and Cubs) that year alone. Many other contemporary championship teams had pairs who won more than 43% of their team's victories; the 1944 Tigers, who just missed the pennant, got 64% of their 88 wins from Hal Newhouser (29) and Dizzy Trout (27), but as far as we know, no one wrote a rhyme about them.

Award-winning researcher and analyst Tom Ruane points out that, even during the stretch drive, the S&S boys were no more effective than the rest of the staff. In the last 28 games of the season, Spahn and Sain combined for an impressive 12–4 record and 2.47 ERA. But the rest of the team's pitchers went 9–3 with a 1.77 ERA.

According to Bill James's "Win Shares" (WS) system, the 1948 Braves were led by Sain's 28 WS, followed closely by third baseman Bob Elliott's 27. Others who matched or exceeded Spahn's 14 were shortstop Alvin Dark (20), injury-plagued left fielder Jeff Heath (20), right fielder Tommy Holmes (19), second baseman Eddie Stanky (14), and first sacker Earl Torgeson (14). Not far behind were pitchers Bill Voiselle (12) and Vern Bickford (11) and center fielder Mike McCormick (11). Heath (.319), McCormick (.303), and

Holmes (.325) formed an all-.300 outfield. Defending MVP Elliott was the power man (23 homers, 100 RBI, .283), also leading the NL with 131 walks. Dark batted .322 as a rookie, finishing third in MVP balloting. Late-season acquisition Nels Potter pitched brilliantly (5–2, 2.33) down the stretch, and Vern Bickford (11–5, including 4–0 in September through October), Bobby Hogue (8–2), and Clyde Shoun (5–1) also contributed fine records in limited roles.

Spahn and Sain actually had bigger impacts on their team's win totals in two surrounding seasons, accounting for 49% of the Braves' wins in both 1947 (42 of 86) and 1950 (41 of 83). So, it was when the Braves *weren't* a two-man team that they won the pennant.

The Indians Could Have Had Aaron, Mays, and Banks

Larry Doby became the first black player in the AL in 1947, and he starred for the Cleveland Indians for the next eight years. Had management listened to Doby's scouting tips, the Indians might have dominated the major leagues throughout the 1950s and 1960s, according to a story included in Russell Schneider's *Cleveland Indians Encyclopedia* (1996), and reprinted in *USA Today Sports Weekly* in December 2002:

> When Hank Greenberg became the Indians' farm director in 1949, Doby recommended three Negro leagues players he had played against. Greenberg sent his scouts to check them out. That spring, Doby asked Greenberg what the scouts thought of the three. "Their reports were not good," Greenberg said. "[Hank] Aaron has a hitch in his swing and will never hit good pitching. [Shortstop Ernie] Banks is too slow and didn't have enough range, and [Willie] Mays can't hit a curveball."

A problem with this story is that Doby last played in the Negro National League (with Newark) in 1947, at which time Banks and Mays were 16 years old, and Aaron was 13. Mays began his Negro leagues' career in 1948, Banks in 1950, and Aaron in 1952. In other words, Doby never played against any of the three men in the Negro leagues, nor were Banks or Aaron available for scouting in the spring of 1949.

Ted Williams Lost the Closest Batting Race in History

In 1949, Ted Williams had a chance to set a record by winning his third Triple Crown. Williams topped the AL, with 43 home runs, and tied teammate Vern Stephens for the RBI lead, with 159. And Williams batted .343, the same as Detroit's George Kell. But when statisticians carried out the decimals another place to break the tie, it was reported that Kell edged out Williams, .3429 to .3427, to win the batting title in the closest batting crown finish in major league history.

Actually, the race was even tighter than reported: .3429 to .3428. But, there was an even closer one in the same league just four years before, and recent research has discovered the new record holder for closest batting race of them all.

In the days before computers or even calculators, the statisticians computed batting averages by hand and then rounded up or down as necessary to three decimal places. In 1945, the Yankees' Snuffy Stirnweiss and the White Sox' Tony Cucinello both averaged .3085—but, in rounding, Stirnweiss moved up to .309, while Cucinello dropped to .308, making it appear to be a clear-cut victory for Snuffy. But, it actually takes five decimal places to break the tie between the two, .30854 to .30846.

The 1910 AL batting race was the most controversial of all time. Prior to that season, Hugh Chalmers, president and general manager of the Chalmers Motor Company, announced that he would present a Chalmers "30" roadster to the major leaguer who compiled the highest batting average (minimum 100 at bats for pitchers, 250 for catchers, and 350 for all other players). It became a two-man race between Detroit's detested Ty Cobb (who already owned a Chalmers 30) and Cleveland's popular Nap Lajoie. There were various charges of favoritism by official scorers, and the consensus of the press was that Cobb's selfish pursuit of the car had cost his team the pennant (although they finished 18 games out). Cobb sat out the Tigers' last game, owning a seemingly safe .383 to .376 lead, but Lajoie went 8-for-8 in a season-ending doubleheader to apparently edge ahead, .384 to .383. Included among Lajoie's output were seven bunt hits—remarkable for a slow-footed slugger, until we learn that the Browns' Jack O'Connor, the opposing manager, had ordered Red Corriden, his rookie third baseman, to play ridiculously deep when Lajoie came to bat. AL president Ban Johnson relieved O'Connor of his duties (but did not implicate Lajoie or Corriden) and awarded the bat crown to Cobb, citing an error in the records, whose correction raised Cobb to .385. Chalmers gave automobiles to both players and, the next year, started what is recognized as the first MVP Award, rewarding players for perceived value rather than statistics (and Cobb won yet another car).

Subsequent researchers have discovered errors in the 1910 records of both Cobb and Lajoie. Most recently, Trent McCotter's exhaustive research of the records of the two players reveals that Lajoie actually edged Cobb by the narrowest of margins, .38345 to .38340. Subsequent research also erased what was long thought to be the closest race. In the NL, in 1892, Cleveland's Cupid Childs and Brooklyn's Dan Brouthers were listed in a virtual tie at .335, although Childs (185-for-552, .33514) was a hair ahead of Brouthers (197-for-588, .33503). But Childs is now listed at 177-for-558, a mere .317, giving Big Dan a comfortable margin. Table 3.6 presents the batting title races in which less than one point separated the first- and second-place (and, in one case, third-place) finishers.

Table 3.6. Closest Batting Races, 1871–2011

Year	LG	Players, Teams	AB	H	AVG	DIFF
1910	AL	Nap Lajoie, CLE	592	227	.38345	
		Ty Cobb, DET	506	194	.38340	.00005
1945	AL	Snuffy Stirnweiss, NY	632	195	.30854	
		Tony Cuccinello, CHI	402	124	.30846	.00009
1949	AL	George Kell, DET	522	179	.34291	
		Ted Williams, BOS	566	194	.34276	.00016
2003	NL	Albert Pujols, SL	591	212	.35871	
		Todd Helton, COL	583	209	.35849	.00022
1931	NL	Chick Hafey, SL	450	157	.34889	
		Bill Terry, NY	611	213	.34861	.00028
		Jim Bottomley, SL	382	133	.34817	.00072
1970	AL	Alex Johnson, CAL	614	202	.32899	
		Carl Yastrzemski, BOS	566	186	.32862	.00037
1886	AA	Guy Hecker, LOU	343	117	.34111	
		Pete Browning, LOU	467	159	.34047	.00064
1935	AL	Buddy Myer, WAS	616	215	.34903	
		Joe Vosmik, CLE	620	216	.34839	.00064
1982	AL	Willie Wilson, KC	585	194	.33162	
		Robin Yount, MIL	635	210	.33071	.00092

KEY: LG = league; AB = times at bat; H = hits; AVG = batting average; DIFF = differences in batting averages. Note: Discrepancies in the "DIFF" column result from rounding.

Hoyt Wilhelm Homered and Tripled His First Two Times Up and Then Never Hit Another Homer or Triple in His 21-Year Career

On April 23, 1952, New York Giants' rookie reliever Hoyt Wilhelm came to the plate for the first time. Facing the Braves' Dick Hoover, Wilhelm knocked a ball into the Polo Grounds seats, helping himself toward his first big league victory, 9–5. Wilhelm went on to pitch in 21 major league seasons, but he never hit another home run.

Legend has it that Wilhelm also tripled his next time up and never hit another triple. While it's true that Wilhelm hit only one big-league three-bagger, it wasn't in his second time up. In fact, it was more than a year later, in his 50th career at bat.

Wilhelm's triple came on June 4, 1953. In the seventh inning, he drove a ball into center field and made it all the way to third base, knocking in Ray Noble with the go-ahead run. The Giants went on to win, 11–3, and Wilhelm again earned the victory.

Wilhelm could have left his bat in the dugout after the 1953 season. In the last 19 years of his career, he came up 361 times and collected just 27 hits—26 singles and a double—good for a .078 slugging percentage.

Willie Mays Caught a 480-Foot Drive in the 1954 World Series

The most famous catch in World Series history occurred in Game One of the 1954 Fall Classic. Willie Mays made the catch on a drive hit by Vic Wertz. The ball was hit anywhere from 450 to 480 feet, depending which source you trust. Trust this source: The ball traveled about 415 feet.

The heavily favored Cleveland Indians—winners of an AL-record 111 games during the 154-game regular season—were locked in a 2–2 tie with the New York Giants. The game was played at the Polo Grounds, whose wall in dead center field was listed at 483 feet from home plate (in other years, the distance was listed at anywhere from 475 to 505 feet, with no explanation for the changes). In the top of the eighth, Cleveland's first two batters reached base, bringing up the hot-hitting Wertz. The Indians' first baseman would finish the day 4-for-5, including a double and a triple. The three-bagger hit the right field wall and brought home both of Cleveland's runs.

This time, Wertz blasted a ball toward deep center field, threatening to break the game wide open. But Mays, the 23-year-old phenom, was off on contact. After a long run, Mays hauled the ball in with a spectacular over-the-shoulder catch in front of the fence, then spun and threw the ball back to the infield. Larry Doby advanced to third on the catch, but Cleveland failed to score. The Giants went on to win the game in extra innings and then sweep the demoralized Indians in four games.

Virtually every published source claimed the drive went at least 450 feet. "The ball had traveled 460 feet," according to the *Sporting News*, while New York's *Newsday* described it as "a 470-foot poke." Fred Lieb, in *The Story of the World Series: An Informal History* (1949), takes the cake:

> Wertz greeted lefty reliever Don Liddle with a terrific line fly to deepest center— in front of the 480-foot marker. It looked like two sure runs and a triple for Wertz. However, Mays was off with the crack of the bat and made a miracle catch, taking the ball as it came over his shoulder only a few inches from the wall. Willie was running at full speed, with his back to home plate. Only an agile person such as Mays could have checked himself without crashing into the wall. The writer regards it as one of the greatest catches he has seen in a half-century of World Series coverage.

So we've seen 450, 460, 470, and now a few inches shy of 480 feet. Where does it stop? Speaking of stopping, how does someone "running at full speed" come to a complete stop in the matter of a few inches, without hitting a barrier?

Mays caught the ball a little in front of the wall, but it was *not* the 483-foot wall at the deepest part of the park. Rather, it was the wall to the right of the center field enclosure, at the corner of the bleachers. According to Phil Lowry's original *Green Cathedrals: The Ultimate Celebration of All Major League Ballparks* (2006), the bleacher corners measured 425 feet from home plate, although that distance—like all of the Polo Grounds' published dimensions—are subject to question (New York sportswriter Leonard Koppett told one researcher that the correct unmarked distance was 435 feet). Either way, the ball traveled less than 425 feet before settling in Mays's glove. We have to allow for the three braking steps he took before wheeling and throwing the ball. The third step landed him in the warning track, which was about eight feet wide.

John Pastier, an architecture critic and baseball historian, has studied this issue for decades. His methodology has included studies of photographs and park diagrams and the application of architectural calculation methods. "I'm not yet positive about the correct distance," Pastier says, but "I've never seen a published estimate of the distance that wasn't wildly overstated. . . . I'd give the range for the catch as 405 feet to 420 feet."

Ron Selter, another baseball historian and a ballpark student, has also invested considerable time into this subject. Selter believes that the bleacher corners were actually about 432 feet from home, and his work convinced Lowry to change the dimensions in the revised *Green Cathedrals*. Selter estimates the distance of Wertz's fly ball "in the range of 415 to 420 feet."

The ball would have been a home run in almost any other big-league park. It would have been a triple against almost any other outfielder. The situation and the play itself warrant its label as the greatest World Series catch ever. We needn't hyperbolize it by adding 65 feet to the distance.

While we're at it, there are a couple of other myths associated with this event. Don Liddle was the pitcher brought in to face Wertz, and he was promptly relieved by Marv Grissom. As legend has it, Liddle threw just the one pitch, resulting in the long drive miraculously turned into an out. As he left the field, Liddle reportedly quipped to pitching coach Fred Fitzsimmons, "Well, I got *my* man."

In fact, Liddle threw four pitches to Wertz. The first was a ball, high and tight, and the second was a called strike on the outside corner. Then, Wertz fouled off a *sacrifice bunt* attempt (imagine how history would have changed), before flying out to Mays. And, according to Liddle, the quip came after the game was over. "That was no laughing matter. We were still in a tough spot. I wouldn't joke like that in the situation we were in during a World Series game," said Liddle years later. It was after the game, when the team was celebrating in the Giants' clubhouse, that Liddle went up to Mays and manager Leo Durocher with the famous quote.

A Racist Manager Prevented
Brooks Lawrence from Winning 20 Games

According to former Cincinnati slugger George Crowe, longtime manager Birdie Tebbetts was a racist whose views affected his job. Crowe claimed that,

> We had a manager who didn't want to win the pennant. We had a pitcher named Brooks Lawrence who won 13 straight games. But Birdie Tebbetts came out one day and told someone, "Ain't no black man's going to win 20 games for me." And he refused to pitch Lawrence after he got 19 wins.

It was in 1956 when Lawrence ran off his string of victories but wound up one short of the 20-win plateau. Over the last 11 days of the season, Lawrence got into only one game, a two-inning stint on September 25. But the facts point to a pitcher who was lucky to have the record he had and did not pitch effectively enough to keep his spot in the rotation.

Lawrence was 12–0 at the All-Star break that year, and he extended it to 13–0 by July 17. But he had enjoyed a goodly amount of run support and luck to get there; his ERA was a modest 3.58 (the NL's was 3.78 that year), and he had just 50 strikeouts against 45 walks in 123⅓ innings. During the next two weeks, he pitched well, although he absorbed his first two losses. Through August 1, Lawrence was 15–2 with a 3.30 ERA in 152⅔ innings—just six innings fewer than his career high to that point.

Over the next 45 days, including his 19th win on September 15, Lawrence got hammered. He pitched 61⅓ innings with a 4–7 record and a 5.72 ERA. That seems a valid reason for a contending team to remove him from the starting rotation. Bear in mind that Lawrence was primarily a reliever before 1956 (53 relief outings versus 28 starts), and he was used out of the pen 14 times in 1956 before September 15.

Lawrence actually pitched in each of the next four contests, all reasonably close games. On September 17, he pitched the ninth inning of a game that was tied 4–4 when he entered. He gave up a homer, another hit, and a walk to earn the 5–4 loss. In the four games, he pitched 2⅔ innings, walked four, and had a 6.75 ERA. Again, a seemingly valid reason for a contending team to try someone else. If I were a manager trying to prevent a pitcher with 19 wins from reaching 20, I wouldn't put him into close games in four straight days, and I sure as hell wouldn't put him into a 4–4 game in the ninth.

Fidel Castro Was a Pro Baseball Prospect

Fidel Castro ruled communist Cuba with an iron hand for almost half a century, from 1959 to 2008. It is said that he was a professional baseball prospect before that, starring as a right-handed pitcher for the University of Havana, and signing (or almost signing) a minor league contract for the Washington Senators (or the New York Giants, or the New York Yankees). Senators' scout Joe Cambria and Giants' bird-dog Alex Pompez were always on the lookout for Latin American talent, and they reportedly gave Castro serious consideration. How history might have been changed had Castro stuck with pitching instead of dictating.

Castro *was* a basketball, track, and table tennis star in Cuba, but he never signed a contract in organized pro baseball, and he never played that sport at the University of Havana (although he tried out for the team). According to Latin American baseball expert Peter Bjarkman, Castro's only documented pitching experiences were as a high school senior in 1945, and for pickup teams after he came into power in 1959.

The story of Castro's prowess may have grown from a tale told by major league player Don Hoak. In a June 1964 *SPORT* magazine article, Hoak claims to have faced Castro in a 1950–1951 winter league game. With Hoak at bat, the game was interrupted by a student demonstration on the field of play. Castro, the student leader, supposedly marched to the mound in his street clothes, seized the ball, and ordered Hoak back to the batter's box. After Hoak fouled off a couple of wild fastballs, order was restored, and Castro left the field "like an impudent boy who has been cuffed by the teacher and sent to stand in the corner." The story was reprinted in Charles Einstein's *The Third Fireside Book of Baseball* (1968) and *The Baseball Reader: Favorites from the Fireside Books of Baseball* (1986), and John Thorn's *The Armchair Book of Baseball* (1985), and repeated in many other sources, none questioning its veracity.

The Hoak hoax was dismantled by the late Everardo J. Santamarina in the Society for American Baseball Research's (SABR) 1994 *National Pastime*. Santamarina describes many inaccuracies and inconsistencies in the Hoak story, but the biggest are that Hoak played winter ball in Cuba only in the winter of 1953–1954—and Castro was in the midst of a two-year stint in prison at the time.

The 1955–1960 Kansas City Athletics Gave Away Their Talent to the Yankees

> Kansas City had been the location of a minor league Yankee farm team for 18 years, and its management never seemed to understand that their role had changed when they were granted a major league franchise.
>
> —*The Baseball Trade Register* (1984)

After 54 seasons in Philadelphia, the Athletics moved to Kansas City prior to the 1955 season. Arnold Johnson, a business associate and close friend of New York Yankees' coowner Del Webb, bought a controlling interest in the team from the Mack family and moved the team west. The team soon became known as the "Yankee Farm Club." As explained in *The Baseball Trade Register* (1984),

> Kansas City had been the location of a minor league Yankee farm team for 18 years, and its management never seemed to understand that their role had changed when they were granted a major league franchise. In the first five years of its existence, Kansas City made 16 trades with New York involving 59 players. . . . The worst of these abuses were halted when Charlie Finley bought the team from Arnold Johnson's estate in the winter of 1960–1961.

Johnson had died on March 10, 1960.

Aided mightily by Kansas City castoffs, particularly Roger Maris and Ralph Terry, the Yankees continued to win pennant after pennant: every year from 1955 to 1964, except 1959. Meanwhile, the A's never had a winning season before moving to Oakland after the 1967 season. The perception remains that the A's gave away their best players to the Yanks. While there is no doubt that something fishy was going on between the two teams from 1955 to 1960, the fact is that Kansas City did pretty well overall in these dealings—and arguably got the better of them.

Bill James devised a system to evaluate trades more than three decades ago, publishing the results in SABR's 1978 *Baseball Research Journal*. James disregarded transactions involving cash and decided that five years was a reasonable period to evaluate trades (stopping the count if a player was subsequently sold or released). He used a crude player evaluation system he called "Approximate Value"; I am substituting his more precise "Win Shares" (WS) to evaluate the Kansas City–New York deals of 1955 through 1960:

- March 30, 1955: The A's purchased first baseman Dick Kryhoski and pitchers Ewell Blackwell and Tom Gorman. Kryhoski and Blackwell did virtually nothing for Kansas City, but Gorman went on to become a valuable member of their pitching staff. He went 7–6, with 18 saves (second in the AL), for a 1955 team that was 63–91 and accumulated 38 WS by 1959. However, this deal is not rated because it was a straight cash deal.
- April 28, 1955: The Athletics bought pitcher Lou Sleater. Sleater did little the rest of his career, totaling ten WS. Again, this deal is not rated.
- May 11, 1955: The A's acquired outfielder Enos Slaughter and pitcher Johnny Sain in exchange for pitcher Sonny Dixon and cash. Slaughter went on to bat .302 in 199 games for the A's before being sold back to the Yanks in 1956; Sain did little, and Dixon pitched just four innings for New York. Score: Kansas City 18, New York 0.
- June 14, 1956: Kansas City got outfielder Lou Skizas and first baseman Eddie Robinson in trade for pitcher Moe Burtschy, outfielder Bill Renna, and cash. Skizas went on to bat .316 in 83 games as a rookie and hit 18 homers as a sophomore before flaming out; neither Burtschy nor Renna ever played for New York. Score: Kansas City 19, New York 2.
- August 25, 1956: The Yankees purchased outfielder Enos Slaughter for the waiver price. Slaughter went on to have 16 WS the rest of his career; the deal was for cash, thus it is not rated.
- October 16, 1956: The A's bought outfielder Bob Cerv. Cerv went on to have a monster year for Kansas City in 1958 (38 homers, 104 RBI, .305), contributing to 66 WS over the five-year period. He was dealt

back to New York in 1960. As a straight cash deal, the 1956 transaction is not rated.

- February 19–June 4, 1957: In their biggest and most successful deal of the period, the Yanks got pitchers Bobby Shantz, Art Ditmar, and Jack McMahon, and infielders Clete Boyer, Wayne Belardi, and Curt Roberts; they gave up pitchers Tom Morgan, Jack Urban, Mickey McDermott, and Rip Coleman; infielders Billy Hunter and Milt Graff; and outfielder Irv Noren. Although three of the new acquisitions never played in pinstripes, Shantz and Ditmar became valuable staff members for the Yankees, and Boyer anchored their hot corner for most of the next decade. Morgan and Urban went on to fashion winning records for the A's, but they hardly made up for the mismatch. Score: New York 119, Kansas City 60.
- June 15, 1957: In the aftermath of the Copacabana incident, the Yankees unloaded infielder Billy Martin, along with pitcher Ralph Terry and outfielder Woodie Held, for pitcher Ryne Duren and outfielder Jim Pisoni. Duren went on to become New York's bullpen ace for a couple of years, but all three new A's accumulated more WS during the period, with Held proving to be the best of the bunch (and helping KC land Roger Maris a year later). In the most lopsided deal of them all, the A's prevailed, 155–43.
- June 15, 1958: In their second straight trading deadline deal, the A's got pitcher Bob Grim and outfielder Harry "Suitcase" Simpson in exchange for pitcher Duke Maas and Virgil Trucks. Score: Kansas City 27, New York 13.
- August 22, 1958: The Athletics traded pitcher Murry Dickson for outfielder Zeke Bella and cash; neither player made a tangible contribution thereafter (score 0–0).
- April 8, 1959: In another scoreless deal, the A's swapped pitchers with the Yankees, Jack Urban for Mark Freeman.
- April 12, 1959: The Athletics acquired outfielder Russ Snyder and shortstop Tommy Carroll for infielder Mike Baxes and outfielder Bob Martyn. Neither Baxes nor Martyn ever played again in the majors, but Snyder went on to be a solid utility player until 1970. Score: Kansas City 48, New York 0.
- May 9, 1959: The Yankees purchased pitcher Murry Dickson. Dickson never appeared in another major league game. This was the last of five straight cash deals between the two clubs during this period; although they are not rated, the A's got 114 WS out of the transactions, the Yankees only 16.

- May 26, 1959: The Yankees got pitcher Ralph Terry and outfielder Hector Lopez in trade for second baseman Jerry Lumpe and pitchers Tom Sturdivant and Johnny Kucks. Terry posted records of 16–3 and 23–12 for New York in 1961–1962, while Lopez proved to be a valuable role player. But Lumpe quietly emerged as the most valuable of the bunch, almost evening out the score: New York 120, Kansas City 116.
- December 11, 1959: In the most visible and criticized swap of them all, the Yankees got outfielder Roger Maris and infielders Joe DeMaestri and Kent Hadley for outfielders Norm Siebern and Hank Bauer and pitcher Don Larsen. With the others contributing little, the trade essentially boiled down to Maris for Siebern, and we all know what Maris went on to do: back-to-back MVPs, including the record-breaking 61-homer season of 1961. But Siebern was hardly chopped liver, as he earned three All-Star selections and had one of the best seasons in Kansas City A's history in 1962: 25 homers, 117 RBI (second in the AL), and a .308 average (fifth), good for seventh in MVP voting. Score: New York 136, Kansas City 116.
- May 19, 1960: New York acquired outfielder Bob Cerv for third baseman Andy Carey. Score: New York 12, Kansas City 11.

Final score: Kansas City Athletics 570, New York Yankees 445 (and if you add in the sales, it's 684–461). Not bad for a farm team.

Jerome Holtzman Invented the Save

When longtime Chicago sportswriter Jerome Holtzman died in 2008, practically every obituary named him as the "inventor" or "father" of the save, giving statistical recognition to relief pitchers. But Holtzman himself shunned such titles. "Three people were keeping track of saves before I came along in 1957," Holtzman told me in a 1993 interview, naming "Irving Kaze at Pittsburgh, Jim Toomey at St. Louis, and Allan Roth at Brooklyn. But, by their criteria, all a pitcher had to do was finish a winning game. What I did was develop a formula."

Holtzman's original definition of a save demanded that a reliever not only preserve someone else's victory, but face the potential tying or lead run during his tenure on the mound. Holtzman proposed to compile saves on a daily basis himself, reporting the results. He wrote to *Sporting News* publisher J. G. Taylor Spink with his proposition and was eventually rewarded with a "100 or 200 dollar bonus" and hired to keep track of the pen men. The result was the "Fireman of the Year Award," given annually starting in 1960 to the relief pitcher in each league with the highest combined total of wins and saves. As reported in the 1961 *Sporting News Baseball Guide*, "Pitching saves had been compiled by some club statisticians for several years on a helter-skelter basis, but under the *Sporting News*'s rules, save (sic) were credited only under specific circumstances." Holtzman's definition was later expanded to include appearances in which a reliever pitched at least one perfect inning while preserving a two-run lead (1961), and those in which he pitched two-plus innings to finish a game in which he inherited a three-run lead (1964).

Saves were considered a "very minor stat," says Holtzman. "Nobody paid much attention at first." But, by 1969, the save had grown in importance to the point that the Rules Committee felt obliged to make it an official statistic, the first new one in nearly a half century. They did not adhere to Holtzman's definition, however, requiring only that a reliever preserve a lead and not get removed during an inning (he did not even have to finish the game). The rule was made much stricter in December 1973, and then set at its current definition in December 1974.

CHAPTER FOUR

~

Timeless Myths

Some baseball legends can't really be tied to any specific era; they are myths for all seasons.

A Hit That Bounces over the
Fence Is a Ground Rule Double

We've all seen it: a batter hits a fair drive that lands deep in the outfield and then bounces over the fence. The announcer matter-of-factly informs us that it's "a ground rule double." But he's wrong.

The New Dickson Baseball Dictionary (1999) defines "ground rules" as a "set of special rules unique to the specific conditions and dimensions of a given ballpark." These were more common in early baseball, when parks were very different from one another, and special circumstances (like spectators overflowing onto the field) had to be addressed. They still apply to some modern situations, such as the possibility of a batted ball hitting the roof of a domed stadium.

But all other situations are governed by the Official Rules of Major League Baseball. Rule #6.09 (e) states that, "A batter becomes a runner when a fair ball, after touching the ground, bounds into the stands, or passes through, over, or under a fence . . . in which case the batter and the runners shall be entitled to advance two bases." This applies in every major league park. Incidentally, this rule went into effect in 1930 (1931 in the National League). Before that, fair balls that bounced over a fence were ruled home runs.

So, when a batter hits a fair ball that bounces over the fence, it is a rule-book double, not a ground rule double.

The Curveball Is an Optical Illusion

The September 15, 1941, issue of LIFE magazine contains a seven-page article "proving" that a baseball could not really be made to curve. LIFE "assigned its high-speed photographer, Gjon Mili, to investigate the matter pictorially. . . . His evidence fails to show the existence of a curve, raises once more the possibility that this standby of baseball is after all only an optical illusion." The article is accompanied by more than a dozen time-lapse photos of pitches thrown by two aging hurlers, Hall of Famer Carl Hubbell and journeyman Cy Blanton (both known to throw screwballs rather than traditional curves), who went on to combine to win just 15 more big-league games. LIFE concludes that "no pitcher, it seems, has a strong enough finger and wrist motion to put the necessary spin" to curve a baseball.

The article's hypothesis was soon after debunked by articles in the New York Daily News and Look magazine. They included photos of another aging pitcher, Freddie Fitzsimmons, throwing a curveball around three wooden stakes placed in a straight line. The pitch started on the left side of the first stake, curved around the right side of the second, and completed its journey back on the left side of the third. This repeated similar tests done decades earlier and merely confirmed what anyone who had ever seriously played or watched baseball already knew. As early as October 1877, right-hander Tommy Bond and southpaw Bobby Mitchell proved the ability to curve pitches in an experiment in Cincinnati.

But the damage was done. LIFE's conclusions became "fact" to many readers and were echoed as such in numerous other books and publications. To this day, there are those who believe that the curveball is an optical illusion.

"I Got Stan Musial Out 49 Times in a Row"

Throughout history, players have been notorious for telling tall tales about their careers. The problem for us was that many, if not most, of these stories defied documentation, because record keeping was sketchy and haphazard until relatively recently. Enter Retrosheet, an offshoot of the Society for American Baseball Research. Retrosheet's mission is to collect and computerize the scoresheet for every game in major league history. An ambitious project, to be sure, but Retrosheet has managed to document more than 80%

of the 160,000-plus major league games since 1900 (it should be noted that their entries have not all been proofed at this point, thus there may be some minor errors in the data). And their holdings can help us disprove some of these stories, like the following:

- "I can remember things and pitches I made and the hitters. Do you know I got Stan Musial out 49 times in a row? Somebody counted and told me. I'd curve him and jam him with the sinker."—Clem Labine, in *The Boys of Summer* (1971)

  The truth: Labine faced Musial 48 times in his career and retired him in 32 of those occasions. Musial was 10-for-42 (.238) against Labine, with a double, a triple, a homer, three RBI, six walks, and three strikeouts. Un-Man-ly numbers, for sure, but a far cry from 0-for-49.

- "I faced [Mickey Mantle] 63 times and he got one hit—that home run—off me. Believe it or not, I struck him out 47 times."—Dick Radatz, in *The 500 Home Run Club* (1999)

  The truth: Radatz faced Mantle only 19 times in his career, striking him out on 12 occasions. Mantle was 3-for-16 (.188) against Radatz, with a double, a homer, two RBI, and three walks. Dick may have had Mick's number, but he sure didn't have his own numbers straight.

- "For years, whatever reputation I had as a player was based entirely on my label as a 'good defensive catcher who only needs a chance to play,' and on my ability to hit . . . Sandy Koufax. Koufax? *That* Sandy Koufax? Right. I hit him. I hit him hard. Neither one of us ever figured out why."—Bob Uecker, in *Catcher in the Wry* (1982)

  The truth: Uecker went a measly 7-for-38 lifetime with just two RBI against Koufax, batting even lower (.184) than against other pitchers. Included were two doubles and a homer, plus three walks and eight strikeouts.

- "Willie Mays . . . threw out hundreds of runners at home plate."—Ahmad Rashad, in a 2000 Coors beer commercial

  The truth: Mays had a total of 195 outfield assists in his career. Of those, 143 are documented by Retrosheet, with 52 resulting in outs at home plate. That projects to about 71 runners that Mays threw out at home plate—129 short of "hundreds."

- "With the Pirates, I had the distinction of batting behind Gus Bell and Ralph Kiner. Hitting back-to-back home runs was not unusual for those two. The pitcher would be so upset he'd knock me down. I could never understand it since I rarely hurt a pitcher with a bat in my hands."—Joe Garagiola, in *Just Play Ball* (2007)

The truth: Bell and Kiner, teammates from 1950 to 1952, *never* hit back-to-back homers. This research was supplied not by Retrosheet, but by award-winning researcher Herman Krabbenhoft.

- "I did that a lot [stopped at first base on a likely double so that Willie McCovey wouldn't be walked intentionally] . . . I wanted Mac to hit all the time. So if I hit a ball in the gap that might be a triple or double or something, I wouldn't go, I'd let him hit. In San Diego one day, Clyde King says, 'Why don't you go to second?' Well I said, 'I want Mac to hit.' So the next time Mac comes up, he hits the scoreboard in San Diego, that's way out there. He knocks in three runs."—Willie Mays, in a September 2010 interview with the *San Francisco Chronicle*

  The truth: The Giants played only 12 games in San Diego while Clyde King was manager. Mays and McCovey batted back-to-back in only six of them, and Mac drove in Mays only once, on a two-run double (with Mays on first and Ron Hunt on second), on June 30, 1969. This is also based on research by Krabbenhoft.

- "Boog Powell was 1-for-61 against Mickey Lolich."—Earl Weaver, in *Weaver on Strategy* (2002)

  Explaining his rationale for playing certain players and sitting certain others, even if it defied logic, Weaver makes this and other claims in the book based on detailed index cards he kept during his regime as Orioles' manager.

  The truth: Powell was 16-for-90 lifetime against Lolich, 13-for-66 (.197) with two homers while Weaver was his manager.

- "Mark Belanger hit well over .300 against . . . Nolan Ryan."—Earl Weaver, in *Weaver on Strategy*

  The truth: Belanger was 11-for-45 (.244) with just one extra-base hit and 15 strikeouts lifetime against Ryan; all but one at bat came while Weaver was Belanger's manager.

- "Tug McGraw, against whom I consistently hit lasers for base hits."—Tim McCarver, in *Tim McCarver's Baseball for Brain Surgeons and Other Fans* (1998)

  The truth: McCarver had just five hits in 22 at bats against McGraw, a .227 average. Two of the hits were singles, three were doubles; it is not known how many were lasers.

The moral of the story: If it sounds impossible to believe, don't.

Abbott and Costello Are in the Baseball Hall of Fame

A time-honored baseball trivia question asks, "What two people are in the Baseball Hall of Fame, despite having nothing to do with baseball?" The supposed answer is "Abbott and Costello." In reality, everyone enshrined in the Hall *did* have something to do with baseball, either as a player, manager, umpire, executive, or pioneer of the game. And Abbott and Costello are no more members of the Hall of Fame than Batman and Robin.

Although it is generally referred to as simply the Hall of Fame, the official name of the institution in Cooperstown is the "National Baseball Hall of Fame and Museum." The Hall of Fame—the one-room gallery of bronze plaques, depicting elected members of the Hall—was an afterthought to the museum and occupies only 6.5% of its exhibit space, according to longtime curator Ted Spencer. The rest is devoted to the museum and library, which commemorate the history of the national pastime. This is where you will find Joe Jackson's shoes and Pete Rose's uniform, and pictures and artifacts relevant to hundreds of other non–Hall of Fame members. The Hall of Fame is part of the museum, but the museum is not part of the Hall of Fame.

This is also where Bud Abbott and Lou Costello come in. The duo made their mark in baseball with their hilarious "Who's on First?" comedy routine—actually, an anonymously penned skit that had floated around vaudeville for years before Abbott and Costello popularized it in their 1945 film, *The Naughty Nineties.* In 1956, the comedy team donated a gold record of the routine to the Hall of Fame, and, for years, it was displayed in the museum, along with a picture of the pair. Although this display was taken down many years ago, a video clip of the routine is shown continuously in various places in the museum. So, Abbott and Costello indeed have their places in the National Baseball Museum, but they are not members of the Hall of Fame.

And, while we're at it, the participants in the All-American Girls' Professional Baseball League that spanned from 1943 to 1954 are not members of the Hall, either. A special exhibit honoring these individuals, and other women connected to baseball, was unveiled in a 1988 ceremony, but this, again, did not constitute "induction" of the women. Furthermore, this exhibit is made up of just one display window, not an entire floor, as the 1992 movie *A League of Their Own* might have you believe.

There Are Writers' and Broadcasters' Wings at the Baseball Hall of Fame

How often have you heard someone referred to as a member of the "Writers' Wing" or "Broadcasters' Wing" of the Baseball Hall of Fame? Fans, the media, and even many of the honorees themselves are convinced that these writers and broadcasters are full-fledged members of the Hall (writer Jack Lang once even asked me to show him where his plaque was). They are not. Check the Hall of Fame's list of members, and see if you find Harry Caray or

Grantland Rice listed anywhere. Go to Cooperstown, and see if you can find bronze plaques for any of these people. You won't. Writers and broadcasters are simply not eligible for the Hall.

The confusion stems from two prestigious awards that, until 2011, were presented each year during the Hall of Fame induction ceremonies: the J. G. Taylor Spink Award, and the Ford C. Frick Award. (They are now presented in a separate ceremony on the day before the inductions.) The Spink Award recognizes "meritorious contributions to baseball writing." As early as 1944, the Baseball Hall of Fame's administrators had suggested that some sort of "Roll of Honor," distinct from actual Hall of Fame induction, be established for distinguished baseball writers. Following the December 7, 1962, death of the *Sporting News's* longtime publisher, J. G. Taylor Spink, such an award was created. Spink was the first winner of the award bearing his name. Each year since then (except one), between one and three writers have been nominated by a committee of members of the Baseball Writers' Association of America. Until recently, the winners were announced in the fall and honored the following summer; now, the electing and honoring takes place in the same year.

The Frick Award—for a broadcaster's "major contributions to the game of baseball"—began in 1978. Frick, who died on April 8 of that year, had done some broadcasting early in his career, although he was better known for his roles as NL president and commissioner of baseball. A special committee of baseball personalities makes the annual selection. One announcer has been honored each year since 1978. As with the Spink Award, there is no 75% vote required—it's just "Whose turn is it this year?"

As mentioned, the awards were presented during the annual Hall of Fame induction ceremonies, and the winners give acceptance speeches just as the inductees do. This no doubt accounts for most of the misconception in this matter. However, unlike the Hall's actual inductees, the Spink and Frick Award winners have no individual plaques. There is one plaque for each award, tucked away in the Hall's library building, listing the winners of each honor. With the completion of the library's expansion project in 1994, a formal writers' and broadcaster's section—including photographs of these honorees—was added to dress up these two plaques. This "Scribes and Mike-Men" exhibit is the closest you will find to a writers' or broadcasters' "wing" at the Hall.

The Hall of Fame does little to clarify this matter, not wanting to offend the honorees, some of whom shamelessly refer to themselves as Hall of Famers. In 2010, a longtime employee of the Hall attempted to set the record straight on the "wings" in his baseball blog. This angered at least one winner of the Spink Award, and the employee was promptly fired. But the Hall's current president, Jeff Idelson, has made the distinction clear. In an August 31, 2004, letter, Idelson writes,

> While we don't agree with award winners being referred to as Hall of Famers, we also don't have plans to outwardly stem that action, which really would not be in the museum's best interest. We will, however, continue to remind the winners that they are award recipients and not Hall of Fame members. . . . Our museum does not have wings.

It is fair to say that winning the Spink or Frick Award is as near to Baseball Hall of Fame election that a writer or broadcaster can get, but, to call winners of them Hall of Fame inductees is just plain bad journalism. Table 4.1 gives the winners of the Frick and Spink Awards.

The Headfirst Slide Is Dangerous

The preference is to avoid headfirst slides because injury possibilities are larger.

—Yankees' general manager Brian Cashman

After Derek Jeter was injured during a collision at third base on Opening Day 2003, Yankees' general manager Brian Cashman said, "The bottom line with headfirst sliding is . . . you're risking too much. The preference is to avoid headfirst slides because injury possibilities are larger." Analyst Tim McCarver agrees, writing in *Tim McCarver's Baseball for Brain Surgeons and Other Fans* that, "My least favorite sliding method is the injury-risking hands-first slide."

Before the 1991 season, Mets' manager Bud Harrelson ordered Howard Johnson to switch from the headfirst slide to the feetfirst version, because he didn't want his star player getting hurt. Harrelson, like Cashman and McCarver, was following conventional wisdom, which states that sliding headfirst is dangerous, but dispensers of this wisdom never back it up with any evidence. The evidence that we do have indicates that sliding headfirst is actually not only more effective, but safer.

Johnson is a case in point. He had averaged 153 games per season, with an 80% success ratio in steal attempts between 1987 and 1990. In 1991, HoJo didn't get hurt, but his steal percentage dropped to 65%. And that was the last year he played in more than 100 games in a season.

Table 4.1. Winners of the Ford C. Frick Award and J. G. Taylor Spink Award

The Ford C. Frick Award

Year	Name	Year	Name	Year	Name
1978	Mel Allen, Red Barber	1993	Chuck Thompson	2008	Dave Niehaus
1979	Bob Elson	1994	Bob Murphy	2009	Tony Kubek
1980	Russ Hodges	1995	Bob Wolff	2010	Jon Miller
1981	Ernie Harwell	1996	Herb Carneal	2011	Dave VanHorne
1982	Vin Scully	1997	Jimmy Dudley	2012	Tim McCarver
1983	Jack Brickhouse	1998	Jaime Jarrin		
1984	Curt Gowdy	1999	Arch McDonald		
1985	Buck Canel	2000	Marty Brennaman		
1986	Bob Prince	2001	Rafael "Felo" Ramirez		
1987	Jack Buck	2002	Harry Kalas		
1988	Lindsey Nelson	2003	Bob Uecker		
1989	Harry Caray	2004	Lon Simmons		
1990	By Saam	2005	Jerry Coleman		
1991	Joe Garagiola	2006	Gene Elston		
1992	Milo Hamilton	2007	Denny Matthews		

The J. G. Taylor Spink Award

1962	J. G. Taylor Spink
1963	Ring Lardner
1964	Hugh Fullerton
1965	Charles Dryden
1966	Grantland Rice
1967	Damon Runyon
1968	H. G. Salsinger
1969	Sid Mercer
1970	Heywood C. Broun
1971	Frank Graham
1972	Dan Daniel
	Fred Lieb
1973	J. Roy Stockton
	Warren Brown
	John Drebinger
	John F. Kieran
1974	John Carmichael
	James Isaminger
1975	Tom Meany
	Shirley Povich
1976	Harold Kaese
	Red Smith
1977	Gordon Cobbledick
	Edgar Munzel
1978	Tim Murnane
	Dick Young
1979	Bob Broeg
	Tommy Holmes
1980	Joe Reichler
	Milton Richman
1981	Bob Addie
	Allen Lewis
1982	Si Burick
1983	Ken Smith
1984	Joe McGuff
1985	Earl Lawson
1986	Jack Lang
1987	Jim Murray
1988	Bob Hunter
	Ray Kelly
1989	Jerome Holtzman
1990	Phil Collier
1991	Ritter Collett
1992	Leonard Koppett
	Bus Saidt
1993	John Wendell Smith
1994	(no nominee)
1995	Joseph Durso
1996	Charlie Feeney
1997	Sam Lacy
1998	Bob Stevens
1999	Hal Lebovitz
2000	Ross Newhan
2001	Joe Falls
2002	Hal McCoy
2003	Murray Chass
2004	Peter Gammons
2005	Tracy Ringolsby
2006	Rick Hummel
2008	Larry Whiteside
2009	Nick Peters
2010	Bill Madden
2011	Bill Conlin
2012	Bob Elliott

Pete Rose used the headfirst slide for 24 big-league seasons and played in more games than any other player. Rickey Henderson used the headfirst slide for 25 years and survived more steal attempts than any other player. Joe Morgan, Tim Raines, and Roberto Alomar had long, successful careers using the headfirst slide. Were they just lucky?

Henderson says that he was told early on by Lou Brock that those who slide feetfirst wear out their legs. Rickey says that people get hurt sliding headfirst only when they don't do it right; the proper way is to stay low going into the slide. Incidentally, both Henderson and Rose preferred the feetfirst slide when going into home plate.

Figure 4.1. Pete Rose Beats a Throw Home with His Characteristic Headfirst Slide (1972).
Source: National Baseball Hall of Fame Library, Cooperstown, New York

In 1979, Rose authored a ten-part series on baseball fundamentals for the Gannett News Service. On sliding, Rose says the following:

I think the headfirst slide is the best way to go into second or third base. It is the fastest way, the safest way . . . if you go in like an airplane landing, there is no way you can lose momentum.

How many times have you seen a player slide into second feetfirst, lose sight of the ball, and not be able to get up and take another base should it be bobbled? If you go headfirst, your peripheral vision will pick the ball up, you can quickly jump up and keep going on to the next base.

I also think the headfirst slide is the safest. . . . We all know that a leg injury is harder to overcome than an arm or hand injury.

Indeed, most serious baserunning injuries result from spikes getting caught on a feetfirst slide, snapping a runner's leg at the ankle. According to *Baseball: The Biographical Encyclopedia* (2000), early twentieth-century infielder Terry Turner "claimed that sliding feet first hurt his ankles—and so pioneered the use of the headfirst slide." Around the same time, in 1909, Roy Thomas told the *Sporting Life* that feetfirst slides should be banned from baseball, saying, "A ballplayer without good legs isn't a good ballplayer."

The following are some notable sliding injuries in major league history:

- July 9, 1888: Detroit's Hardy Richardson, 33, and bucking for his second home run title, was out for the season after breaking his leg at the ankle. The *Sporting Life* reports that, "Hardie found it necessary to slide into second. In so doing, he caught his left foot in the base bag and was carried from the field." Richardson returned to play in four more seasons.
- April 20, 1891: Fred Dunlap, a former .400-hitter, saw his 12-year career end on the base paths. Dunlap, just 32, "broke the small bone of his left leg while stealing third base," according to the *Sporting Life*.
- May 10, 1893: Giants' rookie Willie Keeler, 21, who had hit a single, double, and triple in the previous game, sprained his right ankle sliding. By the time he returned on July 3, the Giants had no room in the outfield for him. After four games in the Giants' infield, Keeler wound up shuttling to Binghamton, Brooklyn, and Baltimore all within a year. He went on to emerge as a star with the 1894 Orioles, going on to a 19-year Hall of Fame career.
- May 22, 1902: Giants' star George Van Haltren, 36, snapped a small bone near his right ankle while stealing second base. Van Haltren was out for the season and played only 84 more big-league games.
- July 11, 1902: The Pirates' Lefty Davis, 26, in stealing second, "broke his leg in the same manner Van Haltren did two months ago on the

same spot," per the *Sporting Life*. Davis, a .287 hitter with 45 steals in 171 big-league games under his belt, was out for the season. He returned but batted only .234 with 20 thefts in 177 more games.

- April 27, 1903: Red Sox' catcher Duke Farrell, hitting .563 in his first seven games of the season, fractured his leg while stealing second. Farrell, 36, remained out until August 18, and he played only ten more games that year and 85 more in his career.

- April 10, 1906: Promising Reds' rookie John Siegle broke a small bone directly above his left ankle while sliding into second base in a spring training game. He didn't appear in another game until June 23 (a fruitless pinch hitting effort, in which he supposedly stepped up to the plate with the aid of a cane) or return to the lineup until July 10. After limping to a .118 average in 22 games, Siegle disappeared from the majors.

- April 27, 1906: The Pirates' Otis Clymer, who had batted .296 with 23 steals in 96 games as a rookie the year before, broke his leg at the ankle in the third inning. Clymer, 30, was out for the season, but he returned to play parts of four others. The *Sporting Life* points out that, "Apropos to Otis Clymer's broken ankle, due to sliding into second, it is noted that three other Pittsburg players have sustained similar accidents in the past. They were Bierbauer, Van Haltren and (Lefty) Davis."

- May 15, 1906: The Giants' Mike Donlin, batting .339 for the season and .338 for his eight-year career, "turned his ankle (sliding into third base) and had to be carried off the field," according to the *Sporting Life*. "A late report has it that his ankle is broken and that the injury is so serious that he may be out of the game for several months." He did not return until August and went only 1-for-12 the rest of the season. Donlin, 28, had been among the league's top four in runs, hits, doubles, triples, homers, total bases, batting, and slugging in 1905, but he went on to play only one more full season after 1906.

- May 9, 1907: Tigers' star left fielder Matty McIntyre, 26, "broke a bone in his right ankle sliding into a bag and will be out of the game for at least a month," per the *Sporting Life*. He was actually out for 11 months, missing the rest of the year. McIntyre returned to have his best season in 1908, and he played through 1912.

- September 19, 1907: Brooklyn Dodgers' star outfielder Harry Lumley, 26, ended his season early on an unfortunate slide. According to the *Sporting Life*, "Lumley broke his leg in the eighth inning, sliding into second base. . . . It is a hard thing for a man of his size to put on the brakes while running to the bases. He must have thrown a great strain on his leg to snap in the manner that he did. He couldn't short step easily enough, and away went the bone when all the weight of his body struck the weak spot." Lumley had been one of baseball's top players during his first four seasons in the majors, batting .291 during the Deadball Era, leading the NL in triples and home runs as a rookie in 1904, and topping the circuit in slugging in 1906. He could run, too, as evidenced by his average of 13 three-baggers and 26 stolen bases per season. But he wasn't able to rebound from the injury. Lumley batted just .223 with five steals in 190 games over three seasons after the injury and was through at the age of 29.

- October 1, 1910: "Johnny Evers, in sliding to the plate in the fifth inning, broke a bone in the right ankle," per the *Sporting Life*. The injury cost the Hall of Famer the last two weeks of the regular season and the World Series, which his Cubs lost to the Athletics. Evers, 29, went on to play in only 46 games the following year before rebounding in 1912.

- May 23, 1911: Phillies' outfielder John Titus, 35, "had his ankle broken sliding to the home plate in the fifth inning," according to the *Sporting Life*. "An examination of Titus's ankle after that Tuesday's game revealed a Potts fracture, which required about eight weeks to heal." Titus had been off to a fast start, batting .298 and slugging .545 for the season to that point. He was out until July 8 and didn't return to the field until August 6. He slugged only .357 after returning. Titus came back to have two strong years before retiring after the 1913 season.

- August 4, 1911: White Sox' sophomore infielder Rollie Zeider "sprained his right ankle sliding home in the first game and will not be able to play for a month," per the *Sporting Life*. Except for one unsuccessful pinch hitting appearance, Zeider remained out until September 11. He came back to play seven more seasons.

- September 1, 1913: The Cardinals lost 24-year-old rookie outfielder Ted Cather for the rest of the season. According to the *Sporting Life*, "In the fourth inning Cathers (sic), sliding into second base on a steal, broke his right leg just above the ankle and was carried off the field." Cather went on to return the next season, but he played in just 129 more big-league games.

- September 21, 1913: Boston Braves' rookie outfielder Joey Connolly, 29, "broke his right ankle while sliding into second base in the third inning of the first game and was removed to a hospital," per the *Sporting Life*. Connolly was done for the year, but he returned for two more good seasons and one bad one before losing his job at 32.

- October 6, 1914: In the final game of the regular season, 24-year-old Red Smith "broke an ankle sliding into second base, thus depriving the Braves of a valued player in the World's Series," according to the *Sporting Life*. The Braves went on to win without him, and Smith recovered to play in five more seasons, but he never made it to a Fall Classic.

- July 3, 1916: The first-place Yankees' promising right fielder Frank "Flash" Gilhooley, who "had developed into the best leadoff man in the league," broke his right ankle sliding into third base and was carried off the field. According to an unidentified newspaper account, "as his spikes struck the canvas they caught, and the full weight of his body was thrown on his ankle. It snapped; Gilhooley fell back helpless. Manager [Bill] Donovan, who was coaching at third, ran over to him and found that Gilhooley's ankle was turned so that his foot hung loosely. A doctor was called from the stands, and, after he had one look at the injured ankle, he ordered the player removed to the hospital." Gilhooley did not play again that year, and the Yankees finished fourth. Gilhooley, 24, played in just 214 more big-league games, and he claimed that the injury cost him his effectiveness. "From then on I was just a step slower," Gilhooley said years later, "and a step in baseball means the difference between a hit and a putout."

- April 15, 1917: Vic Saier of the Cubs started to slide home, changed his mind, and stumbled and fell, catching his spikes and breaking his right leg. Saier, 26, was out until the final game of the season on September 30, and he played just 58 more big-league games after that.

- May 4, 1919: The Phillies' Dave Bancroft, 28, was carried off the field after breaking his right leg at the ankle while sliding into a base. He remained out of action until July 1. In 1920, the Phils traded Bancroft to the Giants, with whom he went on to have his best seasons en route to the Hall of Fame.

- September 8, 1920: Yankees' center fielder Ping Bodie, 32, injured his ankle sliding during an exhibition game in Pittsburgh. Initially described as a sprain, it was later called a break. Bodie, a .295-hitter that year, was out for the season and, after going just 15-for-87 (.172) in 1921, for his career as well.

- May 25, 1920: Reds' pitcher Rube Bressler, 25, was "injured in sliding into second, and an x-ray taken showed that a small bone in his ankle was broken," per the *Sporting News*. Bressler remained out until July 28 and pitched only six more games, but he spent the next 12 years as a .311-hitting outfielder/first baseman.

- June 15, 1924: Yankees' rookie Earle Combs, batting .412 in 23 games, was practically done for the season. Combs dislocated and broke his right leg at the ankle in a slide home, and—except for a fruitless pinch hit appearance in September—he did not play again in 1924. Combs, 25, returned to carve out a Hall of Fame career.
- March 15, 1925: Cubs' Hall of Famer Rabbit Maranville, 33, broke a bone near his right ankle while sliding into third base in an exhibition game. Maranville's foot caught under the bag and twisted under him. He remained out until May 24. After averaging .283 over the previous four seasons, Maranville slipped to .233 in 1925.
- June 25, 1926: The Yankees' Bob Meusel, the league's defending home run and RBI champion at the age of 29, "suffered a leg injury while sliding into second and was carried from the field by two of his teammates," according to the *Boston Globe*. Meusel, batting .365, stayed out of action with a broken left ankle until August 11, and he went on to hit only .229 the rest of the season. He played with diminished effectiveness through 1930.
- June 21, 1927: Cardinals' shortstop Tommy Thevenow, a key player on the 1926 world championship team, suffered a fractured leg at the ankle when he slid into second. Thevenow, 23, remained out until September 14 and went 0-for-6 the rest of the year. He went on to play 11 more seasons, mostly as a backup.
- July 4, 1928: Cards' 25-year-old rookie sensation, Wally Roettger, batting .341, was out for the season. According to the *Sporting News*, "St. Louis fans who gathered at Sportsman's Park on the Fourth of July saw a great career snapped at its zenith, when, sliding into third base in the second game against the Cubs, outfielder Wally Roettger's spike caught in the dirt, and the player suffered a broken leg—broken in two places, and the ankle dislocated. There is no question about his being out for the balance of the season, but there is about his ever being able to play baseball again or, at least, play it as he was when the most unfortunate accident took place." Roettger returned the next year, but he batted just .253 in 79 games. He played only 526 contests, batting .277, after the injury.
- May 30, 1930: Rogers Hornsby, with 2,731 hits and a .362 career average at the age of 34, suffered an injury that effectively ended his reign as the NL's best hitter. Per the *Sporting News*, "Hornsby broke his ankle in the same way that a dozen others have suffered similar mishaps. He started to slide and didn't go through with it. . . . Going into the [third base] bag, he started the feetfirst slide, then remembered that

his [troublesome] right heel needed protection and tried to go into the bag standing up. As he changed his mind his legs curled up under him, he twisted around, and the left ankle snapped." Missing most of the league's greatest offensive season of the century, the defending MVP went on to collect only six more hits that year and 199 more in his career.

- July 9, 1931: Giants' Hall of Famer Fred Lindstrom, 25, broke a bone near his left ankle while sliding into third base. Lindstrom remained out of action until September 10, appearing in just five more games. After hitting .300 plus for six straight seasons, including .379 in 1930, Lindstrom plunged to .271 in 1932, precipitating a trade to Pittsburgh. Lindstrom, who had followed Ty Cobb as only the second man ever to amass 1,000 hits before his 25th birthday, finished with just 1,747.
- August 7, 1932: Braves' sophomore outfielder Red Worthington, a .297-lifetime hitter at the age of 26, went out as a regular. According to the next day's *Boston Globe*, "In the first inning of the second game, 'Red' Worthington, sliding into third base, broke two bones above his left ankle." He collected only 23 more hits in his career.
- March 29, 1933: In an exhibition game, the Cubs' Kiki Cuyler "set out for second base," according to the *Sporting News*. "He made a clean steal of the bag, but in hook-sliding nipped the bag with his right foot. In twisting from left to right, the bone snapped three inches above the ankle. Players sitting in the Cub dugout almost 90 feet away heard it. . . . Cuyler was carried to the clubhouse, an ambulance summoned, and . . . x-ray pictures revealed the extent of his injury [he had splintered the fibula of his left leg]." Except for an unsuccessful pinch hit appearance, the 34-year-old Cuyler remained out until July 7, but he played through 1938.
- March 28, 1934: Rabbit Maranville, now with the Braves at the age of 42, again broke a leg sliding in a spring training exhibition, and he missed the entire season. This time it was his left leg in an attempted steal of home, the victim of a collision with Yankees' catcher Norman Kies. Maranville collected only ten more big-league hits before his career came to a close.
- September 17, 1935: Cardinals' 23-year-old rookie center fielder Terry Moore, a defensive wizard and .287-hitter, broke a bone in his leg and was out for the season. The Cards, even with the Cubs in the loss column at the time, wound up losing the pennant to them by four games. Moore returned to play ten more seasons.

- April 23, 1936: The Dodgers' Randy Moore, having won the team's right field job, broke his right leg at the ankle while attempting to steal second base. Moore was out of action until July 28, and he played in only one more game on the field before August 27. After batting .103 in 1937, his ten-year career ended at the age of 31.
- August 10, 1937: Cubs' All-Star Ripper Collins, 33, cracked a right ankle bone during an awkward slide home. Per the *Sporting News*, Collins "started to slide, changed his mind, and then changed it again," causing his right foot to turn under him. Collins reamined out of the lineup until September 17, and he played only one more full season.
- March 27, 1938: Sliding into second base in spring training, White Sox' Hall of Famer Luke Appling fractured two bones in his lower right leg. "Old Aches and Pains," 30, didn't return to shortstop or get his first hit of the season until July 8, but he remained in the majors until 1950.
- May 8, 1939: The Cubs' Phil Cavarretta, 22, broke a leg at the ankle sliding. Out until July 25, Cavarretta went on to appear in only seven more games that season, all as a pinch hitter.
- July 17, 1940: Phil Cavarretta [again] suffered a leg injury sliding, and he went on to have only five more at bats [with no hits] all season. He recovered to play for 15 more years.
- March 8, 1941: Promising Boston Bees' [Braves] outfielder Chet Ross, 23, broke his ankle sliding into second base in Boston's first exhibition game of the season. According to the *Sporting News*, "Ross suffered a ruptured literal (sic) ligament in the left ankle making a slide into second base in the ninth inning [and] probably will be out of action for a month or more." He spent a week in the hospital and struggled after his return to the team in May, until another sliding injury in July ended his season. Again, per the *Sporting News*, "The Braves lost Chet Ross for the balance of the season when he suffered a recurrence of the training camp accident of last spring in the first game of the Boston-Pittsburgh doubleheader of July 18. The injury was described as a fractured fibula and a severe strain of the ligaments of the left ankle." After batting .283 with 15 triples in 160 games before the first injury, Ross went on to hit just .206 in 253 games the rest of his career. His career ended at the age of 27.
- May 30, 1942: "Mike McCormick broke his left leg just above the ankle sliding into second base," according to the *Sporting News*. The Reds' third-year outfielder, 25, returned in August to play in just five more games, going 0-for-10, and never lived up to his 1940–1941 promise (.294 in 220 games).

- April 19, 1945: The Red Sox' Joe Cronin, 38, ended his Hall of Fame career on the base paths. Per the *Sporting News*, Cronin "started to slide for second base, changed his mind, caught his spike in the bag, and suffered a severe fracture of his right leg."

- September 26, 1946: The Dodgers' Pete Reiser "fractured fibula in left leg, catching foot in bag in sliding back to first," according to the *Sporting News*. Reiser, at 27 a two-time NL stolen base champion with a .310 lifetime average, missed the rest of the season, including the pennant-deciding playoff loss against the Cardinals. He went on to have more than 60 hits or four stolen bases in a season only once more in his career.

- April 8, 1947: Giants' 20-year-old phenom Whitey Lockman fractured his fibula six inches above the ankle sliding into second on a double play in a preseason game. He went on to play only two games all season, both pinch hitting appearances in late September, but he recovered to play 13 more seasons.

- August 28, 1948: Phillies' rookie sensation Richie Ashburn, using his "characteristic headfirst slide," fractured a finger sliding into second base and was out for the season. Ashburn, 21, recuperated to have a Hall of Fame career.

- September 29, 1948: The Braves' Jeff Heath, a four-time All-Star at the age of 33, broke his left leg sliding home. Heath broke the bone two and a half inches above the ankle, also dislocating the joint. He missed what would have been his only World Series and played in just 36 more major league games before another ankle injury ended his career.

- July 23, 1949: Cardinals' All-Star rookie Eddie Kazak, hitting .302, wrenched and fractured his leg at the ankle sliding into second base. Kazak, 29, played just five more games that year—all September pinch hitting appearances—and collected only 60 big-league hits after 1949.

- April 28, 1951: The Cubs' Roy Smalley Sr. fractured his right ankle and remained out until July 1. The 24-year-old shortstop had played in all 154 games the previous season, collecting 21 homers and 85 RBI. He never again played more than 92 games in a season.

- October 3, 1951: Overshadowed by the pennant-winning homer hit by teammate Bobby Thomson moments later, Don Mueller saw his season come to an end on the bases. Mueller broke his leg at the ankle sliding into third base, costing the Giants one of their hottest hitters for the World Series. The Giants went on to lose to the Yankees, four games to two. Mueller, 24, recovered to play eight more seasons.

- March 12, 1952: The Yankees' Billy Martin "broke two bones in his [right] ankle while going through some sliding antics for a kinescoped television program soon to be started by Joe DiMaggio to boost a spaghetti foundry," per the *Sporting News*. Martin remained out of action until May 14.
- April 2, 1952: Monte Irvin, the Giants' defending league RBI champion, "suffered a broken ankle in a needless slide into third base" in a spring training game, according to the *Sporting News*. "Irvin's ankle was so badly broken that the bone was protruding." Some observers thought Irvin was checking his slide, since there was no throw to third, although he denied it. The Giants' Bill Rigney said that, "On the bench, we could hear the ankle pop like a paper bag." Irvin, 33, was out until July 27 and wouldn't return to the regular lineup until August 24. He played four more seasons.
- June 14, 1952: Hal Bevan, a 21-year-old rookie who batted .333 in nine games, broke his leg. Per the *Sporting News*, "Bevan, on the heels of [George] Kell, caught batter Ferris Fain's signal—that no slide was necessary—too late. Having committed himself, he slid—and his spikes stuck. Momentum carried him across the plate, but his right leg was folded up so painfully behind him that . . . he could not get up." Bevan was out for the season and played only six more major league games.
- July 6, 1952: Jerry Priddy, a solid second baseman batting .283 for the Tigers, broke his right leg as his spikes caught in the ground on what the *Sporting News* calls an "unnecessary slide." This ended Priddy's season and his streak of 386 consecutive games played. Priddy returned in 1953 to bat .235 in 65 games and concluded his career at the age of 33.
- March 13, 1954: The Braves' new acquisition, Bobby Thomson, 30, broke his right leg at the ankle sliding in an exhibition game, paving the way for rookie Hank Aaron to break into the lineup. According to Aaron, "Thomson's leg folded under him as he slid into second base." It was called a "trimalleolar fracture," meaning broken in three places. The three-time All-Star didn't return to the lineup until August 22, and he never again approached his preinjury success.
- March 24, 1954: The Indians lost two players to sliding injuries during a spring training game with the Cubs. According to the *Sporting News*, "The fibula in [Mickey] Grasso's left leg was broken at the ankle when he attempted to slide into second base in the fifth inning. . . . He checked himself slightly, and the break, quite audible, resulted. . . . [Harry] Simpson was hurt in the seventh inning of the same game when he attempted to reach home on a wild pitch. . . . Simpson slid feet first, but his body

seemed to twist at a right angle to the foul line, his face and left arm in the dirt. He suffered a bruised face and a bloody nose, and his arm was so painful it required a splint. X-rays taken the next day showed a break just beyond the wrist." Grasso, 33, went on to collect only two more big-league hits. Simpson, 28, was sidelined the entire year, but he returned to play five more seasons. Commenting on the rash of sliding injuries that spring, the *Sporting News* editorialized, "How many hundreds of times have players moaned, as they were being carried off the field with broken legs, that their 'spikes caught'?"

- September 5, 1954: As Hank Aaron recalls, "I was sliding into third for a triple when I broke my ankle the same way [Bobby] Thomson broke his in Florida." Aaron, 20, missed the rest of the season and a shot at the Rookie of the Year Award. He recovered to have a respectable career.

- June 23, 1957: Braves' slugger Joe Adcock broke his right fibula six inches above the ankle and tore ligaments in his right knee, when his spikes got caught in second base during a slide. "I was trying to slide so I wouldn't hurt my knee again," said Adcock. "When my foot hit the bag, I heard a snap." Adcock, 29, was out until September, but he lasted another nine seasons before turning to managing.

- March 25, 1961: Cubs' popular 28-year-old rookie Cuno Barragan went down in an exhibition game in Mesa, Arizona. Per the *Sporting News*, Barragan "became a serious casualty . . . on March 25 when he suffered a severe fracture of the right ankle. The injury . . . was caused when Barragan tried to check his slide while going into third base. . . . The injury was described by Dr. George Truman, the club physician . . . as a backward dislocation and fracture of the fibula an inch and a half above the right ankle. A cast [was] necessary for six to eight weeks." Barragan's major league debut was delayed until September 1, and his big-league career lasted only 69 games.

- March 5, 1962: Cincinnati's Gene Freese, 28, suffered a severe right leg fracture and torn ligaments in an intrasquad game. Freese, a key contributor to the 1961 NL pennant (26 homers, 87 RBI, .277), "tried to hold up on a slide into second base," according to the *Sporting News*. Out until August 17, Freese collected only six hits all year and never again played regularly.

- May 1, 1965: Dodgers' two-time batting champ Tommy Davis, 26, suffered a fractured right leg at the ankle and torn ligaments sliding into second. "I was undecided whether to slide, so I didn't go down like I should have," said Davis. "I looked down, and my ankle was out in right field." The *Sporting News* said Davis's "spikes caught in the cement-hard [Dodger Stadium] base-path, and he rolled over like a fighter who had been hit on the button." Except for a pinch hitting appearance on the last day of the regular season, Davis was done for the year, including the World Series. Although he went on to play for another 11 seasons, he never again approached his preinjury success.

- March 30, 1967: In spring training action, per the *Sporting News*, the Dodgers' Willie Davis got a "chipped inside ankle bone on his left leg, which he suffered when his spikes caught in the eighth inning of a game with the Athletics in Bradenton. He was making a successful steal of second at the time." Davis, 26, didn't return to the lineup until May 2.

- March 19, 1970: Indians' slugger Ken Harrelson, coming off back-to-back 30-homer seasons at the age of 28, had his career derailed. According to the *Sporting News*, Harrelson "suffered a fractured fibula bone, torn ligaments, and also tendon damage when his ankle was dislocated in a game against the Athletics. . . . The injury happened, according to Harrelson, when he launched a late slide into second base and his spikes caught in the dirt. . . . 'My spikes caught and flipped me over. I knew right away it was bad because I heard the pop, and I saw my foot turned around the wrong way. . . . I knew the bone was broken.'" Harrelson remained out until September 6, and he went on to hit only six more big-league homers.

- July 22, 1973: The Reds' Dave Concepcion lost his opportunity to fulfill his first All-Star selection. Per the *Sporting News*, "Concepcion suffered a dislocated left ankle and a fracture of the fibula, sliding safely into third base. . . . 'It was a sickening sight, seeing Concepcion lying there on the ground, his distorted ankle staring me in the face,' said [Alex] Grammas, the third base coach." Concepcion, 25, was out for the rest of the year, but he returned to play 15 more seasons and earn eight more All-Star selections.

- July 26, 1973: For the second time in four days, a star NL shortstop went down with a broken leg. According to the *Sporting News*, "Frustration struck hard at the Phillies the other night when their shortstop, Larry Bowa, suffered a fractured left ankle. . . . He was attempting to steal second . . . when he was thrown out, then carried out with the injury." Bowa, 27, remained out until September 3, but he rebounded to play 12 more years, five as an All-Star.

- April 18, 1975: Bill Buckner, who had helped the Dodgers to the 1974 World Series with 31 stolen bases and a .314 average, severely sprained his ankle sliding into second. He returned May 16, but with diminished mobility and effectiveness (eight steals, .243), before submitting to season-ending surgery on September 1. Buckner, 25, rebounded to play 15 more seasons, but he was bedeviled by leg problems throughout the remainder of his career.

- August 18, 1976: The Tigers lost two infielders within 11 days, both as the result of slides into second base. Shortstop Tom Veryzer injured his knee and was fitted with a cast. He was out for the season and dipped to .197 in 1977.

- August 29, 1976: Third baseman Aurelio Rodriguez became the second Detroit sliding casualty of the month. Rodriguez, 28, severely tore the ligaments in his right ankle "and was immediately scheduled for tentative surgery," per the Sporting News. Rodriguez was also done for the year.

- April 26, 1977: Barely recovered from the previous year's injury, Aurelio Rodriguez went down again. According to the Sporting News, Rodriguez "apparently caught his spikes while making an unnecessary slide home" and badly sprained the same right ankle. He remained out until June 15.

- August 21, 1977: Pittsburgh's Rennie Stennett, batting .336 for the season and .285 for his career, broke his right leg at the ankle sliding into second base. Stennett, 26, missed the rest of the season (falling 12 plate appearances short of qualifying for the batting title, won by teammate Dave Parker at .338), and he never again hit higher than .244.

- May 12, 1978: Baltimore's Al Bumbry, 31, broke his leg sliding into second base. Except for five pinch hitting appearances in September, he remained out for the rest of the season.

- July 1, 1979: Boston speedster Jerry Remy, 26, "suffered hyperextension of his left knee in a freak sliding incident," per the Sporting News. Out until August, he appeared in just seven more games, with two hits, the rest of the season. After averaging 35 stolen bases a year over his first four seasons, Remy never again swiped more than 16 sacks in a season.

- June 10, 1980: George Brett, just starting to heat up with the bat, went out for a month. According to the Sporting News, a "hard slide into second base against Cleveland June 10 resulted in a foot injury to All-Star third baseman George Brett [who] tore a small [knee] ligament on an attempted steal of second base. . . . 'I slid too hard and too late,' said Brett." Brett returned July 10 and went on to bat an incredible .421 the rest of the year.

- June 23, 1982: Carney Lansford, Boston's defending batting champ, severely sprained his left ankle while sliding. Since he missed "only" a month, this injury doesn't quite measure up to most of the others on this list, except for a historical footnote. Lansford's injury opened up a lineup spot for a rookie who had accumulated only eight hits so far that season—but Wade Boggs went on to add another 3,002 hits before he finished up in the majors.

- April 3, 1986: The Dodgers' 29-year-old slugger Pedro Guerrero, sliding during an exhibition game, ruptured the tendon that held his left kneecap in place. Per the *Sporting News*, "as he started his slide into third base he had a change of mind, his spikes caught in the dirt, and he tumbled over the bag." Guerrero didn't return until August or get his first hit of the season until September. It is noted that Pedro had suffered several previous sliding injuries. He fractured a leg at the ankle in the Pacific Coast League, missing the last four months of the 1977 season. He also damaged ligaments in his left knee sliding into second in 1980. He tried sliding headfirst for a while and injured his shoulder. "I guess the best thing to do is not to slide," reflected Guerrero, who played through 1992.

- March 21, 1997: Robin Ventura of the White Sox severely dislocated his right ankle and suffered a compound fracture in his lower leg. Ventura, 29, was sliding home in an exhibition game, trying to protect a bruise on his left calf, when his spikes got caught. A pin was inserted into his leg, and he was out until July 24, but he recovered nicely.

- April 19, 1997: Milwaukee's Fernando Viña, 28, broke his left leg at the ankle while sliding into second base. Viña, off to a hot start (.321 batting average and .500 slugging percentage in 13 games) remained out until July 18, but he came back with an All-Star season in 1998.

- August 15, 1999: Oakland's Tony Phillips broke his left fibula on a slide. The injury ended his 18-year career at the age of 40.

- August 26, 2000: The Cubs' Rondell White, 28, dislocated his left shoulder sliding headfirst into second base and was out for the season. He returned for another .300-plus season in 2001.

- March 6, 2001: The Orioles' Luis Matos, 22, dislocated his left shoulder in a feetfirst slide into third base during a spring training game. Matos remained out until August 26 and went on to play only 31 big-league games the rest of the season.

- May 11, 2002: Boston superstar Manny Ramirez, 29, fractured his left index finger "with an ill-advised headfirst slide into home plate. . . . Flesh jammed into shin guard, and shin guard won," according to the

Boston Globe. Ramirez remained on the disabled list until June 25, but he returned to win the AL batting title.

- June 28, 2010: The Phillies' Chase Utley, 31, trying unsuccessfully to stretch a single into a double against the Reds, suffered a strained ligament in his right thumb on a headfirst slide. Utley remained out of action until mid-August.

This is by no means a complete list of serious sliding injuries, but it encompasses more than 60 of the worst and most significant ones I could find (to qualify, an injury had to be season-ending or disabling for at least 30 days, and result from the slide itself more so than a collision with another player). And all but four resulted from a feetfirst slide.

The June 1, 1999, edition of *Family Practice News* reports on a study of sliding in 637 collegiate baseball and softball games (3,889 slides). According to the findings, they

> estimated that the injury risk is ten per 1,000 slides for headfirst sliding and nine per 1,000 slides for feetfirst sliding. But the injuries associated with feetfirst slides were more severe. The two worst injuries were shoulder dislocations and occurred during feetfirst slides with arms extended out to the side.

So, where is the evidence that sliding headfirst is more dangerous?

A Star Relief Ace Is as Valuable as Any Other Great Player

Relievers are in the bullpen for a reason: They can't start.

—former closer Todd Jones

Belief in this section's title is reflected in all aspects of baseball. Salaries? In 2005, three relievers—Mariano Rivera, Billy Wagner, and Eric Gagne—pocketed at least $10 million apiece for their services. Beset by injury, Gagne worked a total of 13⅓ innings all year, thus averaging three-quarters of a million dollars per inning pitched.

Awards? Up until 1947, relievers had been categorically ignored in MVP voting, but, Joe Page's outstanding season (56 games, 141 innings, 14 wins, 17 saves, 2.48 ERA) appeared crucial to the Yanks' pennant, and the writers took notice: They gave him seven first-place MVP nominations toward a strong fourth-place finish in the voting. A precedent had been set. Two years later, Page saved a record 27 games and placed third in the voting. In 1952, rookie relievers Joe Black (Dodgers) and Hoyt Wilhelm (Giants) finished three-four in the NL poll. And, in between, Jim Konstanty—a one-year wonder for Philadelphia's "Whiz Kids"—was overwhelmingly named the NL's MVP for 1950. The success of these men changed the perception of relief pitchers for good: They could be not only valuable staff members, but *most* valuable.

Until the 1970s, although several had received MVP support, no relief pitchers were getting serious consideration for the Cy Young Award (established in 1956). Of 322 votes cast through 1969, only one went to a reliever. Apparently, writers had accepted that a reliever could be a most valuable *player*, but not a most valuable *pitcher*. The 1970 adoption of the 5–3–1 voting system (permitting voters to list three candidates instead of one) opened the doors for bullpen aces to at least get mentioned, and one in particular moved right up the ladder.

Mike Marshall put together three brilliant bullpen seasons in a row for the Expos and Dodgers. He finished a distant fourth in the NL Cy Young balloting in 1972, moved up to a strong second in 1973, and became the first reliever ever to win the award in 1974 (the season Marshall amassed the phenomenal totals of 106 games and 208 innings out of the pen). Once again, a precedent had been set; since 1974, relievers Sparky Lyle (1977), Bruce Sutter (1979), Rollie Fingers (1981), Willie Hernandez (1984), Steve Bedrosian (1987), Mark Davis (1989), Dennis Eckersley (1992), and Eric Gagne (2003) have won Cy Youngs, with Fingers, Hernandez, and Eckersley also capturing league MVP Awards. And, of course, relievers have had their own awards, including the *Sporting News*'s "Fireman of the Year," and the Rolaids Relief Man Award.

So, let's get back to the original question: Do they deserve all this attention? Can a relief ace—who toils for perhaps 75 innings per season—indeed be as valuable as a starting pitcher (who pitches 225) or an everyday player (who plays in 1,400)? Let's look at just the pitchers. For the 75-inning closer to be as valuable as the 225-inning starter, you have to believe that the closer's innings are three times as important as the starter's. Bill James, after simulating thousands of games, concludes that, "The real value of a run saved by a modern reliever is 73% to 89% greater than that of a run saved by a starting pitcher." In other words, current relievers' innings are not three times as important as starters', but "only" about 1.8 times as important, partly because relief aces aren't put in true pressure situations as much as they used to be.

Researcher Mark Armour summarizes today's trend, saying, "The modern closer is a role designed to avoid, at all possible costs, pitching in the most difficult situations." It used to be that the relief ace was brought into the game when it was on the line—be it the fourth or the ninth inning. It could have been when the team was up a run or two, tied, or even down a run or two—and his job was to maintain the team's chance to win. And he often pitched two or more innings in a game. Now, the closer comes in almost exclusively at the start of the ninth inning, only when the team is ahead, often by two or three runs.

As Tim McCarver writes in *Tim McCarver's Baseball for Brain Surgeons and Other Fans*,

> Currently, when the weak middle men start to get battered around, few managers are bold enough to bring in their star closers because agents are insistent that their clients pitch only an inning or an inning and a third each appearance. . . . Today's agents aren't going to allow their closer clients to be used frequently in nonsave situations.

In *Total Baseball* (2004), Bill Felber analyzes whether this new strategy is more effective. Felber examined all games in the 1952, 1972, and 1992 seasons in which a team had a lead of one, two, or three runs after seven or eight innings to see how often the teams won. There was little difference between the three seasons, but the biggest difference was with a one-run lead after eight innings, the most crucial closer situation. In 1952, those teams won 89.1% of the time, and, in 1972, 89.4% of the time. But in 1992, with the multimillion dollar closer going against the other team's mop-up guy, the teams won only 85.3% of the time in this situation.

Felber paid special attention to Dennis Eckersley, the American League's Cy Young and MVP Award winner in 1992. Eck was credited with 51 saves that year—but only 12 times did he face the tying run, and 37 of those 51 saves were vultured while working with at least a two-run lead. His manager, Tony LaRussa, often said that he preferred to bring his ace reliever in only in the ninth inning with no runners on base. Eckersley was the best in the business—but the business was nowhere near as important as it used to be, or as people still believe it to be.

As Armour says,

> Once LaRussa did it with Eckersley, everyone else said, "Hey, I don't want to have to think during a game either, I want one of those guys." . . . There is still this perception that pitching in the ninth inning with a two-run lead takes a certain mental toughness, whereas entering in the eighth inning of a tie game does not.

Retrosheet founder David Smith did a similar (but much more exhaustive) study to Felber's, presenting it at the Society for American Baseball

Research's (SABR) 2004 convention and summarizing the results in the Fall 2009 *Baseball Research Journal*. Smith examined the scoring patterns in 122,906 games. As fellow researcher David Vincent summarizes, Smith

> researched late-inning leads . . . from 1944 to 2003, and an additional 14 seasons prior to that span. What he found is that the winning percentage for teams who enter the ninth inning with a lead has remained virtually unchanged over the decades. Regardless of the pitching strategy, teams entering the ninth inning with a lead win roughly 95% of the time. That was the exact rate in 1901, and that was the rate 100 seasons later. In fact, the rate has varied merely from a high of 96.7% in 1909 to a low of 92.5% in 1941. But I know what you're thinking. That study applies to all leads, including big ones. But what about the slim leads, the ones defined as "save situations"? Glad you asked. Because Smith looked at those leads as well. And what he found is winning rates for those leads have also remained constant—one-run leads after eight innings have been won roughly 85% of the time, two-run leads 94% of the time, and three-run leads about 96% of the time.

James points out that,

> Each run saved in a tie game has more than eight times the impact of a run saved with a three-run lead. If you use your relief ace to save a three-run lead in the ninth inning, you'll win that game 99% of the time. But if you don't use your ace in that situation, you'll [still] win the game 98% of the time.

Another baseball author, Gabriel Schechter, has done extensive research on relief pitching. In one project, he compared the first ten seasons of the save rule (1969–1978) with the ten most recent seasons at the time (2000–2009), checking every game in which the starting pitcher finished the seventh inning with a lead of one, two, or three runs. In the former period, the starter finished the game 51.5% of the time; in the latter, only 9%. Yet the results, in the form of team winning percentages, were almost identical: .850 in 1969–1978 and .846 in 2000–2009.

In 2006 Schechter wrote the following:

> The way I see it, the save rule has devolved into a rationale for managers approaching pitching deployment in an ass-backwards way. It used to be that the manager relied on his starter to go as far as he could, using relievers only when necessary. Today, when [then-Yankees' manager] Joe Torre (to use just one example out of a possible 30) goes to the ballpark, he is hoping that he will wind up using Mariano Rivera in the ninth inning. He's also hoping that he'll use his best setup guy in the eighth inning. And he's depending on

several other relievers, including the lefty-lefty specialist, to get him through the seventh inning. In other words, today's manager is managing from the end of the game backward toward the start, instead of the other way around as it was 30 or 40 years ago. The starting pitcher is no longer expected, trained, or conditioned to give his manager more than six or seven innings. I think that's a big mistake in philosophy. When we ask for less, we get less; when we accept mediocrity, we foster mediocrity. The study I presented at the [2006 SABR] convention demonstrated that using a bevy of relievers after the seventh inning to do the job that the starter used to do by himself does not generate more wins. All it generates is jobs for more relievers with less talent than the pitchers they replace.

If you think about it, relief pitchers are, by and large, guys who aren't good enough to be starting pitchers (see page 33–34). If somebody had the ability to give you 225 quality innings, why would you use him for only 75? You wouldn't, which should remind you that a reliever is just a role-player: important, but not to be confused with the best pitchers in the game. Does anyone think that guys like Randy Johnson, Pedro Martinez, or Roy Halladay wouldn't have been dominant as closers, if management were foolish enough to waste them in that role?

Occasionally, a team has tried to convert a star reliever into a starter, with poor results:

- After a monster year in the White Sox' bullpen in 1975 (a league-leading 26 saves and a 1.84 ERA over 142 innings), Goose Gossage became a starter in 1976. He went 9–17 with a 3.94 ERA, which ranked 39th of 43 ERA title qualifiers. He never started another game and carved out a Hall of Fame career as a reliever.
- After three strong seasons in the Braves' bullpen, Steve Bedrosian was given 37 starts in 1985 and went 7–15 with 111 walks and a 3.83 ERA, which ranked 34th of 37 ERA qualifiers. He returned to the pen for the rest of his career and won the 1987 Cy Young Award.
- Between 1999 and 2002, the Reds' Danny Graves averaged 30 saves with an 8–5 record each year. Converted into a starter in 2003, Graves went 4–15 with a 5.33 ERA. Back in the bullpen in 2004, he saved 41 games and made the All-Star team.

Sporting News columnist Todd Jones, who was credited with more than 300 saves during his pitching career, makes no pretense about the value of his former role. In the January 19, 2009, issue, he writes,

Relievers are in the bullpen for a reason: They can't start. . . . Most relievers either throw hard or have a trick pitch. Their command doesn't need to be as sharp as a starter's. Because relievers usually see a hitter only once a game, they don't have to worry as much about setting him up. By the time the hitter knows a reliever isn't locating well or doesn't have his good stuff, the inning often is already over. Another reason relieving is easier than starting: It's much easier to have one clean, scoreless inning three days a week than it is to go six or seven good innings once every five days. Think of it this way: Do you have a better chance of beating Tiger Woods on one hole or outlasting him for 18? I'll take my chances on one hole. That logic worked for me for 16 seasons.

Jim Kaat, who started 625 big-league games and relieved in 273 others, expresses similar sentiments, saying,

As a starter, you're a pitcher. As a reliever, you're a thrower. . . . Most of the time, your relievers are specialty pitch pitchers. They come in, and they throw that one pitch, time after time, and they only have to do it for an inning or two. . . . As a starter, you'll have four pitches, and you've got to learn to use them all and change speeds.

The aforementioned Mike Marshall also minimizes the modern role of closer. Marshall once told *Sports Business Daily* the following:

If you pitch fewer innings, [the hitters] don't get to see what you do as often, and it's hard for them to make adjustments. So, pitching 80 innings one inning at a time with a lead? That's a walk in the park. Billy Beane made a point. He said that if you want to get something for nothing, find a guy that can throw a little bit good and throw strikes, use him in a closing role and pump up a lot of saves, and then you can sell him for something very valuable because that's not a very difficult man on your team to replace. He's right! It's the easiest gig in baseball.

Journalist John Shiffert analyzed relief aces in the 2001 to 2005 time frame, noting that the Yankees were the only team to have the same closer (Rivera) in each of those five years. Pitcher after pitcher stepped into the role for different teams—the average club had 4.9 different closers in the five years—and the majority of the closers had success. Shiffert concluded that, "In fact, practically anybody can close."

The Dodgers' Greg Gagne received deification for his record of 84 consecutive saves converted between 2002 and 2004 (disregarding his blown save in the 2003 All-Star Game, which cost the NL home-field advantage in that year's World Series). Gagne is a fine example of a relief star who was a failure as a starting pitcher: After going 10–13 with a 4.70 ERA in parts of three seasons as a starter, he was demoted to the pen and suddenly emerged as baseball's best closer. But his record streak, as remarkable as it was, encompassed just 87 innings, less than ten full games' worth. I'd put it in the same class as records for consecutive errorless chances at various positions—notable, but not the kind of thing that gets a guy to Cooperstown.

Getting back to Mariano Rivera, many people thought he was the Yankees' key player during their 1996 to 2001 dynasty, making him a viable Hall of Fame candidate. But who was building up all those leads for Rivera to protect? The Yankees were successful because they scored an average of 883 runs per season during that period and allowed only 732, as compared to the league average of 827. Yes, Rivera was part of the reason that the Yankees allowed fewer runs than average, but only a part. The Yankees had 8,680 innings on defense in those six years, and Rivera pitched 467 of them. Per season, that's 1,447 innings for the Yanks, 78 for Rivera—5.4%. He had eight other guys helping him while he was out there, and he contributed zero to the Yankees' offense. I'm not singling out Rivera or Gagne; they are or were outstanding at what they do. But what they do, in my opinion, is overrated by most baseball fans and the media.

Figure 4.2. Mariano Rivera, the Best of the Modern Closers.
Photograph by Keith Allison

Artificial Turf Increases Batting
Averages and Shortens Careers

Line drives don't take bad hops.

—Pete Rose

Old-timers and "purists" like to claim that artificial turf increases batting averages, some even suggesting that Pete Rose's career hit record was achieved only because of turf. But the numbers tell a different story. Sure, there is an occasional high hopper that becomes an infield single on turf, or a double that becomes a triple because the ball reaches the gap more quickly. But, for every "Ping-Pong hit" produced by the ersatz grass, there is at least one potential bunt hit or slow-rolling infield single that becomes an infield out on Astroturf. Otherwise, players would indeed have higher batting averages on turf.

But they don't. From 1984 through 1989, when the number of stadiums with artificial turf was at its peak, all major league players combined had 85,170 hits in 332,001 at bats on the fake stuff—an average of .2565. But, on natural grass, they had 136,301 hits in 527,493 trips—an average of .2583, two points higher than on turf.

And Pete Rose? Research by David Frank shows that Rose's performances on natural grass and artificial turf were almost identical, requiring the carrying out of batting averages to *six decimal places* to find a difference. For his career, Rose was 2,133-for-7,043 (.302854) on turf, and 2,123-for-7,010 (.302853) on grass. As Rose often remarked, "Line drives don't take bad hops."

Artificial turf has also been blamed for shortening careers, with the likes of Vince Coleman, George Brett, and Frank White going on record to that effect. Bill James set about to test this theory, publishing the results in his 1986 *The Bill James Historical Baseball Abstract*. Using his "similarity scores," James analyzed 48 pairs of similar players from the 1973 season, each pair containing one man who played his home games on artificial turf, the other on grass. From 1974 through 1985, the 48 "turf" players averaged 957 games apiece, while the 48 "grass" players averaged only 691. James concluded that,

> This study strongly suggests that if artificial turf has important durability effects, then those effects tend on balance to make careers longer. In other words, it appears to help more than it hurts . . . if anything, artificial turf has reduced injuries in baseball, and tends to make careers longer.

A Team with a 91–71 Record Is 20 Games over .500

It has become common in recent years to express teams' (or pitchers') performances in terms of "games over .500." For example, when the 2001 Seattle Mariners finished with a won-lost record of 116–46, most everyone said that the M's were 70 games over .500 (116 minus 46). They weren't. I say they were 35 games over .500.

The fact is, a game includes both a win and a loss. *The New Dickson Baseball Dictionary* (1999) defines "games back/games behind," concluding that, "It is expressed as a combination of whole and half numbers, with each victory or loss counting as half of a game." The logical syllogism is that "games ahead/games above/games over" would follow the same rules. In the same book, definition number 2 of "game" says the following:

> Unit of measurement used to determine a team's exact place in the standings. This unit is expressed in terms of full and half games. . . . To compute the number of games a team is ahead or behind, you add the difference in the number of wins and the difference in the number of losses and divide by 2.

So, to figure out how many games a team is over .500, choose any won-lost record that works out to .500, and apply the above formula to that team's won-lost record:

Mariners = 116–46
.500 = 81–81
$[(116 - 81) + (81 - 46)] / 2 = (35 + 35) / 2 = 70 / 2 = 35$ games over .500.

So the M's were not 70 games over .500, but "only" 35 games over.

Look at it another way: Suppose the second-place Athletics had finished with an 81–81 record. Everyone would agree that Seattle finished 35 games ahead of Oakland. So, how could the M's be 70 games over .500, but only 35 ahead of a .500 team?

Of course, I realize that there's a different principle at work here. The difference between teams alludes to how many games one would have to beat the other head-to-head to catch up. In the example above, if the Athletics beat the Mariners 35 games in a row, the two teams would be even in the standings, but the M's would still be safely above .500. You can say that the Mariners were 70 *wins* above .500. But, if you say they were 70 *games* over .500—no matter how many learned people say it along with you—you are confusing the issue.

The Quality Start Is a Meaningless Statistic

The term *quality start* drives me nuts. . . . Who came up with three runs
for six innings being a quality start? That means the ERA would be 4.50.

—Tim McCarver, in *Tim McCarver's Baseball for Brain Surgeons and
Other Fans*

In the mid-1980s, the term *quality start* came into usage, and it has since
become a widely used statistic, abbreviated QS. It refers to an outing by
a starting pitcher in which he hurls at least six innings and gives up three
earned runs or fewer. Critics of the statistic point out that a pitcher could go
six innings and allow three runs every time out, all "quality starts," yet have
a mediocre 4.50 ERA to show for them. It is just another meaningless stat,
they say.

Well, sure. You can conjure up extreme examples to "prove" that just
about any stat is meaningless. A closer could come in with a three-run lead in
the ninth every time out, give up two runs every time, and wind up with 60
saves despite an 18.00 ERA. A batter could ground out with the bases loaded
once a game and drive in 162 runs despite a .000 batting average.

As Bill James writes in his 1987 *The Bill James Historical Baseball Abstract*,
"If a baseball statistic is meaningless to you, that is simply because you do not
know what it means." James elaborates, saying the following:

All player statistics in baseball, without any exception I am aware of, are
flawed; they are all subject to outside influences. . . . At the same time, all
baseball statistics, with very minor exceptions, bear some relationship to some
baseball ability. . . . *All baseball statistics are in one way or another related to wins
and losses; thus no statistic is 100% meaningless.*

In reality, QS are a fine indicator of a pitcher's effectiveness. From 1984
to 1991, pitchers had a 1.91 ERA and .674 winning percentage in QS, but a
7.50 ERA and .311 winning percentage in all other starts. And, less than 6%
of all QS resulted from exactly six innings and three earned runs.

Pick any season, look at the QS leaders, and see how they fared in the
more traditional measures of success. In 2007, for example, the AL's leaders in QS were Dan Haren (28), Fausto Carmona (26), and C. C. Sabathia
(26). All three also excelled in the more widely accepted pitching categories:
Carmona was second in the league in ERA, Haren was third, and Sabathia
was fifth. Carmona (19–8) and Sabathia (19–7) were tied for second in the
circuit in victories; Haren was 15–9. The NL's 2007 QS leaders were Jake

Peavy (28), Brad Penny (26), and John Smoltz (26). Peavy led the NL in ERA, Penny was third, and Smoltz was fourth. Peavy (19–6) was also tops in victories, while Penny (16–4) led in win percentage; Smoltz was 14–8.

Derek Jeter Is a Great Clutch Hitter

> Derek Jeter is the reason I believe. I know in big situations he takes bet-
> ter at bats. He shrinks his strike zone. That's what makes him so good.
>
> —former Yankees' teammate Jason Giambi

Derek Jeter doesn't really have much to do with this section. It's the whole idea of "clutch" players—guys who seem to rise to the occasion, raising their games to a higher level when the game is on the line.

Clutch and Math

Study after study (by such baseball statistical heavyweights as Richard Cra-mer, Pete Palmer, Tom Ruane, and Phil Birnbaum) has shown that clutch hitting is not a provable skill. If it were, the same hitters would rank among the leaders in clutch hitting every year, but they don't. Some hitters do bet-ter than expected in clutch situations, some do worse, but their performances fall within the scopes of random variation.

For example, say you had 100 people each flipping a coin 100 times and you decide that landing "heads" is a favorable outcome. Naturally, most people would get around 50 heads out of 100, but some would get more or less just by luck. Based on the rules of random chance, about 16 of the 100 people would get more than 55 heads, and two or three would get more than 60. Maybe coin number 73 would emerge as the leader, with 63 heads. Does that make it a good clutch coin? Of course not; if we tried the same test again, coin number 73 would probably wind up with, oh, about 50 heads.

The same pattern emerges when analyzing so-called clutch hitters. In any given year, some players do better than expected in clutch situations, and some do worse. The next season, we'll have different sets of players who do better or worse than expected, with some of last year's "clutch" hitters looking like "chokers" this year, and vice versa. To illustrate, Palmer plotted the clutch stats of 330 players from 1979 to 1989. Based on the laws of random chance, one of the 330 players would be expected to differ from his norm in clutch situations by three standard deviations (50 to 60 points of batting average), and 16 players would be expected to exceed by two standard deviations. In fact, one player differed by three standard deviations, and 14 differed by two.

The Great American Baseball Stat Book (1992) defines a clutch-hitting situation as seventh inning or later with a one-run lead; a tie; or the tying run on base, at bat, or on deck (typically called "late-inning pressure situations," or LIPS). David Grabiner examined 245 player seasons from 1991 and 1992 using those parameters, concluding that the "correlation between past and current clutch performance is .01, with a standard deviation of .07. In other words, there isn't a significant ability in clutch hitting; if there were, the same players would be good clutch hitters every year."

As top baseball researcher Mike Emeigh puts it, "A player's performance in clutch situations does not vary significantly from his performance in all other situations. In other words, there are players who hit well in the clutch—but those players hit well in *all* situations." Another baseball statistician, Cyril Morong, did an exhaustive study of player performances over a 15-year period, from 1987 to 2001, which supports Emeigh's statement. Morong checked every player with at least 6,000 plate appearances over that span, 71 players in all. He found that the players who hit best in clutch situations were, by and large, the best hitters, period. For example, the highest overall career batting averages during this period were achieved by Tony Gwynn (.342), Edgar Martinez (.319), Frank Thomas (.319), Wade Boggs (.317), Paul Molitor (.316), Larry Walker (.315), Mark Grace (.307), and Roberto Alomar (.306). The top six batting averages with runners on base? Gwynn (.357), Thomas (.327), Grace (.324), Alomar (.319), Walker (.317), and Boggs (.317). The same pattern emerges when looking at other stats, like on-base percentage or slugging percentage. Some players did a little better in so-called clutch situations, some did a little worse, but 52 of the 71 players were within 5% of their expected results in "late and close" situations. That 5% is the difference between a .300 and .315 batting average, which is one or two extra or fewer hits a year in clutch situations.

Since there are relatively few "clutch" situations in a typical player's season, it is not unusual for someone to exhibit gaudy clutch stats in one year. For example, according to the Elias Sports Bureau, the best single-season clutch performance between 1974 and 2003 was by the forgettable Manny Trillo. Trillo batted .466 (27-for-58) in what Elias defined as "late-inning pressure situations" in 1981. But Trillo's career LIPS average in other seasons was a mere .245 (more in line with his .263 overall career average), so his 1981 performance was obviously a statistical fluke.

Yet Elias has castigated those who say clutch hitting is a mirage. In the 1989 *Elias Baseball Analyst* they write that,

As in the past, we feel it's our duty to demonstrate that clutch hitting isn't simply a random trait of a player's profile. To most of us, of course, that's obvious, and has been as long as there have been baseball fans to notice it. Nevertheless, a small group of shrill pseudo-statisticians has used insufficient data and faulty methods to try to disprove the existence of the clutch hitter. . . . When the clutch-hitting data is analyzed properly, the trends are undeniably apparent except to those who choose not to see.

ESPN.com's Rob Neyer responded, saying the following:

Also in 1989, Elias finally gave us what they hadn't . . . earlier, a list of the greatest clutch hitters of the previous decade, the 25 major leaguers whose batting averages in late-inning pressure situations were more than 25 points better than in other situations. . . . Twenty-five points? That's not much, is it? No, it's not. And hold on another minute, because it gets better. You only needed 250 LIPS at bats to qualify for the list, and 250 at bats isn't much, either. What kind of numbers would be reasonable? Well, how about 35 points of batting average, and 400 LIPS at bats? You wanna guess how many great clutch hitters that left? Two (Tim Raines and Steve Sax). From 1979 through 1988, Tim Raines batted .352 in so-called "pressure situations" and .296 the rest of the time. Even if you use Elias's limits (250 at bats), Raines remains at the top of the list, just ahead of—are you ready for this?—Jeff Newman, Garth Iorg, Glenn Hoffman, Thad Bosley, and Larry Milbourne. And that is, I suspect, exactly why Elias never went out of their way to publicize this particular metric. For the most part, it tells us that the great clutch hitters are not the players we lionized as great clutch hitters, but rather a bunch of stiffs like Jeff Newman and Larry Milbourne. That list—the "Newman/Milbourne List"—was printed in the *Analyst* without comment. None of the haughty pronouncements that accompanied their earlier analyses of clutch hitting. This time, just a chart in the back of the book, like a poor student slouching at his desk in the corner, hoping not to be called upon.

Neyer concludes that, "If you look, really look, at the 'evidence' of clutch hitting as a true ability rather than happenstance, you find out that, at best, it's a bunch of blurry photos, in the form of poorly constructed studies presented by people who desperately want to believe."

Sports Illustrated addresses the phenomena of "clutch hitting" in its 2004 Baseball Preview issue. Some numbers crunchers are quoted as saying that it doesn't exist. "That could be the dumbest thing I've ever heard in my life," replies Reggie Jackson, the self-proclaimed "Mr. October." Jeter, or "Captain

Clutch" to his admirers, adds, "You can take those stats guys and throw them out the window."

"Derek Jeter is the reason I believe," asserts Jason Giambi. "I know in big situations he takes better at bats. He shrinks his strike zone. That's what makes him so good." Nike apparently agreed, designing the "Jeter Clutch" sports shoe in 2008.

This raises a crucial question about this issue: If there really are players who are capable of performing better in the late innings or the big games, wouldn't that mean that they aren't really giving 100% the rest of the time? When I

Figure 4.3.   Derek Jeter, aka Captain Clutch.
Photograph by Keith Allison

was in high school, the final exam for each course counted for one-third of the grade for the year. Talk about late-inning pressure: You carry a 96% average for nine and a half months, miss the bus on the day of the final, and wind up failing the course. Many of my classmates got very stressed out about these exams. Not me—I thrived on them. I typically got better grades, sometimes much better, on my finals than my averages for the year to that point, boosting them nicely. Was this because I was a great clutch performer? No, it was because I hated school, slacked off most of the year, and then turned it on at the end. Which makes me wonder, even if someone could be proven to have clutch ability, what would it tell us? Perhaps that he doesn't give maximum effort except in high-profile situations. And that's supposed to be an attribute?

Noted author John Updike was more eloquent on this topic, in referring to Ted Williams's reputation as a choker in the clutch (based on nine games of his 2,300-game career). Wrote Updike,

> For me, Williams is the classic ballplayer of the game on a hot August weekday, before a small crowd, when the only thing at stake is the tissue-thin difference between a thing done well and a thing done ill. Baseball is a game of the long season, of relentless and gradual averaging-out. Irrelevance—since the reference point of most individual games is remote and statistical—always threatens its interest, which can be maintained not by the occasional heroics that sportswriters feed upon, but by players who always *care*; who care, that is to say, about themselves and their art. Insofar as the clutch hitter is not a sportswriter's myth, he is a vulgarity, like a writer who writes only for money.

Clutch Legends

But what about Reggie and Derek? Everyone knows that Jackson excelled in World Series play: a .357 batting average and .755 slugging percentage with ten homers in 27 games. But his performance in League Championship Series (LCS) games, which many people believe are bigger clutch situations (after all, if you don't win the LCS, you don't even get to play in the World Series), was putrid: a .227 batting average with just six homers in 45 games. Add his League Championship and World Series numbers together and you have a .276 batting average and .521 slugging percentage, only a little better than his regular-season numbers (.262, .490). And Jackson's regular-season clutch numbers? According to Retrosheet, Jackson batted .263 and slugged .481 with runners in scoring position; in "close and late" situations, the numbers were just .251 and .452.

And Jeter, through 2009, was a career .317 hitter and .459 slugger overall, including .308/.429 averages with runners in scoring position and .295/.423 marks in "close and late" situations, plus .313/.479 averages in postseason play. He is a good hitter in the clutch simply because he is a good hitter.

Another player reputed to come up big in the tight spots was Harold Baines. Playing mostly for the White Sox, Baines batted .289 and slugged .465 over 22 seasons—but those numbers didn't tell the whole story, according to Chicago executives. "When the game was on the line," said Sox chairman Jerry Reinsdorf, "Harold was awesome." General manager Ken Williams agreed, saying, "Personally, I've never seen a more clutch player." But Baines's numbers at crucial moments were about the same as in all other situations. In "late and close" situations (using the same definition as *The Great American Baseball Stat Book*), Baines batted .284 and slugged .474. With two out and runners in scoring position, he hit .280 and slugged .448.

Another with a big clutch reputation was David Ortiz, who went through an amazing run of late-inning heroics for the Red Sox in 2005–2006. Team owner John Henry presented him with a plaque calling Ortiz "The Greatest Clutch Hitter in the History of the Boston Red Sox." But, his relative clutch performance in other years has been ordinary at best, and through 2009, Ortiz had batted .282 and slugged .545 overall for his career, and .273/.547 in "late and close" situations.

You get pretty much the same results over a long career no matter which clutch legend you check. Brooks Robinson? He batted .267 and slugged .401 overall, .267/.401 with runners in scoring position, and .270/.396 close and late. Tony Perez? .279 and .463 overall, .284/.470 with runners in scoring position, .300/.488 close and late.

The Other Side of the Coin

If there are clutch hitters, aren't there also clutch pitchers? If a batter succeeds in a crucial situation, is it because he is a good clutch hitter, or because his opponent is a poor clutch pitcher? Many people believe there are, indeed, clutch pitchers: men who win significantly more games than expected, because of some unusual ability to pitch to the score and emerge victorious in the close games. Pete Palmer took on this theory by examining every pitcher (501 in all) with at least 200 starts and 200 decisions between 1876 and 2006, checking how many runs were scored on his behalf, how many he gave up, and what his record "should" have been based on that data. The results were published in the 2006 *Baseball Research Journal*. They showed that pitchers win about as many games as they can be expected to win, given their overall runs–runs allowed records, with deviations falling within the scope of random chance. Even hurlers reputed to be "big game pitchers" were within a few wins of projection: Bob Gibson (251 wins versus 250 projected wins), Sandy Koufax (165–161), Curt Schilling (207–210), and John Smoltz (193–201). That's right, Schilling and Smoltz won *fewer* games than they should have.

Timing Is Everything

As author David Kaiser says,

> The argument [whether clutch performance exists] depends on the idea that a run in the eighth or ninth inning is worth more than a run in the first or second; but in fact, all runs are equal. . . . If Bobby [Thomson] had hit his famous three-run homer in the first inning of the third game of the 1951 playoff, the Giants would have won 5–4, just the same as they actually did. *The bottom of the ninth wouldn't even have been played.* But the home run wouldn't have gone down in history as the greatest clutch hit of all time. The ability to hit a home run in a late-inning, close situation may earn you immortality; but it has nothing to do with the ability to win ball games, which is measured by your average performance in every at bat you have.

Author Merritt Clifton puts another spin on the matter. Clifton notes that the defense is often forced to play differently in "clutch" situations: holding on runners at first base (making for a bigger gap on the right side), playing deep in the infield in hopes of a double play (increasing the chances for an infield hit), and playing shallow in the outfield in hopes of holding a runner at third base or throwing him out at home (increasing the chances of a deep fly falling for an extra-base hit). Someone who has the ability to put the ball in play is most apt to take advantage of such defensive aberrations, thus gaining a reputation as a clutch hitter, even though he is hitting the ball the same way as he does in nonclutch situations. As Clifton concludes, "A 'clutch hitter,' in short, is an opportunist."

Finally, when you think about it, every major league batsman has proven himself to be a clutch hitter. Each time, an at bat occurs against pitchers firing 90-plus mph missiles, in front of tens of thousands of spectators, with hundreds of thousands of dollars of salary on the line. Those who can't handle these pressures get weeded out in college and the minors, if not earlier. So, if a player can't perform reasonably well in the clutch, he will have no data points in the major league sample, and we won't even be talking about him.

CHAPTER FIVE

~

The Expansion Era

After six decades of essentially the same 16 teams, major league baseball began to expand in 1961, nearly doubling the number of teams over the next four decades. This gave twice as much opportunity for mythology.

Stu Miller Was Blown Off the Mound in the 1961 All-Star Game

At Candlestick Park, on July 11, 1961, Stu Miller entered the All-Star Game in relief of Sandy Koufax. There were none out in the ninth inning, and the National League was clinging to a 3–2 lead with two on base. Miller was promptly called for a balk—the first of his career—when the San Francisco winds literally blew him off the mound, according to lore.

But Miller's quote in *Baseball: The Biographical Encyclopedia* (2000) indicates that the story is exaggerated: "All of a sudden the wind pushed my shoulder forward. My feet didn't move, so I didn't get blown off the mound as the story goes. Each time it gets told, I get blown farther off the mound." Miller gives more details in *Inside Pitch* (1996), by John Skipper, saying the following:

> I relieved in the ninth inning, and the wind was really blowin' up a storm. I'd never seen it worse. It was coming in out of left field and was circling around. There were men on first and second. I tried to anchor myself, but just as I went into my motion, a real whoosh came and I swayed. I'm hearing "Balk!"

147

coming from the American League dugout, and of course it was. But the umpires didn't say anything, so I just continued on and threw the pitch. Rocky Colavito swung and missed. Then Stan Landes, the home plate umpire, calls the balk and motions the runners up a base. I went up to him and said, "You know, Stan, the wind shoved me." And he says, "I know it did, but rules are rules and that was a balk."

Practically forgotten is the rest of Miller's day. Despite three errors behind him and a dropped foul pop in front of him, Miller hurled one and two-thirds hitless innings, striking out four, and earning the victory when the NL scored two in the tenth. It would appear that the only ones blown away while Miller was pitching were the American League hitters.

Roger Maris's Home Run Record Was Marked with an Asterisk

Whether I beat Ruth's record or not is for others to say. But it gives me a wonderful feeling to know that I'm the only man in history to hit 61 home runs. Nobody can take that away from me.

—Roger Maris

Babe Ruth's record of 60 home runs in 1927 was once considered the record of all records. When Roger Maris broke it in 1961, it was considered a fluke. Yet, Maris's record of 61 homers in a season wound up standing longer than Ruth's did.

It was commonly believed that Maris's achievement was marked with an asterisk. The AL schedule had been increased from 154 to 162 games in 1961, giving Maris an extra eight games to set the record. Other fans pointed out advantages that *Ruth* had over Maris and for three decades lobbied to get the demeaning asterisk removed. Their efforts were rewarded on September 4, 1991, when a "statistical accuracy committee" led by commissioner Fay Vincent (along with Seymour Siwoff, David Voigt, George Kirsch, Jerome Holtzman, and Jack Lang)—amid much pomp—expunged the infamous asterisk from the record books. It was an easy job: The asterisk never existed.

Maris's record *was*, from 1962 until 1991, listed separately from Ruth's: Roger's as the standard for a 162-game season, Babe's for a 154-game schedule. This situation came about on July 17, 1961, when—with Maris (35) and teammate Mickey Mantle (33) threatening Ruth's record—commissioner Ford Frick (a former ghostwriter for the Babe) made the following proclamation:

Any player who may hit more than 60 home runs during his club's first 154 games would be recognized as having established a new record. However, if the player does not hit more than 60 until after his club has played 154 games, there would have to be some distinctive mark in the record books to show that Babe Ruth's record was set under a 154-game schedule and the total of more than 60 was compiled while a 162-game schedule was in effect.

We also would apply the same reasoning if a player should equal Ruth's total of 60 in the first 154 games: He would be recognized as tying Ruth's record. If in more than 154 games, there would be a distinction in the record book.

Frick never actually defined "some distinctive mark." In the press conference afterward, New York writer Dick Young suggested an asterisk, but no such mark ever actually accompanied the record in either of the leading record books, *The Sporting News's One for the Book*, or the Elias Sports Bureau's *Little Red Book of Baseball*. Each had only the footnote, "If the accomplishment was directly benefited by an increase of scheduled games the record will be annotated with the phrase (162-game schedule)."

It was the first time a commissioner had ever made a ruling involving a baseball record, and many people thought he was out of line, especially since most of the season had already been played. "I think the commissioner shouldn't have made any 154-game ruling when he did," said Maris. "But if Mick breaks it, I hope he does it in 154. The same goes for me." A poll of sportswriters showed support of Frick's ruling by a 37–18 margin; however, after a Baseball Writers' Association of America (BBWAA) meeting on October 3, the writers went on record to protest the commissioner's involvement. The writers had already established a Records Committee, and Frick's move threatened to make it irrelevant.

Frick and the writers seemed to have forgotten that the matter was discussed less than a year earlier. In the *New York Times* of October 23, 1960, Arthur Daley raised the possibility of Ruth's and other records being challenged under the expanded schedule, which at the time was not planned until 1962. Frick responded that he didn't think that the "great marks we treasure will even be approached, despite the eight extra games." He added that,

> I intend to ask the rules committee to study this problem and try to soften the impact wherever necessary. My own idea is that some records might deserve to be listed in two categories—the one made during a 154-game schedule, presuming that the 162-game one surpasses the 154-game record.

Actually, if *anyone* deserves an asterisk next to his achievement, it is *Ruth*. The Babe never had to play a night game, hit a slider, or face a fireballing relief ace. Moreover, while Maris was batting against the best pitchers in the nation, Ruth had been facing only the best *white* ones.

Maris got off to a slow start in 1961, failing to homer in his first ten games and managing only three dingers (compared to Mantle's ten) in the Yankees' first 28 contests. But Roger went on a tear starting May 17, hitting an incredible 24 round-trippers in 38 games. By the end of June, Maris had 27 homers, and Mantle had 25. It was 40–39 after July, and 51–48 after August. Mantle was still in the hunt as late as September 10, with 53 homers to Maris's 56, but a hip abscess soon knocked Mickey out of the race. He finished with 54.

All eyes were on Maris on September 20, the Yankees' 154th game of record. Maris hit his 59th homer that day but failed in three more tries for number 60. Roger tied Ruth in game number 159 and hit number 61 in the final game of the season. As Maris later pointed out, he *had* hit his 61 homers in 154 games: the *last* 154 games.

"Whether I beat Ruth's record or not is for others to say," said Maris after the game. "But it gives me a wonderful feeling to know that I'm the only man in history to hit 61 home runs. Nobody can take that away from me."

Incidentally, Maris hit another homer during the 1961 season. It came at Baltimore on July 17, ironically the same day Frick made his ruling (in another irony, it was also the day Ty Cobb—Ruth's perpetual challenger for the title of "Greatest Player Ever"—died). On that day, with two out in the fifth inning—just short of official status—the game was rained out, canceling homers by both Maris and Mantle.

In December 1961, noted writer Dan Daniel approached Frick on behalf of the BBWAA. "I told the commissioner that the writers resented his involvement in baseball records," Daniel wrote, "and that if his office wanted to continue this involvement, the writers would relinquish custodianship of the records." Frick stood his ground, allowing only that, "I should have made no mention of Ruth, and announced that all baseball records made in 162 games would be so listed. I never said anything about asterisks in the record book."

The following are some other myths about Maris's record and the facts to dispel them:

- *Maris hit 61 only because he was a dead pull hitter aiming at a 296-foot foul line.* While Yankee Stadium's short right field porch certainly didn't hurt Maris (or Ruth, either, for that matter), Roger actually hit more home runs on the road (31) than he did at home that year.
- *Maris feasted off expansion pitching to get the record.* Two new teams, the Angels and Senators, were added to the AL in 1961. But, while the

Yankees played 22% of their games against these teams, Maris hit only 21% of his homers against them.

- *Maris was booed by even his own fans for breaking Ruth's record.* Although Yankees' fans may have been pulling more for Mantle (in his 11th year with the team) than Maris (in his second) to break the record, they were proud that the record belonged to a Yankee one way or the other, and they *were* rooting for Roger. It wasn't until 1962, when Maris proved human, that he fell out of grace with the press and then the fans. Although he led the 1962 Yanks in homers (33) and RBI (100), en route to another world championship, Maris didn't get a single point in the MVP poll. "If a vote were taken," said an October 1962 *Sporting News* article, "Roger Maris undoubtedly would be elected flop of the year."
- *Ruth's "60" had been considered the ultimate achievement.* As storied as the record was, it was under siege from the beginning. As longtime baseball writer Dan Daniel put it, "we of the press box felt that (Ruth) would be on his way to 65 in 1928 or 1929." Indeed, Ruth was ahead of his 1927 homer pace for most of the next season, amassing 30 by the end of June and 41 by the end of July 1928, before finishing at 54. Ruth again had 30 by the end of June 1930, the same year Hack Wilson belted 56 to set the NL record. Jimmie Foxx smashed 58 in 1932. Six years later, Hank Greenberg also clubbed 58, while Foxx hit another 50. Between 1947 and 1956, Ralph Kiner (twice), Johnny Mize, Willie Mays, and Mantle each topped 50 homers.

In contrast, Maris's record was not seriously threatened for 35 years: No one hit more than 52 homers in a season between 1962 and 1996. By the time Mark McGwire (and Sammy Sosa) decimated it in 1998, the record had outlived Ruth's 60 by three years. It had even outlived its own mythical asterisk.

Sandy Koufax Suddenly Matured to Become Great

Over his first seven seasons (1955–1961), the Dodgers' Sandy Koufax was mostly a struggling young pitcher. Despite great promise and flashes of brilliance, his record at that point was an uninspired 54–53, his ERA 3.94. In his next—and last—five seasons, it was an entirely different story: Koufax was a phenomenal 111–34, with a 1.95 ERA, winning three Cy Young Awards and five straight ERA titles.

What caused this dramatic transformation? Conventional wisdom says Koufax suddenly "matured" at the age of 25, learning to pitch rather than just throw (Koufax's example is even cited as proof that left-handers mature late). In his autobiography with Ed Linn, Koufax credits Dodgers' catcher Norm Sherry with the transformation. Before a meaningless 1961 spring training game, Sherry convinced Koufax to "let up and throw the curve and try to pitch to spots"—in other words, take a little off his blazing fastball and work on control. Koufax hurled a seven-inning no-hitter. "That day in Orlando was the beginning of a whole new era for me," said Koufax. "I came home a different pitcher from the one who had left."

In reality, Koufax's "maturity" was largely the product of two environmental changes: first, the Dodgers' 1962 move from hitter-oriented Los Angeles Coliseum (and Ebbets Field before that) to Dodger Stadium, one of the best pitchers' parks in baseball history, and, second, the 1963 to 1968 rule change that increased the height of the strike zone by approximately eight inches.

Koufax's home-road breakdowns (see table 5.1) illustrate the first argument. Koufax posted a 4.09 ERA at cozy Ebbets Field (343 feet to the left field foul pole, but just 384 to center and 297 to right); a 4.43 mark at the cozier Coliseum (252–420–300); but an incredible 1.37 figure at Dodger Stadium, with its huge foul territory and built-up mound (measured at an illegal 18 inches by umpire Ken Burkhart on April 30, 1965). In his last two years with the Coliseum as his home, Koufax posted a fine 2.88 ERA on the road, but a bloated 4.58 mark at home. In his first two years after the move to Dodger Stadium, Koufax had a similar road ERA (2.71), but cut his home ERA by two-thirds (1.53). This suggests that Koufax was just as good a pitcher in 1960–1961, when he was 26–26 with a 3.64 ERA, as he was in 1962–1963, when he went 39–12 with a 2.13 mark. His talents had simply been disguised by a hitter's haven. And, for some reason, southpaws at Dodger Stadium got an even bigger boost than righties. According to Retrosheet's 1963 data, all left-handed pitchers, *excluding* Koufax, posted a 2.75 ERA in Los Angeles, but a 3.90 ERA elsewhere, almost a 30% bonus. To put it into full perspective, Koufax had a 1.37 career ERA at Dodger stadium, 3.38 at all other parks.

In 1963, the strike zone was redefined to encompass the *top of the batter's shoulders* (imagine that today!) to the bottom of his kneecaps. Prior to that, it had extended from the armpits to the top of the kneecaps, so the net effect was about one square foot more strike zone for the pitchers to work with. ERAs and batting averages plunged dramatically until the former strike zone was restored in 1969. The big-league strikeout-to-walk ratio ballooned to 2.00 from 1963 to 1968, as compared to 1.56 in 1961–1962 and 1.65 in 1969–1970.

Table 5.1. Sandy Koufax's Major League Statistics at Home versus at Other Ballparks

Year	G	IP	W-L	SO	BB	H	ER	ERA
Sandy Koufax at Home								
1955	7	24	2–0	22	10	16	6	2.25
1956	8	18	0–2	8	11	28	15	7.50
1957	18	57	3–1	68	23	48	24	3.79
Ebbets	33	99	5–3	98	44	92	45	4.09
1958	17	62.2	2–6	53	49	55	39	5.60
1959	16	80.1	5–2	98	41	64	28	3.14
1960	19	70	1–7	71	49	63	41	5.27
1961	21	132.1	9–8	145	51	119	62	4.22
Coliseum	73	345.1	17–23	367	190	301	170	4.43
1962	13	102.2	7–4	118	25	68	20	1.75
1963	17	143.2	11–1	144	23	83	22	1.38
1964	15	127.2	12–2	124	18	82	12	0.85
1965	20	170	14–3	208	31	89	26	1.38
1966	21	171.1	13–5	160	45	124	29	1.52
Stadium	86	715.1	57–15	754	142	446	109	1.37
Total	192	1,159.2	79–41	1,219	376	839	324	2.51

Year	G	IP	W–L	SO	BB	H	ER	ERA
Sandy Koufax on the Road								
1955	5	17.2	0–2	8	18	17	8	4.08
1956	8	40.2	2–2	22	18	38	17	3.76
1957	16	47.1	2–3	54	28	35	21	3.99
	29	105.2	4–7	84	64	90	46	3.92
1958	23	96	9–5	78	56	77	40	3.75
1959	19	73	3–4	75	51	72	41	5.05
1960	18	105	7–6	126	51	70	35	3.00
1961	21	123.1	9–5	124	45	93	38	2.77
	81	397.1	28–20	403	203	312	154	3.49
1962	15	81.2	7–3	98	32	66	32	3.53
1963	23	167.1	14–4	162	35	131	43	2.31
1964	14	95.1	7–3	99	35	72	31	2.93
1965	23	165.2	12–5	174	40	127	50	2.72
1966	20	151.2	14–4	157	32	117	33	1.96
	95	661.2	54–19	690	174	513	189	2.57
Total	205	1,164.2	86–46	1,177	441	915	389	3.01

KEY: G = games pitched; IP = innings pitched; W-L = won-lost record; SO = strikeouts; BB = bases on balls (walks) allowed; H = hits allowed; ER = earned runs allowed; ERA = earned run average

Who benefited most from the 1963 to 1968 zone? Power pitchers with control problems, like Koufax, who tend to miss high. Koufax averaged 4.44 walks per nine innings before 1963, 1.95 afterward. A bigger strike zone means not only fewer walks, but more advantageous situations: Instead of throwing a 3–1 meatball, the pitcher can come in with a 2–2 money pitch.

This is not to demean Koufax's achievements, merely to put them into a broadened context. He was better than he seemed before 1962, and not quite as good as he seemed afterward. Rather than experiencing a sudden metamorphosis, Koufax made the best of some changes in his habitat, turning a mediocre career into a Hall of Fame one.

Bill DeWitt Gave Away Frank Robinson, Calling Him "An Old 30"

The time to trade a star player is when you feel he has reached the twilight of his career.

—Hall of Fame executive Branch Rickey

On December 9, 1965, the Baltimore Orioles made a blockbuster deal, swapping nondescript pitchers Milt Pappas and Jack Baldschun and outfield prospect Dick Simpson to the Cincinnati Reds in exchange for future Hall of Famer Frank Robinson. Reds' owner Bill DeWitt, defending the trade, supposedly called Robinson "an old 30." Robby went on to make DeWitt eat his words by having a Triple Crown season to lead the Orioles to the world championship, the first of four AL titles in Robinson's six years with the team. But DeWitt's remark was made four months after the trade and did not even contain the word "old." And the deal, at the time, seemed a good one for the Reds to many observers.

Quoted in the newspapers of April 3, 1966, responding to a question as to whether there was anything personal about the trade, DeWitt said, "Nothing personal at all. Robinson is not a young 30. If he had been 26, we might not have traded him." Rather than a jab at Robinson, it seemed to be a commentary on the fact that most players of that era peaked in their mid- to late 20s, and were in decline by 30.

In fact, trading Robby at this stage of his career seemed a savvy move to many pundits. As Cincinnati scribe Earl Lawson writes,

Perhaps, too, DeWitt was guided by an old saying of the late Branch Rickey [who, ironically, died on the day of the trade]—"The time to trade a star player is when you feel he has reached the twilight of his career." Robby, now 30, is approaching that stage. He was at his peak in 1961 and 1962.

The numbers seemed to bear that out: In 1961–1962, Robinson had averaged 38 homers, 130 RBI, and a .333 batting mark each year, but, in the three years since, the averages had dipped to 28–100–.289. Besides the decline in his numbers, Robby had been involved in some on- and off-field incidents that embarrassed the Reds. Even Harry Dalton, the Orioles' new director of player personnel, admitted that the move was a "gamble."

The players the Reds got were not chopped liver, either. Pappas, just 26 years of age, already had a 110–74 record to his credit (compare that with three Hall of Fame pitchers at that time: Bob Gibson, age 30, was 91–69; Gaylord Perry, 28, was 24–30; Phil Niekro, a month older than Pappas, was 2–3). Baldschun, 29, had been one of the NL's top relievers over his five big-league seasons, appearing in 65-plus games each year and ranking fourth in the league in saves over that period. And Simpson, 22, had slugged .626 in the California League in 1962 and .523 in the Triple-A Pacific Coast League in 1965 (the Orioles had acquired both Baldschun and Simpson in separate deals just days before the Robinson trade). As DeWitt said, "A top-flight starter and a top-flight relief hurler was just too attractive a package to turn down." The 1965 Reds, despite leading the league in runs scored by a wide margin, had finished in fourth place, so their new focus was on pitching.

It was Robinson who introduced the "o" word when he responded to DeWitt's April quote. "That comment about me being an old 30 is hitting below the belt," said Robby. "It was uncalled for. It seems I suddenly got old last fall between the end of the season and December 9."

We all know now that, while Robinson continued to excel, Pappas had a mediocre 99–90 the rest of his career, Baldschun crashed and burned, and Simpson failed to pan out in the majors (although he did go on to help land Alex Johnson for the Reds in a later trade). But, when the deal was made, it looked like a reasonable swap, and nobody but Frank Robinson himself used the adjective "old."

Tony Conigliaro Was the Youngest Man to Hit 100 Homers

Tony Conigliaro was a tragic figure. The Boston slugger's blossoming career was, for all intents and purposes, ended by a fastball to the skull when he was 22 years old; his life was over at 45. Tony C burst into the major leagues at the age of 19 in 1964. Despite suffering a broken forearm when hit by a Pedro Ramos pitch on July 24, putting him out of action for six weeks, Conigliaro hit 24 homers, the all-time record for a teenaged player. In 1965, despite again being shelved by a hit-by-pitch injury (this time a fractured wrist on July 28, courtesy of Wes Stock), Conig hit 32 homers, enough to lead the AL and make him the youngest home run champ of all time.

Table 5.2.   Youngest Players to Hit 100 Homers, 1876–2011

Player	Date of Birth	Date of Homer	Age (Years, Days)
Mel Ott	3/02/1909	7/12/1931	22, 132
Tony Conigliaro	1/07/1945	7/23/1967	22, 197
Eddie Mathews	10/13/1931	8/01/1954	22, 292

Conigliaro had a solid season (28 homers) in 1966, and was en route to another (20 homers) when tragedy struck on August 18. A pitch by the Angels' Jack Hamilton nailed Tony in the left temple, nearly killing him (this was before the days of earflap helmets). His cheekbone was fractured in three places, his jaw was dislocated, and he had a hole in his retina that left his vision at 20/300 in that eye. Conigliaro missed the rest of the season, the World Series, and the entire 1968 campaign as well. He was stuck on 104 career home runs for a year and a half.

Conigliaro came back to have two strong seasons before recurring vision problems forced him to retire midway through the 1971 season. Another comeback attempt in 1975 failed, and he finished with 164 career homers. On January 9, 1982, at the age of 37, he suffered a massive heart attack and lapsed into a coma. He finally died on February 24, 1990.

Through his tribulations, many people reported (and still do) that Conigliaro had been the youngest player to reach 100 career home runs, and it seemed plausible. In fact, Hall of Famer Mel Ott holds this honor. The Giants' slugger hit one homer at the age of 18, 19 homers at 19, 42 at 20, and 25 at 21, before connecting for number 100 midway through the next season. Ott was 65 days younger than Conig, as shown in table 5.2.

Several other players hit their 100th homers at the age of 23: Alex Rodriguez, Andruw Jones, Johnny Bench, Albert Pujols, Hank Aaron, Ken Griffey Jr., Frank Robinson, Mickey Mantle, Jimmie Foxx, Ted Williams, Juan Gonzalez, Joe DiMaggio, and Orlando Cepeda. So, Tony C is in some good company—but he's not number one.

Curt Flood Pioneered Free Agency

> After 12 years in the major leagues, I do not feel I am a piece of property to be bought and sold irrespective of my wishes.
>
> —Curt Flood

Free agency came to major league baseball in 1975, starting the shift of power between management and players. Curt Flood is often cited as the pioneer who made it all possible, but, in truth, he had virtually nothing to do with it.

Until the 1970s, team owners had all the leverage when it came to negotiating with players (who had no agents to do their bidding, either). Under baseball's reserve clause, a club had exclusive rights to a contracted player's services until it traded or released him. As noted writer F. C. Lane put it, the "player is at a disadvantage in a salary wrangle with his club. If he delays signing a contract beyond a certain date, he becomes automatically blacklisted. . . . His only real recourse is to quit the game, [but in so doing] he 'cuts off his nose in spite of his face.'" Players who did not sign contracts by March were called holdouts. There were many celebrated holdout incidents over the years, but the owners generally prevailed.

When the Cardinals traded Flood to the Phillies after the 1969 season, Flood refused to report or sign a contract. "I am [not] a piece of property to be bought and sold irrespective of my wishes," he wrote to commissioner Bowie Kuhn, asking to be declared a free agent. Kuhn refused, so Flood filed suit, hiring former Supreme Court justice and secretary of labor Arthur Goldberg to represent him. The lower court dismissed Flood's case, and, by a 5–3 vote, the Supreme Court upheld its decision in 1972. Justice Harry Blackmun recognized that "Professional baseball is a business, and it is engaged in interstate commerce." He referred to baseball's antitrust immunity as an "exception," an "anomaly," and an "aberration," but concluded that after a half century, any change must come from Washington:

> The Court has emphasized that since 1922, baseball, with full and continuing congressional awareness, has been allowed to develop and to expand unhindered by Federal legislative action. Remedial legislation has been introduced repeatedly in Congress, but none has ever been enacted. The Court, accordingly, has concluded that Congress as yet has had no intention to subject baseball's reserve system to the reach of the antitrust statutes. . . . If there is any inconsistency or illogic in all this, it is an inconsistency and illogic of long standing that is to be remedied by the Congress and not by this Court.

The dissenting justices responded that, "The unbroken silence of Congress should not prevent us from correcting our own mistakes," but four decades later neither the Court nor Congress has done so. Major League Baseball has relied on the Flood decision to shoot down a variety of antitrust claims, including umpires' allegations that they were illegally dismissed for union activity and a minor league team's challenge to the rules governing player assignment and franchise location. After Flood, however, baseball's antitrust status faded into the background for two decades as free agency created new legal problems.

It was another Cardinal, Ted Simmons, who unwittingly paved the way for free agency in the same year that Flood lost his case. Simmons, who had received just $17,500 while batting .304 in 1971, wanted more than the $25,000 the club offered him in 1972, and refused to sign. But instead of holding out, Simmons just kept coming to work every day. This forced the Cards to invoke the little-known "renewal clause," permitting a club to unilaterally renew a player's contract from the previous season (at up to a 20% cut) if a new one had not been signed by March 10. Simmons played most of the year under this arrangement, finally signing a two-year pact worth a reported $75,000 on July 24. Had he held out a couple of months longer and tested the system, he might have become baseball's first free agent, three years before Andy Messersmith and Dave McNally. "I'm no crusader," Simmons admitted. "I don't even have a lawyer. All I want is more money."

The baseball world wondered what would have happened had Simmons completed the entire season without a contract, and it would soon find out. In 1973, six players (Mike Andrews, Stan Bahnsen, Dick Billings, Jerry Kenney, Fritz Peterson, and Rick Reichardt) started the season without contracts in place, but each was either signed or released before the campaign ended. In 1974, the Yankees' Sparky Lyle waited until the final day of the season to ink a pact, and the Padres' Bobby Tolan played the whole year before signing in December. Finally, pitchers Messersmith (Dodgers) and McNally (Expos) went the distance in 1975 (the Pirates' Richie Zisk had finally signed during the postseason). Messersmith received $115,000 but played without a written contract. The Players' Association filed a grievance, claiming that the two pitchers were entitled to "free agent" status. In a landmark decision on December 23, 1975, arbitrator Peter Seitz agreed. Seitz said that the renewal clause created only a one-year right of renewal, after which the club had no further claim to the player. McNally had already retired, but the arbitrator's decision allowed Messersmith to sell his services to the highest bidder. He soon signed a three-year, $1,000,000 contract with the Braves.

This opened the floodgates. Twenty-four players became part of the sport's first mass-market free agent reentry draft a year later, and huge, multiyear pacts soon became commonplace. Between 1976 and 2001, the average player salary increased from $51,501 to $2,138,896 per year—a 4053% increase! The owners didn't accept the changes quietly. They were found guilty of collusion against free agents in the 1980s, and poor relations between owners and players caused five work stoppages between 1980 and 1995.

A good case can be made that Flood's action indirectly led to the Seitz decision. When the topic came up on the Society for American Baseball Research's Listserver in 2005, Stew Thornley wrote, "I don't believe that there would have been the 1972 strike [the first in baseball history] had not Curt Flood stood up against the reserve clause beforehand. No strike means no arbitration clause in the 1973 [Major League Basic Agreement]. No arbitration clause means no Peter Seitz." Jules Tygiel noted that players' negotiator Marvin Miller, in his autobiography, writes that, "what Flood versus Kuhn really accomplished was . . . raising the consciousness of everyone in baseball: the writers, the fans, the players—and even perhaps some of the owners." Attorney Richard Zitrin writes, "The case made headlines. It got everyone thinking about the unfairness of the reserve clause. It created a synergy for change."

Yet, there is no direct link. Flood was a courageous, principled man, who basically lost his livelihood because of his challenge of baseball's reserve clause. But he lost, leaving it up to others to find the key to free agency.

Hank Aaron Rode "The Launching Pad" to the Career Home Run Record

While he had a total of 40 home runs in his first two big-league seasons, it is unlikely that Aaron will break any records in this department.

—Furman Bisher, in an August 4, 1956, *Saturday Evening Post* article

For breaking Babe Ruth's career home run record, Henry "Hank" Aaron was rewarded with hate mail and criticism from all angles. One of the common complaints was that Aaron had the advantage of playing his home games at Atlanta's Fulton County Stadium, aka "The Launching Pad." But, Aaron played only nine of his 23 seasons—from ages 32 to 40—while calling this cozy arena home, and he hit just 190 of his 755 career home runs there. He played most of his career in Milwaukee's County Stadium, a poor homer park. Hank Aaron broke the home run record (subsequently topped by Barry Bonds in 2007), and numerous other records, because he was an enormously talented, consistent, and durable ballplayer.

Aaron played for Milwaukee from 1954 to 1965. Over that span, he batted .320, won three Gold Glove Awards for excellence in the outfield, and became one of the league's top base stealers. Hammerin' Hank hit line drives to all fields, and the home run was only one weapon in his arsenal. While most players hit more homers in their home parks, Aaron did most of his damage on the road. In his rookie season, Hank managed only one dinger at Milwaukee, but 12 abroad. In his MVP season (1957), the breakdown was 18–26; the following year, it was 10–20; in 1962, it was 18–27; and, in 1963, it was 19–25. Overall, Aaron hit 185 four-baggers at home, as compared to 213 on the road in those dozen seasons.

When the Braves moved to Atlanta in 1966, Aaron decided that he could help the team more by *trying* for homers. He led the NL with 44 that year, while his average slipped to .279. He topped the league again in 1967, giving him 481 lifetime homers. It was about this time that people finally started realizing that Aaron had a chance to reach Ruth's career record of 714, and that his home park would be an asset in that quest.

Aaron took full advantage of The Launching Pad, especially in 1971, when 31 of his career-high 47 homers were hit there. He then returned to Milwaukee for his final two seasons, finishing his career with 385 homers at home, 370 on the road. Until Bonds (383) passed it in his final season, Aaron also held the all-time record for most career *road* home runs.

Pete Rose Ruined Ray Fosse's Career in a Meaningless Game

Probably the most memorable All-Star Game play occurred on July 14, 1970. The game was tied, 4–4, with two out in the bottom of the twelfth inning. Hits by the Reds' Pete Rose and the Dodgers' Billy Grabarkewitz put runners on first and second. Then, the Cubs' Jim Hickman singled to center. Kansas City's Amos Otis hurriedly fielded the ball in shallow center and heaved it toward the plate as Rose barreled around third. Rose then bowled over Indians' rookie catcher Ray Fosse to score the winning run and end the game. It was the eighth straight win for the NL.

Over the years, a lot of people have put their own spin on the story. It was a dirty play by a dirty player, they say; Rose ruined Fosse's career in a meaningless game. Let's review exactly what happened in the play. Rose was approaching home plate with the potential winning run. He started to go into his characteristic headfirst slide, but then he realized something: Fosse, three inches taller, 20 pounds heavier, and covered with protective gear, had the plate blocked as he awaited the ball—which, incidentally, could be ruled "obstruction." Rose could either (a) go facefirst into Fosse's shin guards and get tagged out; (b) tiptoe around Fosse and get tagged out; or (c) go through him to win the game. Rose chose "c," aborting his slide and laying out Fosse to end it. It was a clean play, a winning play, and neither player criticized the other then or later—in Fosse's own words, it was a "couple of aggressive ballplayers doing their jobs."

As longtime catcher Tim McCarver writes in *Tim McCarver's Baseball for Brain Surgeons and Other Fans* (1998), "Pete Rose's infamous game-winning 'slide' into Ray Fosse on Jim Hickman's hit in the 1970 All-Star Game was a legitimate play. Anybody who thinks otherwise just doesn't know the catching position. You've just got to take your knocks."

Fosse (along with Indians' pitcher Sam McDowell) had been Rose's houseguest the night before, talking baseball until 3 a.m. After the game, both players involved in the collision were hospitalized, but Fosse was released before Rose. Fosse was right back in the lineup the first game after the break; Rose didn't play again until July 19, five days after the collision, and he didn't hit with authority for several weeks afterward (three extra-base hits in his next 85 at bats, as compared to 58 in 564 the rest of the year).

It has been written that Fosse suffered a separated shoulder in the collision, but that it went undiagnosed. Fosse continued to hit for average (he finished the season at .307), but with markedly diminished power—he had 16 homers before the break, but only two afterward. He played through the 1979 season but never really approached his first-year numbers. Of course, that's true of a lot of hotshot rookies. Fosse was an All-Star again in 1971, but his career really went downhill after he suffered a crushed vertebra while breaking up a clubhouse fight in 1974.

As for the "meaninglessness" of the All-Star Game, the original premise was "Let's pick the best players in each league, match them against each other, play for pride and glory, and see which league comes out on top." By the latter part of the twentieth century, it became, "Let's find good players who don't want a three-day vacation, trot them out there for a couple of innings each, encourage them to clown around, and play until they've had enough."

Joe Morgan Became a Superstar
Because He Escaped the Astrodome

Joe Morgan began his career with the Houston Colt '45s two days after his 20th birthday in 1963. He became the team's regular second baseman two years later, leading the NL in walks and finishing second in Rookie of the Year balloting. Over the next six years, Morgan established himself as a solid player, but hardly a spectacular one. He had three 40-steal seasons, earned one All-Star selection, and led the league in triples once, but he never batted higher than .285 or hit more than 15 homers in a season. In six full campaigns in Houston, he averaged 86 runs scored, ten home runs, 46 RBI, 32 stolen bases, and a .264 batting average.

All that changed after November 29, 1971, when Morgan was dealt to the Cincinnati Reds in a blockbuster trade. Morgan spent the next eight years in Cincinnati, piling up enough credentials along the way to become a first-ballot Hall of Fame selection in 1990. In his first six years with the Reds, Morgan earned six All-Star selections, five Gold Gloves, two MVP Awards, and two World Series rings, averaging 113 runs, 22 homers, 84 RBI, 60 steals, and a .301 average each year.

What caused this metamorphosis? Common wisdom says that it was Morgan's escape from the Astrodome, one of the worst hitters' parks in baseball. Morgan's talents had simply been hidden.

Morgan's career home and road breakdowns, shown in table 5.5, give the lie to this theory. Little Joe's numbers improved all-around—*but especially on the road.* Morgan's career home statistics, per 150 games played in both Houston and Cincinnati, look like this:

Table 5.3. Joe Morgan's Career Home Statistics per 150 Games

Team	AB	R	H	2B	3B	HR	RBI	SB	AVG	OBP	SLG
HOU	521	89	141	23	12	7	45	32	.272	.401	.405
CIN	508	108	143	31	3	20	82	53	.282	.418	.473

KEY: AB = times at bat; R = runs scored; H = hits; 2B = doubles; 3B = triples; HR = home runs; RBI = runs batted in; SB = stolen bases; AVG = batting average; OBP = on-base percentage; SLG = slugging average

While his corresponding road numbers look like this:

Table 5.4. Joe Morgan's Career Road Statistics per 150 Games

Team	AB	R	H	2B	3B	HR	RBI	SB	AVG	OBP	SLG
HOU	564	85	141	21	6	14	50	32	.250	.351	.382
CIN	533	105	157	26	4	20	77	53	.294	.420	.468

KEY: AB = times at bat; R = runs scored; H = hits; 2B = doubles; 3B = triples; HR = home runs; RBI = runs batted in; SB = stolen bases; AVG = batting average; OBP = on-base percentage; SLG = slugging average

To summarize, by moving from Houston to Cincinnati, Morgan's home batting average went up ten points, his on-base percentage increased by 17, and his slugging percentage leaped by 68. But, on the road—where the only difference was nine games per year at the Astrodome instead of at Riverfront Stadium—Morgan's batting average jumped 44 points, his on-base percentage grew by 69, and his slugging percentage soared 86 points.

So, if it wasn't the park, what was it? Maturity, partially: Morgan, from the age of 28 to the age of 36, might have been in his prime during his Cincinnati years. But, mostly it seems to have been his teammates. After laboring for eight years for a team whose best won-lost percentage was .500, Morgan suddenly found himself on a squad of superstars, only one year removed from a World Series. Pete Rose was the captain, the elder statesman of a group of players who prodded each other to peak performance, arousing their competitive instincts. From 1970 to 1977, Reds' players won six NL MVP

Table 5.5. Joe Morgan's Major League Statistics at Home versus at Other Ballparks

Joe Morgan at Home

Year	Team	G	AB	R	H	2B	3B	HR	RBI	SB	AVG	OBP	SLG
1963	HOU	8	25	5	6	0	1	0	3	1	.240	.367	.320
1964		7	23	3	3	0	0	0	0	0	.130	.310	.130
1965		80	285	54	82	10	8	4	14	15	.288	.415	.421
1966		63	222	31	67	4	5	3	24	2	.302	.432	.405
1967		69	247	45	73	17	8	2	22	17	.296	.416	.453
1968		5	14	6	5	0	1	0	0	3	.357	.550	.500
1969		72	255	52	66	8	4	7	25	25	.259	.396	.404
1970		73	266	49	72	15	7	4	28	22	.271	.396	.425
1971		79	268	34	59	14	5	4	18	16	.220	.334	.354
1972	CIN	73	259	53	79	12	3	9	35	32	.305	.438	.479
1973		78	278	50	70	17	0	9	34	25	.252	.386	.410
1974		74	257	49	61	12	1	13	39	28	.237	.374	.444
1975		72	237	61	77	15	3	10	49	32	.325	.484	.540
1976		69	231	58	75	18	3	13	57	34	.325	.455	.597
1977		74	246	64	74	14	2	11	38	28	.301	.445	.508
1978		63	203	36	51	14	0	6	39	10	.251	.361	.409
1979		64	210	36	54	16	3	4	19	11	.257	.393	.390
1980	HOU	69	217	32	62	13	3	2	24	11	.286	.428	.401
1981	SF	41	142	24	39	10	0	4	16	5	.275	.408	.430
1982		65	223	28	59	7	0	6	29	9	.265	.383	.377
1983	PHI	54	160	34	41	8	0	9	29	10	.256	.428	.475
1984	OAK	57	180	25	50	9	0	2	18	5	.278	.384	.361
Total		1,309	4,448	829	1,225	233	54	122	560	341	.275	.408	.434

(continued)

Table 5.5. *(Continued)*

Joe Morgan on the Road

Year	Team	G	AB	R	H	2B	3B	HR	RBI	SB	AVG	OBP	SLG
1963	HOU	0	0	0	0	0	0	0	0	0	.—	.—	.—
1964		3	14	1	4	0	0	0	0	0	.286	.286	.286
1965		77	316	46	81	12	4	10	26	5	.256	.336	.415
1966		59	203	29	54	10	3	2	18	9	.266	.389	.374
1967		64	247	28	63	10	3	4	20	12	.255	.341	.368
1968		5	6	0	0	0	0	0	0	0	.000	.143	.000
1969		75	280	42	60	10	1	8	18	24	.214	.339	.343
1970		71	282	53	75	13	2	4	24	20	.266	.373	.369
1971		81	315	53	90	13	6	9	38	24	.286	.372	.451
1972	CIN	76	293	69	82	11	1	7	38	26	.280	.402	.396
1973		79	298	66	97	18	2	17	48	42	.326	.429	.570
1974		75	255	58	89	19	2	9	28	30	.349	.484	.545
1975		74	261	46	86	12	3	7	45	35	.330	.458	.479
1976		72	241	55	76	12	2	14	54	26	.315	.452	.556
1977		79	275	49	76	7	4	11	40	21	.276	.397	.451
1978		69	238	32	53	13	0	7	36	9	.223	.349	.366
1979		63	226	34	55	10	1	5	13	17	.243	.374	.363
1980	HOU	72	244	34	50	4	2	9	25	13	.205	.314	.348
1981	SF	49	166	23	35	6	1	4	15	9	.211	.345	.331
1982		69	240	40	75	12	4	8	32	15	.313	.419	.496
1983	PHI	69	244	38	52	12	1	7	30	8	.213	.336	.357
1984	OAK	59	185	25	39	12	0	4	25	3	.211	.339	.341
Total		1,340	4,829	821	1,292	216	42	146	573	348	.268	.383	.420

KEY: G = games played; AB = times at bat; R = runs scored; H = hits; 2B = doubles; 3B = triples; HR = home runs; RBI = runs batted in; SB = stolen bases; AVG = batting average; OBP = on-base percentage; SLG = slugging average. Note: On-base percentage here does not account for sacrifice flies.

Awards: two apiece by Morgan and Johnny Bench, and one each by Rose and George Foster.

Reds' Manager Sparky Anderson deliberately had Morgan's locker put next to Rose's. As Joe Posnanski writes in *The Machine* (2009), "Sparky hoped that whatever the hell it was that drove Pete Rose to the baseball edge might rub off on Joe Morgan." It worked, and Morgan will be the first to acknowledge it. "Pete has helped me as a competitor to push myself every day," said Morgan. "Pete's not the best player I ever saw. But he plays every game like it's the seventh game of the World Series—and I've never seen anyone else do that. I know it sounds corny, but playing with Pete Rose is inspirational."

So, it could be said that Morgan's metamorphosis was due to a change in surroundings, but, it was the people, not the place.

Ted Simmons Was a Lousy Catcher

What do the following players have in common: Eddie Murray, Eddie Collins, Honus Wagner, George Brett, Carl Yastrzemski, Ty Cobb, Hank Aaron, Walter Johnson, and Ted Simmons? Give up? Until 2007, they were the players at each field position (having played at least half of their games at that position) with the most career hits. Of the nine, eight are in the Hall of Fame.

The other player not only is not a Hall of Fame member, but he failed to get enough votes to even remain on the ballot. In the 1994 BBWAA voting, Ted Simmons received only 17 of a possible 456 votes in his first try. Since Hall of Fame voting rule 4(A) requires that a candidate get at least 5% of the ballots (23, in this case) to remain on the ballot for future elections, this was also Simmons's *last* try (although he is now theoretically eligible via the Veterans' Committee).

The rap on Simmons was that he was a mediocre to poor defensive catcher. Even if that were true, it's hard to imagine it costing the all-time hit leader at his position so much as a second look by Hall of Fame voters. George Brett was a mediocre third baseman, but it didn't stop him from getting 98% of the vote in 1999.

It's hard to quantify a catcher's defense, but Simmons was good enough to catch 1,771 games (more than Johnny Bench, Yogi Berra, and all but a few other backstops in history). He topped his league in errors once and passed balls three times, but he also led in putouts twice, assists three times, and fielding percentage once. Skeptics might say that Simmons got a lot of assists only because base stealers ran wild on him; we'll examine that more closely later. Simmons never won a Gold Glove Award—Bench had something to do with that—but he once (1978) missed that honor by just three votes. Relief ace Clay Carroll, who had spent the better part of a dozen years pitching to Gold Glove catchers Bench and Joe Torre, had high praise for Simmons. "To me, [Simmons] is a real good defensive catcher," Carroll said in 1977. "He knows what he's doing back there . . . I really have confidence in him. I'd put Ted in a class with Bench and maybe even better." Mike Caldwell states unequivocally that Simmons was the best catcher he ever worked with, saying Ted called a good game and displayed a good glove and arm. Cy Young Award winner Pete Vuckovich concurred. "They say he can't catch," Vuckovich once said. "That makes me laugh."

After two cups of coffee with the Cardinals and a stint in military service, Simmons came to the big leagues to stay in 1970. The Cards moved All-Star catcher Torre to third base to make room for the young line drive hitter. "Ted is . . . one of the strongest, most durable players I ever saw," Torre said in later years, calling him the best natural hitter in the league. Defensively, he was tutored by Torre and old-timers Hal Smith and Mike Ryba. "When I came up, I was 20 years old," Simmons later recalled. "I didn't have time to know what a catcher does. It took five years to come to understand it all."

Simmons soon became one of the best-hitting backstops in baseball history. Yet, he was consistently overshadowed by more-famous catchers on more-famous teams. "All you ever hear is Bench and [Thurman] Munson and [Carlton] Fisk," Pirates' manager Chuck Tanner said. "But where can you find a catcher that can do all the things Simmons can do? He hits better than any of them, and he calls a great game. And, who else in the league can catch as many games as he does?" Simmons played in 150 or more games for seven straight seasons, and, in 1973, he played every inning of the Cards' first 91 games. "I feel sometimes I deserve more attention than I get," Simmons confessed. "Then I forget the thought as quickly as it comes. I get paid good money for what I am doing, and I have the respect of my teammates and opposing players. That's what I want more than anything else."

By the time he retired in 1988, Simmons had amassed more hits (2,472) and doubles (483) than any other catcher in baseball history, and his RBI total (1,389) was topped by only Berra's. (Ivan Rodriguez has since surpassed Simmons in both hits and doubles.) Simmons earned eight All-Star selections and topped .300 seven times.

Let's get back to Simmons's defense. The main criticism of Ted was that he couldn't throw, and that base runners took liberties on him. I decided to examine that criticism. I looked at every game in which Simmons caught the entire contest (1,577 in all), checking how many runners stole and how many were caught stealing in each. I also calculated how many stolen bases (SB) and times caught stealing (CS) we could have *expected*, based on the number of games against each team and the respective clubs' baserunning records for each season. For example, in 1972, Simmons caught 11 complete games against Cincinnati. In 154 games that year, the Reds stole 140 bases and were caught 63 times; so, in 11 games, we would expect them to have ten SB and 4.5 CS. In actuality, they had ten SB and *nine* CS against Simmons that year.

The data appears in table 5.6. To summarize, Simmons caught fairly regularly for 14 years (1970–1983). In nine of them, his CS percentage was better than the league average, with a high of 44% in both 1973 and 1976. His worst season in this regard was in 1979, when he threw out just 27% of would-be thieves, but there was a reason. Simmons suffered a broken left wrist on June 24 of that season. After four weeks of inactivity (during which the contending Cards were 11–17), Simmons came back two weeks earlier than recommended and performed with diminished effectiveness. He had trouble backhanding the ball and transferring it to his throwing hand.

The expected number of stolen base attempts during Simmons's career was 1,536, with 530 CS (34.5%). The actual totals were 1,688 attempts and 590 CS (35.0%). While runners, evidently encouraged by his reputation, did try stealing against Simmons 10% more often than expected, they weren't very successful at it. In fact, Simmons had a *better*-than-average success ratio against the running game, especially when we consider that—according to most analysts—base stealers must be successful at least two-thirds of the time for them to benefit their team's offense. Simmons's defense, instead of being a negative factor in his overall evaluation, appears here to be a slightly *positive* one. This would have come as no surprise to longtime player, coach, and manager Harry Walker, or to award-winning writer Jim Murray. "Ted gets rid of the ball about as quickly and accurately as any catcher in the game," said Walker in 1974. Simmons "could throw out Man O' War by ten feet at second or block the plate on a grizzly," wrote Murray in 1977.

This research was done before the availability of Retrosheet data. Using this information, Chuck Rosciam published a study of 1963 to 2004 catchers against base stealers in the 2004 *Baseball Research Journal*. Among the 35 catchers with at least 275 runners caught stealing during this time frame, Simmons ranked in the middle of the pack at number 19, with a .328 CS percentage—better than such Gold Glovers as Benito Santiago (.325), Tony Peña (.323), and Carlton Fisk (.315).

Table 5.6. Ted Simmons versus the Running Game

Year	GC	CGC	Expected Attempts	CS	Pct.	Actual Attempts	CS	Pct.	Runs Saved	CS Rating
1968	2	1	1	0	.435	0	0	.—	.0	.0
1969	4	3	2	1	.273	2	0	.000	-.6	-2.0
1970	79	72	54	18	.343	60	23	.383	2.7	7.1
1971	130	124	84	31	.366	73	31	.425	6.0	11.8
1972	135	129	101	38	.381	120	38	.317	-1.8	-20.4
1973	153	148	110	42	.382	114	50	.439	10.8	16.8
1974	141	132	119	41	.346	143	46	.322	-1.5	-9.9
1975	154	132	113	37	.332	122	34	.279	-6.0	-19.7
1976	113	100	104	36	.346	107	47	.439	10.2	29.0
1977	143	124	150	52	.344	136	50	.368	4.2	9.4
1978	134	110	134	43	.319	165	60	.364	4.5	23.3
1979	122	104	120	41	.339	125	34	.272	-6.9	-24.6
1980	129	113	161	50	.312	156	51	.327	-.9	7.5
1981	75	66	62	24	.380	68	27	.397	3.9	3.0
1982	121	109	104	38	.365	142	55	.387	6.9	8.6
1983	86	80	81	27	.330	109	34	.312	-2.1	-5.9
1984	0	0	0	0	.—	0	0	.—	.0	.0
1985	15	11	10	3	.307	11	3	.273	-.6	-1.2
1986	10	5	7	2	.315	15	2	.133	-2.7	-5.9
1987	15	14	18	5	.293	20	5	.250	-1.5	-3.0
1988	10	0	0	0	.—	0	0	.—	.0	.0
Total	1,771	1,577	1,536	530	.345	1,688	590	.350	24.6	23.0

KEY: GC = games caught; CGC = complete games caught, with all subsequent data based only on these games; Expected Attempts = projection based on number of CGC against each team, and each team's numbers of attempts and times caught stealing, with totals rounded off; Actual Attempts = opposition steal attempts; CS = opposition caught stealing; Pct. = opposition caught stealing percentage; Runs Saved = inverse of Pete Palmer's Linear Weights "Stolen Base Runs" (.6 CS − .3 SB), with a score above zero being above par, while below zero is below par; CS Rating = an adaptation of Jim Weigand's "Stolen Base Rating," with a score above zero being better than average, compared to the league, while below zero is below average.

The Designated Hitter Rule Was Introduced by Charlie Finley in the 1970s

The AL introduced the innovative designated hitter (DH) rule in 1973. Supposedly, it was the brainchild of Oakland A's maverick owner Charlie O. Finley. During Finley's two decades as a team owner (1961–1980), he proposed many outlandish ideas, including orange baseballs, gold bases, and three-ball walks, but most never took hold.

The idea of the pitcher being replaced in the batting order was indeed proposed by the owner of the A's—but it was long before Finley was even born. The February 3, 1906, edition of the *Philadelphia North American* had the following passage:

> The suggestion, often made, that the pitcher be denied a chance to bat, and a substitute player sent up [for] him every time, has been brought to life again. . . . This time Connie Mack is credited with having made the suggestion. He argues that a pitcher is such a poor hitter that his time at the bat is a farce, and the game would be helped by eliminating him in favor of a better hitter.

This is followed by various arguments against this concept, all of them still being used today. (The best argument, however, was at that time a ten-year-old child in a Baltimore reform school.)

It is clear from the wording that the concept was nothing new, even in 1906. In fact, it dates back to at least 1891, when Pirates' president William Chase Temple proposed it. According to the December 19 issue of the *Sporting Life*,

> In a recent conversation with J. Walter Spalding, of the New York Club, President Temple, of the Pittsburgs (sic), brought up the question as to what disposition should be made of the pitcher in the batting order. President Temple favored the substitution of another man to take the pitcher's place at the bat when it came his turn to go there. Mr. Spalding advocated a change in the present system and suggested that the pitcher be eliminated entirely from the batting order and that only the other eight men of the opposing clubs be allowed to go to bat. . . . The matter will in all likelihood be brought to the attention of the committee on rules. . . . Every patron of the game is conversant with the utter worthlessness of the average pitcher when he goes up to try and hit the ball. It is most invariably a trial, and an unsuccessful one at that. If fortune does favor him with a base hit, it is ten to one that he is so winded in getting to first or second base on it that when he goes into the box it is a matter of very little difficulty to pound him all over creation.

Temple, quoted three months later, said that the proposal was voted down, 7–5.

The idea continued to resurface throughout the 20th century. Yankees' manager Miller Huggins alluded to it in 1921, discussing defensively challenged slugger Bob Meusel in the *New York Evening Journal* (March 29): "If we could get them to change the rules so as to let a pinch hitter bat for a pitcher each time, what a job that would be for this big fellow." A few years later, NL president John Heydler proposed it during the winter meetings. According to the December 13, 1928, *Brooklyn Eagle*, "Heydler's idea of an official pinch hitter operating throughout a game for the pitcher has many advocates as well as scoffers. A good many baseball players seem to think well of the proposed innovation, too." Apparently, the scoffers outvoted the advocates at that point. This was still the case when the Triple-A Pacific Coast League proposed such a rule, but it was rejected by the Professional Baseball Rules Committee on March 31, 1961.

With the majors sorely lacking in offense, a version of the DH rule was experimented with by the White Sox during spring training in 1967, and by other teams over the next couple of springs (I find no contemporary indication that Finley was behind the experimentation; White Sox' manager Eddie Stanky was credited with the idea, saying it would be a "great boon for baseball"). Hall of Fame manager Joe McCarthy recalled Heydler's earlier proposal of such a rule, saying, "I was intrigued with the idea then and think it still has possibilities." The DH rule was adopted by the Triple-A International League and American Association, and some other minor leagues, in 1969. Finally, the AL implemented the rule at the major league level in 1973, little knowing that the new idea was even older than their league.

Minnie Minoso Was the Oldest Man to Get a Hit

In September 1976, Bill Veeck and the Chicago White Sox activated coach Saturnino "Minnie" Minoso, who hadn't played in the majors since 1964. They did it so that Minoso would have a chance to break a record: the oldest man to get a hit in the major leagues. Nick Altrock was said to hold the record, having collected a hit three weeks past his 53rd birthday.

Three players before Minoso were known to have collected hits past the age of 50, all in similar late-season stunts. On October 6, 1929, Altrock, the Senators' coach and clown, played an inning in right field and singled in his only at bat. On September 22, 1904, Hall of Famer Jim "Orator" O'Rourke appeared in his first game in 11 years and singled in four at bats; since his birthdate was listed as August 24, 1852, he was 52 at the time. And on September 30, 1934, Browns' coach Charley O'Leary singled as a pinch hitter and scored a run; O'Leary, who had last played in 1913, was reportedly 15 days short of his 52nd birthday.

According to the record books, Minoso was born on November 29, 1922, making him nearly 54 when the Sox penciled him in as DH. On September 12, 1976, Minoso singled off the Angels' Sid Monge, and the record was his. Or, so we thought. It turns out that Minoso was younger than we realized, and O'Leary and O'Rourke were older—and O'Leary is now the record-holder.

In his 1994 biography with Herb Fagen, *Just Call Me Minnie: My Six Decades in Baseball*, Minoso sets the record straight on his age. Some still dispute this claim, but it's hard to ignore Minoso's own testimony:

> The official sources have me listed as being born on November 29, 1922. That would make me 71 years old, and I would not make excuses or apologies. I am actually just 68 years old. I was 19 years old when I arrived in the United States in 1945, but my papers said I was 22. I told a white lie . . . to obtain a visa, so I could qualify for service in the Cuban army. My true date of birth is the 29th of November, 1925. . . . In 1924, Carlos Arrieta married Cecilia Armas, a divorced woman with four children from a previous marriage. The following year, Carlos and Cecilia had a son of their own. Born on the 29th of November, 1925, they named their son Saturnino Orestes.

Meanwhile, O'Rourke was discovered to have been born two years earlier than believed. In 1989, baseball researcher Rich Bozzone consulted Bridgeport, Connecticut, birth records, showing James O'Rourke (with parents Hugh and Catherine O'Rourke, the same names as shown on Jim's death certificate) born September 1, 1850. Bozzone also found guardianship papers prepared when O'Rourke's father died December 31, 1868. It lists James, age 18, which would tie in with the 1850 birth.

And, in a recent find, baseball researchers Cliff Blau and Richard Malatzky learned that O'Leary was born *seven* years earlier than thought. With the help of his World War I draft registration and the 1880 census, it was determined that O'Leary's birthdate was October 15, 1875.

The *ESPN Baseball Encyclopedia* now carries the 1925 date for Minoso, and the 1850 date for O'Rourke. It is expected that their next edition will reflect the new information on O'Leary. In other words, O'Leary was 58 when he got his final big league hit, and O'Rourke 54, while Minoso was a mere 50, bumping him down to fourth place (see table 5.7).

Table 5.7. Oldest Major Leaguers to Get a Hit

Player	Date of Birth	Date of Hit	Age (Years, Days)
Charley O'Leary	10/15/1875	9/30/1934	58,350
Jim O'Rourke	9/01/1850	9/22/1904	54,210
Nick Altrock	9/15/1876	10/06/1929	53,210
Minnie Minoso	11/29/1925	9/12/1976	50,288

Don Sutton Never Missed a Start during His 23-Year Career

Don Sutton was never considered a dominant pitcher, but he was durable and effective for 23 seasons, enabling him to amass 324 victories—the highest total achieved by any right-handed pitcher between World War I and the war in Afghanistan. How durable was Sutton? When he was elected to the Hall of Fame in 1998, his plaque included a commonly reported story: "Did not miss a turn in the starting rotation due to injury or illness."

But, in August 1980, Sutton suffered a broken toe on his right foot, according to the *Sporting News*. Because of it, he missed his scheduled start on August 26 (Rick Sutcliffe pitched in his place) and did not see action between August 21 and August 31.

Disregarding gaps occasioned by All-Star breaks or rainouts, Sean Lahman found a dozen other times in his career that Sutton had at least a week between starts, although Lahman didn't check whether any of those gaps were due to injury. And that doesn't even include the 1988 season, when Sutton spent 41 days on the disabled list before making the final start of his career in August.

Durable? Absolutely. Did not miss a start? Wrong.

Willie Aikens Was Named after Willie Mays

Willie Aikens first came into national prominence with a historic performance during the 1980 World Series. It was widely reported that he was named after the hero of a World Series played just before Aikens was born: Encyclopedias still list his full name as Willie Mays Aikens. In fact, Aikens has no official middle name, and he was named after a family member.

Aikens was born October 14, 1954, in Seneca, South Carolina. His mother named him after his uncle, Willie. The doctor who delivered him suggested the middle name "Mays," predicting that the newborn would become a "famous ballplayer." No doubt the doc was inspired by the MVP season just completed by the Giants' Willie Mays, capped off by his spectacular World Series catch of a Vic Wertz drive on September 29; however, Mays was never officially added to Aikens's birth certificate.

Pete Rose Broke the Career Hit Record Only Because He Was a Manager, Permitting Himself to Play

Pete Rose broke Ty Cobb's career hit record in 1985, as a 44-year-old player-manager. Rose, a perennial .300 hitter in his prime, saw his averages tumble to .271, .245, .286, .264, and .211 in his final five seasons, from 1982 to 1986. He was a first baseman with no power, not a good combination. By modern accounts, Rose was playing only because he was also a manager, selfishly penning himself into the lineup day after day, hurting his team, until he finally broke the record.

People forget that Rose did not become a manager until August 16, 1984, and that he broke the record just one year and 26 days later—so this is the only period subject to the scrutiny of his so-called selfishness. And, in fact, both Rose and his team did very well during this span.

From August 16, 1984, through September 11, 1985, Rose—platooning himself with 43-year-old Tony Perez—played in 131 games, came to bat 455 times, and had 131 hits for a respectable .288 batting average. More significantly, Pete also drew 79 walks and was hit by five pitches, bringing his on-base percentage to an excellent .397. The only National Leaguers with higher on-base precentages (minimum 200 times reached base) during that period were All-Stars Jack Clark, Pedro Guerrero, and Tim Raines. While Rose was deficient in power, the 1985 Reds were a team that had only two players who hit more than eight homers; it wasn't as if Pete was burying Lou Gehrig on the bench just so he could play.

The Reds had finished dead last in both 1982 (61–101) and 1983 (74–88), and fifth (70–92) in 1984. Rose brought them all the way up to second place (89–72) in 1985, no small feat; in recognition, he finished second in Manager of the Year voting, just one point behind Whitey Herzog, 86–85.

For the Reds in 1984–1985, Rose did what a number-two hitter is supposed to do: get on base and move runners along. And he did what a manager is supposed to do: set the tone for the team and maximize the talent at his disposal. And, along the way, he broke a record that most observers had thought was unbreakable.

Bill Buckner Lost the 1986 World Series for the Red Sox

Red Sox' fans still hiss at the mention of Bill Buckner's name. After all, it was Buckner who lost the 1986 World Series for them when he let Mookie Wilson's ground ball roll between his legs. People forget that the Sox had already blown their two-run lead before the error, that they still had another chance to win the world championship the next game, and that it takes more than one man to win or lose a baseball game.

The Sox led the Mets, three games to two, as October 25 dawned at Shea Stadium. Boston took a 2–0 lead, but New York tied it in the fifth inning. The Red Sox retook the lead, 3–2, in the seventh, but the Mets retied it in the eighth. The game remained deadlocked after nine, but Boston seemingly put it away with two runs in the top of the tenth. Relief ace Calvin Schiraldi then retired Wally Backman and Keith Hernandez on fly balls, leaving the Red Sox one out away from the world championship, which had eluded them since 1918. A scoreboard operator prematurely flashed a message: "Congratulations Boston Red Sox, 1986 World Champions."

Analyst Pete Palmer has conducted simulations of tens of thousands of baseball games, using World Series play-by-play data as a model. Based on this, he has calculated team's chances of winning a game in every possible situation. According to his data, with two out and nobody on, and a two-run lead in the final inning, the Red Sox' chances of winning the game were 98.7%, or .987. Then, the following happened:

- Gary Carter lined a single to left field, dropping Boston's chance to .960.
- Kevin Mitchell singled to center, putting the tying run on base, and dropping the odds to .912.
- Ray Knight singled to center, scoring Carter, putting the tying run on third and the winning run on first. This cut Boston's chance to .799. Schiraldi was lifted, having essentially cost his team .188 wins in the space of three batters.
- Bob Stanley came in and uncorked a low, sailing inside pitch—some say a spitball—that got past catcher Rich Gedman. This allowed Mitchell to score the tying run and put the winning run in scoring position. "The ball grazed my glove, and anything that hits my glove I should catch," said Gedman, but it was scored a wild pitch. The Sox' chances nosedived to .378, a cost of .421 wins, on that one pitch.
- Finally came Wilson's chopper down the first base line, scoring Knight with the winning run. That, of course, dropped Boston's chances of winning to .000, a cost of .378 wins.

Based on this data, if any one man deserves the goat horns for this loss, it is Stanley, not Buckner. It is also interesting to note that, had Buckner retired Wilson, the Sox chances would have improved to only .500. And, if Wilson had beaten Buckner to the bag (he would have had to, since Stanley failed to cover first), they would have dropped to .357, assuming Knight stopped at third. "I knew I had a 90% chance of beating Buckner to the bag," said Wilson, and a look at the videotape supports that claim. "Now that I've seen the films," said Buckner, "I know that we were not going to get Mookie Wilson at first anyway."

Incidentally, the guy the second-guessers would have replaced Buckner with—defensive specialist Dave Stapleton—had a .993 career fielding percentage, compared to .992 for Buckner. And the Red Sox could have made Buckner's error moot simply by winning Game Seven two days later. Instead, they blew a three-run lead in the sixth inning and lost, 8–5.

Pete Rose Was Banned from the Hall of Fame and Jailed for Betting on Baseball

> Any player on Baseball's Ineligible List shall not be an eligible candidate.
>
> —Baseball Hall of Fame voting rule #3(A)

Pete Rose, who collected more hits than any other player in baseball history, saw his career end in disgrace. He was banned from baseball, sent to prison, and made ineligible for the Hall of Fame. It is commonly believed that all three things happened simultaneously, but they didn't. "One of the biggest misconceptions about my sentencing is that people think I went to prison for betting on baseball," wrote Rose. "I didn't. It's not against the law to bet on baseball. It's against baseball rules to bet on baseball."

The charge that got Rose banned from baseball was gambling on his own team to win while he was employed as its manager. While this would not seem to be as serious an infraction as betting on one's team to lose, or helping it to do so, the punishment is the same: placement on baseball's "Ineligible List." Rose was put on the list by commissioner Bart Giamatti on August 24, 1989, after Giamatti received the slanted "Dowd Report" on Rose's gambling activities.

Rose's troubles continued in 1990, when he spent five months in the U.S. Penitentiary in Marion, Illinois, a convicted felon. But the charge had nothing to do with gambling: He was convicted of income tax evasion, due to underreporting income received during memorabilia shows.

While it left him unemployed, Rose's banning did not immediately affect his Hall of Fame eligibility. Having last played in 1986, he was due to go onto the ballot in the fall of 1991, with the results announced in January 1992. There was a lot of speculation as to how Rose would fare. Rose, whom Bill James and others had previously predicted might be the Hall's first unanimous selection, now was expected to receive less than the 75% required for election, at least in his first try. The writers would have to weigh Rose's integrity and character (two little-known and rarely considered criteria for election) with his playing record and contributions to his teams.

Some people, particularly Hall of Famer Bob Feller, started mouthing off on the issue. Rapid Robert said that if Rose were elected to the Hall, he would never return to the annual induction ceremonies (Feller didn't mention that he started coming regularly to the ceremonies only when the Hall's sponsors began paying him $500 per hour to participate in their autograph sessions). This concerned Hall of Fame officials, particularly public relations director Bill Guilfoile. Guilfoile drafted a new voting rule stating that, "Any player on Baseball's Ineligible List shall not be an eligible candidate." He packaged it with another rule designed to appease the writers (making it harder for BBWAA rejects to get voted in by the Veterans' Committee), but nobody would be fooled.

In January 1991, Guilfoile called me over to bounce the proposed voting changes off me, the Hall's senior research associate at the time. If this rule were adopted, Rose could not be elected to the Hall of Fame unless his name was removed from the Ineligible List by the commissioner—the guy that put Rose's name on the list in the first place (true, 1991 commissioner Fay Vincent technically did not put Rose's name on the list, but, as Giamatti's deputy commissioner in 1989, he was instrumental in the process, and Vincent was not about to reverse the decision made by his best friend and mentor). After mulling it over, I sent Guilfoile a memo saying, "While I realize that it may not count for much, I want to go on record as strongly opposed to this proposition. I don't feel that anyone's Hall of Fame eligibility should be left at the mercy of one man."

Guilfoile proposed rule number 3(E), anyway, and, in February, it was approved by the Hall of Fame's Board of Directors—a group that included Fay Vincent. Thus, the "Pete Rose Rule" was pasted into the books just months before he would have become eligible.

This rule change forced the Commissioner's Office to draft up an "Ineligible List," since it apparently existed only in theory before 1991 (at least, they could not locate one in their archives; they asked me who should be on it). Ironically, in the first draft the Commissioner's Office released, they forgot to include Rose. They did name the members of the "Black Sox" charged with throwing the 1919 World Series. So, this officially made Shoeless Joe Jackson—and his .356 career average—ineligible for Cooperstown for the first time, too (he and Eddie Cicotte were the only two of the "Eight Men Out" who played the requisite ten years for Hall of Fame eligibility).

Rose applied for reinstatement in September 1997. Fifteen years later, commissioner Bud Selig had not yet ruled on his application.

Billy Martin Died While Driving Drunk

The legendary Billy Martin died on December 25, 1989. The 61-year-old former World Series hero and brilliant manager was killed in a one-vehicle crash on an icy road only yards from his Fenton, New York, home, after a holiday drinking binge with his buddy, Detroit bar owner Bill Reedy. It seemed only fitting to the press that Billy's life, punctuated by controversial episodes involving alcohol, was ended during his own drunk driving incident—except that, Billy Martin wasn't the driver.

Early reports were fuzzy on the details, but Reedy was soon named as the driver. Then, in April 1990, Reedy claimed otherwise, according to the *Detroit Free Press*. "I'm going to plead not guilty to driving while intoxicated, or even to driving," Reedy was quoted as saying. "I told them [police at the scene] I was driving to try to protect Billy. We've been friends for 20, 25 years." Reedy's defense attorney, Jon Blechman, told jurors that, "When the accident happened, Bill Reedy thought, 'Billy's got himself in trouble again. I've got to help my friend.'" Jurors were unconvinced, finding Reedy guilty of DWI in September 1990, but they let him off the hook on the most serious charges. An appeals court upheld the conviction a year later.

I worked with the man who was the coroner's investigator in Martin's death. Even two decades later, he didn't want his name mentioned in connection with the case, but he gave me his firsthand take on the matter. "It was obvious that Reedy was the driver," he told me. "He had an imprint of the steering wheel on his chest. I recommended that he be charged with vehicular manslaughter, but he wasn't." Instead, Reedy got off with a DWI, a $350 fine, and six months' revocation of his license.

Researcher Frank Russo, coauthor of *Bury My Heart at Cooperstown: Salacious, Sad, and Surreal Deaths in the History of Baseball* (2006), learned the same thing from another source. "I always try to get the truth out about Billy Martin whenever I can," says Russo, a longtime Yankees' fan. "To this day people still assume that Billy was the driver in the pickup truck crash that killed him on Christmas night, 1989. He wasn't the driver, he was the passenger. This was proven by the great forensic pathologist, Dr. Michael Baden, who investigated the case." As explained on Baden's HBO website, the autopsy "revealed that Martin's impact injuries were all on the right side, and the hairs found on the right side of the truck's shattered windshield were Martin's. The conclusion: Reedy, not Martin, was the driver."

Expansion Has Diluted Baseball's Talent

Major league batters went wild after the 1993 and 1998 expansions. Between 1998 and 2001, Mark McGwire hit 70 and 65 homers in a season; Sammy Sosa slugged 66, 63, and 64; and Barry Bonds hit 73. The average number of runs per game skyrocketed, with the AL's ERA reaching 4.86 in 1999. Until the focus shifted to steroids, a common explanation for this phenomenon was that baseball's talent, particularly pitching, had been diluted by expansion. With 30 major league teams, as compared to just 16 of yesteryear, the thinking goes, nearly half of today's pitchers are of minor league caliber.

If the increases in scoring were attributable solely to "expansion" pitchers, we'd expect that the best pitchers of today would compare favorably to their counterparts from previous generations—actually, we'd expect them to be better, because they are facing "expansion hitters." But researcher Mark Armour points out that ERAs have risen even for the better pitchers.

Armour looked at the pitchers with the 15th-best ERA in each league at five-year intervals starting in 1969. That year, Mike Nagy (3.11) and Fergie Jenkins (3.21) were the duo; in 1974, it was Frank Tanana (3.12) and Dock Ellis (3.15). But, by 1999, the numbers were 4.43 (Chuck Finley) and 3.97 (Kent Bottenfield), respectively. In other words, the "good" pitchers were giving up more runs, too.

Armour offers more compelling reasons for increased offense, including the shrinking strike zone, larger players, decreased premium on defensive skill (a typical 1996 middle infielder hit almost three times as many homers as a 1976 middle infielder), and bullpen specialists ("If a manager were to optimize his staff such that his best pitchers pitched the most innings, I believe that scoring would decrease.)" Harvard science professor Stephen Jay Gould, in a seven-page *Discover* article (August 1986), shows how baseball statistics disguise the fact that the level of competition has improved consistently over the years. While league batting averages have stayed fairly stable, the performances of the best and worst players have gotten closer and closer to the mean, indicating that the quality of "average" players has improved. This is the big reason why there are no more .400 hitters.

When people point out the increase from 16 teams to 30, they fail to account for the increase in the talent pool. The main source of major league players is the U.S. population of males aged 20 to 39. In 1901, when the AL joined the majors to make two eight-team leagues, that population was about 12.8 million. By 2000, it was up to 41.1 million. To have the same player-population ratio as in 1901, there should have been 51 teams in 2000. This doesn't even take integration into account. Pre-1947 rosters weren't made up of the best males, only the best *white* males. The game didn't become fully integrated until the mid-1960s, by which time nearly 30% of major leaguers were nonwhite. Nor does it take internationalization into account. In the first half of the 20th century, foreign-born players were few and far between; now, talent comes from all over the world. Of 221 rookie players in 2006, for example, 72—almost one-third—were foreign born.

So, to have a similar level of competition in today's game as we had a century ago, we would have to expand to more than 50 teams, remove all dark-skinned and foreign-born players, and replace them all with white, U.S.-born minor leaguers. If there was ever a dilution of talent, it was then, not now.

The 1991–2005 Braves Were Underachievers

Everyone knows the sad tale of "America's Team," the 1991 to 2005 Atlanta Braves. They won divisional title after divisional title—14 in a row—only to be eliminated in the postseason time after time, with just one world championship to show for it all. People just don't realize how hard it is, especially under today's three-tiered playoff system, for a great team to win the world title. Eight teams of practically equal ability make it to the postseason, and only one can win it all. Anything can happen in a short series, and usually does.

The Braves' improbable run started in 1991, when they went from "worst-to-first" in the NL's Western Division, beat Pittsburgh in the Championship Series, but lost to the Twins, the other worst-to-first team, in a seven-game World Series. In 1992, the Braves again topped Pittsburgh in the National League Championship Series (NLCS), but lost in the Fall Classic, this time to the Blue Jays. In 1993, Atlanta lost to Philadelphia in the NLCS. And, moved to the Eastern Division in 1994, the Braves didn't even finish first. They were six games behind the Expos (!) when the strike ended the season in August, canceling the postseason and, technically, at least in the minds of some, keeping Atlanta's string of divisional titles intact.

The three-tiered system started in 1995, and the Braves won the next 11 NL East Division titles in a row through 2005. From there, they had to play in the National League Divisional Series (NLDS) each year; if they won, the NLCS; and if they won that, the World Series. They won the NLDS in 1995 through 1999 and 2001, the NLCS in 1995–1996 and 1999, and the World Series only in 1995.

But how many titles should we have expected them to win? Based on the laws of random chance, a team that wins its division 11 straight times would be expected to win the LDS 5.50 times, the LCS 2.75 times, and the World Series 1.38 times. Let's round it off to six LDS titles, three LCS titles, and one world championship.

The 1995 to 2005 Braves won precisely six LDS titles, three LCS titles, and one world championship. They won exactly as often as anyone could reasonably have expected them to. During that span, only one world championship team (the 1998 Yankees) had the most wins in baseball, and just two teams won more than one World Series. That one of them was the Florida Marlins should tell you all you need to know about the effects of random chance on postseason series.

Shorter Fences Have Aided Modern Home Run Hitters

Before the steroids witch hunt gathered steam, pundits often tried to explain the increase in home runs starting in the mid-1990s. One of the most common reasons given was "shorter fences," or "smaller ballparks." While the dimensions of a stadium aren't the only factors when it comes to hitting home runs, certainly they are the most obvious ones.

But, these pundits never say what today's fences are shorter than, or ballparks are smaller than. In fact, stadium sizes have not changed much in the past half century, due mostly to official Major League Baseball Rule #1.04 (a) added to the books at that time: "Any Playing Field constructed by a professional club after June 1, 1958, shall provide a minimum distance of 325 feet from home base to the nearest fence, stand, or other obstruction on the right and left field foul lines, and a minimum distance of 400 feet to the center field fence." While there have been minor exceptions granted, almost all existing parks conform to this rule.

Before that, ballpark dimensions were all over the place. In 1925, for example, six of the 15 big-league parks had a center field fence that was more than 460 feet from home plate—but five had a right field fence that was less than 300 feet from home: Yankee Stadium (295), Brooklyn's Ebbets Field (292), Cleveland's Municipal Stadium (290), Philadelphia's Baker Bowl (280½), and New York's Polo Grounds (258).

In Phil Lowry's *Green Cathedrals: The Ultimate Celebration of All Major League Ballparks* (2006), the most thorough history of major league stadiums ever compiled, Lowry lists various known dimensions for every big-league park. Calculating the average home run distances (rounded to the nearest foot) to left, center, and right fields among these parks at ten-year intervals, beginning in 1925, you get what appears in table 5.8.

Table 5.8. Average Home Run Distances (Rounded to the Nearest Foot) to Left, Center, and Right Fields among Major League Stadiums at Ten-Year Intervals

Year	LF	CF	RF
1925	350	452	317
1935	345	434	315
1945	341	425	314
1955	332	424	317
1965	336	415	327
1975	332	405	330
1985	329	404	327
1995	331	404	328
2005	332	404	329

Incidentally, trying to record the distances to the intermediary points was found to be problematic. Some parks had dimensions listed for right-center and left-center (defined as 30 degrees from the foul poles), some to "power alleys" (defined as 22.5 degrees from the poles), some to both, some to neither, and some to various features of the individual parks. The data just wasn't consistent enough to evaluate.

Even so, we can see that ballpark sizes have barely changed since the 1960s, and the distances down foul lines (much more pertinent to home run totals than the distances to dead center field) have hardly changed since Babe Ruth's heyday. If we take an average of the left- and right-field foul lines for each year, the chart looks like what is shown in table 5.9.

So, where are all those shorter fences that everyone talks about?

Table 5.9. Average Distance Down Left- and Right-Field Foul Lines at Ten-Year Intervals

Year	Feet
1925	333
1935	330
1945	328
1955	325
1965	331
1975	331
1985	328
1995	330
2005	330

~

Bibliography

Books

Aaron, Hank, with Lonnie Wheeler. *I Had a Hammer*. New York: HarperCollins, 1991.

Allen, Bob, with Bill Gilbert. *The 500 Home Run Club*. Champaign, IL: Sports Publishing, 1999.

Asinof, Eliot. *Eight Men Out: The Black Sox and the 1919 World Series*. New York: Holt, Rinehart and Winston, 1963.

Broeg, Bob. *Superstars of Baseball*. South Bend, IN: Diamond Communications, 1994.

Bucek, Jeanine, ed. *The Baseball Encyclopedia*. New York: Macmillan, 1996.

Carney, Gene. *Burying the Black Sox: How Baseball's Cover-Up of the 1919 World Series Fix Almost Succeeded*. Dulles, VA: Potomac Books, 2006.

Cobb, Ty, with Al Stump. *My Life in Baseball: The True Record*. Garden City, NY: Doubleday, 1961.

Creamer, Robert. *Babe: The Legend Comes to Life*. New York: Simon & Schuster, 1974.

Deane, Bill. *Award Voting*. Kansas City, MO: Society for American Baseball Research, 1988.

Deutsch, Jordan A., Richard M. Cohen, Roland T. Johnson, and David S. Neft. *The Scrapbook History of Baseball*. Indianapolis, IN: Bobbs-Merrill, 1975.

Dickson, Paul. *The New Dickson Baseball Dictionary*. San Diego, CA: Harcourt Brace & Company, 1999.

Eig, Jonathan. *Luckiest Man*. New York: Simon & Schuster, 2005.

Einstein, Charles. *The Baseball Reader: Favorites from the Fireside Books of Baseball*. 1980. New York: McGraw-Hill, 1986.

———. *The Third Fireside Book of Baseball*. New York: Simon & Schuster, 1968.

Frick, Ford. *Games, Asterisks, and People: Memoirs of a Lucky Fan*. New York: Crown Publishers, 1973.

Garagiola, Joe. *Just Play Ball*. Flagstaff, AZ: Northland Publishing, 2007.

Gillette, Gary, and Pete Palmer, eds. *The ESPN Baseball Encyclopedia*. New York: Sterling Publishing, 2008.

The Great American Baseball Stat Book. New York: Harper Perennial, 1992.

Handrinos, Peter. *The Truth about Ruth*. Chicago: Triumph Books, 2009.

Holway, John. *Blackball Stars: Negro League Pioneers*. Westport, CT: Meckler Books, 1988.

———. *Rube Foster: The Father of Black Baseball*. Washington, DC: Pretty Pages, 1981.

Honig, Donald. *The October Heroes: Great World Series Games Remembered by the Men Who Played Them*. New York: Simon & Schuster, 1979.

Huhn, Rick. *Eddie Collins: A Baseball Biography*. McFarland & Co., 2008.

James, Bill. *The Baseball Book*. New York: Villard Books, 1990.

———. *The Bill James Historical Baseball Abstract*. New York: Villard Books, 1986.

James, Bill, and Jim Henzler. *Win Shares*. Morton Grove, IL: STATS, Inc., 2002.

Justman, Marilyn, typographer. *The Official Rules of Major League Baseball*. Chicago: Triumph Books, 2005.

Kahn, Roger. *The Boys of Summer*. New York: Harper & Row, 1971.

———. *The Era*. New York: Ticknor & Fields, 1993.

Kavanagh, Jack, and Norman Macht. *Uncle Robbie*. Cleveland, OH: Society for American Baseball Research, 1999.

Lane, F. C. *Batting*. Cleveland, OH: Society for American Baseball Research, 2001.

Lieb, Fred. *The Story of the World Series: An Informal History*. New York: G. P. Putnam's Sons, 1949.

Lindberg, Richard C. *The White Sox Encyclopedia*. Philadelphia, PA: Temple University Press, 1997.

Lowry, Philip J. *Green Cathedrals: The Ultimate Celebration of All Major League Ballparks*. New York: Walker and Company, 2006.

McCarver, Tim, with Danny Peary. *Tim McCarver's Baseball for Brain Surgeons and Other Fans*. New York: Villard Books, 1998.

Minoso, Minnie, with Herb Fagen. *Just Call Me Minnie: My Six Decades in Baseball*. New York: Sports Publishing, 1994.

Nash, Bruce M., and Allan Zullo. *The Baseball Hall of Shame*. New York: Pocket Books, 1985.

Neft, David S., and Richard M. Cohen. *The World Series*. New York: St. Martin's Press, 1990.

Neyer, Rob. *Rob Neyer's Big Book of Baseball Legends*. New York: Simon & Schuster, 2008.

Peterson, Robert. *Only the Ball Was White*. Englewood Cliffs, NJ: Prentice-Hall, 1970.

Pietrusza, David, Matthew Silverman, and Michael Gershman, eds. *Baseball: The Biographical Encyclopedia*. Kingston, NY: Total Sports Illustrated, 2000.

Posnanski, Joe. *The Machine*. New York: HarperCollins, 2009.

Quigley, Martin. *The Crooked Pitch: The Curveball in American Baseball History*. Chapel Hill, NC: Algonquin Books, 1984.

Ralph, John J., ed. *The National Baseball Hall of Fame and Museum Yearbook*. Cooperstown, NY: National Baseball Hall of Fame and Museum, 2000.

Reichler, Joseph L. *The Baseball Trade Register*. New York: Macmillan, 1984.

Ritter, Lawrence S. *The Glory of Their Times: The Story of the Early Days of Baseball Told by the Men Who Played It*. New York: Macmillan, 1966.

Robertson, John G. *Baseball's Greatest Controversies*. Jefferson, NC: McFarland & Co., 1995.

Russo, Frank. *Bury My Heart at Cooperstown: Salacious, Sad, and Surreal Deaths in the History of Baseball*. Chicago: Triumph Books, 2006.

Schneider, Russell. *Cleveland Indians Encyclopedia*. Philadelphia, PA: Temple University Press, 1996.

Siwoff, Seymour, Steve Hirdt, Tom Hirdt, and Peter Hirdt. *The 1989 Elias Baseball Analyst*. New York: Collier, 1989.

Skipper, John. *Inside Pitch*. Jefferson, NC: McFarland & Co., 1996.

Society for American Baseball Research. *The Baseball Research Journal*, Vol. 25. Phoenix, AZ: Society for American Baseball Research, 1996.

Spalding's Official Baseball Guide, 1900. Bowling Green, KY: Spalding Athletic Company, 1900.

Spalding's Official Baseball Guide, 1909. Bowling Green, KY: Spalding Athletic Company, 1909.

Sullivan, George. *The Picture History of the Boston Red Sox*. Indianapolis, IN: Bobbs-Merrill, 1979.

Thorn, John, ed. *The Armchair Book of Baseball*. New York: Charles Scribner's Sons, 1985.

Thorn, John, Phil Birnbaum, and Bill Deane, eds. *Total Baseball*. Toronto, Ontario, Canada: SPORT Media Publishing, 2004.

Uecker, Bob, and Mickey Herskowitz. *Catcher in the Wry*. New York: G. P. Putnam's Sons, 1982.

Veeck, Bill, with Ed Linn. *The Hustler's Handbook*. New York: G. P. Putnam's Sons, 1965.

———. *Veeck—as in Wreck*. New York: G. P. Putnam's Sons, 1962.

Waggoner, Glen, Kathleen Moloney, and Hugh Howard. *Baseball by the Rules: An Anecdotal Guide to America's Oldest and Most Complex Sport*. Dallas, TX: Taylor Publishing, 1987.

Weaver, Earl, with Terry Pluto. *Weaver on Strategy*. Dulles, VA: Brassey's, 2002.

Williams, Ted, with John Underwood. *My Turn at Bat*. New York: Simon & Schuster, 1969.

Newspapers, Magazines, and Journals

Atlanta Constitution
Bangor Daily Whig and Courier (Maine)
Baseball Magazine
Baseball Research Journal
Boston Daily Advertiser
Boston Globe
Boston Post
Brooklyn Eagle
Chicago Daily News
Chicago Tribune
Christian Science Monitor
Cincinnati Commercial-Tribune
Cleveland Plain Dealer
CMG Worldwide Report
Des Moines Daily News
Detroit Free Press
Discover
Evansville Courier
Family Practice News
Hibbing Daily Tribune (Minnesota)
LIFE
Look
Los Angeles Times
National Pastime
National Sports Daily
Newark Daily Eagle (New Jersey)
Newark Daily Journal (New Jersey)
New York Clipper
New York Daily News
New York Evening Journal
New York Evening Mail
New York Herald Tribune
New York Journal-American
New York Newsday
New York Sun
New York Sunday Mercury
New York Times
New York World
Philadelphia Inquirer
Philadelphia North American
Poughkeepsie Journal (New York)

San Francisco Chronicle
Saturday Evening Post
Silent Worker
SPORT
Sporting Life
Sporting News
Sports Digest
Sports Illustrated
St. Nicholas Magazine
USA Today
USA Today Baseball Weekly
USA Today Sports Weekly
Washington Evening Star
Yale University Record

Electronic Sources

ESPN   www.ESPN.com
Major League Baseball   www.mlb.com
A Page from Baseball's Past   www.baseballspast.com
Retrosheet   www.retrosheet.org
Sports Business Daily   www.sportsbusinessdaily.com

Other Sources

American League official day-by-day statistics, 1905–2001
Information Concepts, Inc. day-by-day statistics, 1882–1915
Major League transaction cards, 1917–1919
National Baseball Hall of Fame plaques
National League official day-by-day statistics, 1891–2000

Index

About the Author

Bill Deane has been an active member of the Society for American Baseball Research (SABR) since 1982, and served as senior research associate at the National Baseball Hall of Fame from 1986 through 1994. He has authored six previous books and hundreds of book chapters and articles about baseball. He served as managing editor of *Total Baseball* and has performed as a paid consultant to such authors as Roger Kahn and Bill James, and such organizations as Curtis Management Group and Topps Baseball Cards. In 1989, Deane won the SABR-Macmillan Baseball Research Award for his book *Award Voting*. In 2001, he became the youngest honoree ever of the SABR Salute for research that "has contributed significantly to baseball knowledge." And in 2003, Deane won his regional SABR chapter's Cliff Kachline Award. He resides in Cooperstown, New York, the mythical "Birthplace of Baseball."